ROCK ON

MINING FOR JOY IN THE
DEEP RIVER OF SIBLING GRIEF

SUSAN E. CASEY

Published by:
Library Tales Publishing
www.LibraryTalesPublishing.com
www.Facebook.com/LibraryTalesPublishing

Some of the names have been changed to protect privacy

PRINTED IN THE UNITED STATES OF AMERICA

"After the tragic death of her younger brother 'Rocky,' Author Susan Casey takes readers on a harrowing journey from the black river of grief to reclaiming a life with joy and a transformed heart. A licensed social worker, Casey also chronicles the loss of other grief-stricken siblings, who share their heartbreaking and hopeful stories. A must read for anyone who has lost a brother or sister and has embarked on their own healing odyssey." ~ Barbara Walsh, Pulitzer Prize-winning journalist and author of *August Gale: A Father and Daughter's Journey into the Storm and Sammy in the Sky.*

"I loved reading this book! Susan's description of her own journey through grief helped expand on the experiences shared by the siblings she interviewed. Even in the bereavement profession, the grieving sibling is often overlooked or their needs diminished. *Rock On: Mining for Joy in the Deep River of Sibling Grief* is an important book and Susan does a great job of bringing the people and the process to life, even while dealing with the death of her brother." ~ Tasha Walsh, Executive Director at Rockbridge Area Hospice

"*Rock On* details how the loss of a beloved sibling can turn your world upside down. Using personal experience, this book will make you realize that you are not alone, providing hope and support for anyone who is feeling lost in the sea of grief. The heartbreakingly raw and honest account exudes positivity in its messages, telling of how sorrow and heartache can be turned into acts of kindness, emphasizing how important it is to do everything with love and appreciation for life and for our loved ones." ~ Aimee Mckee: a 20 year old who lost her older brother on May 12, 2017 in Belfast, Northern Ireland.

About the Author

Susan E. Casey, MSW, MFA, is a writer, a licensed mental health clinician, a certified bereavement group facilitator, and a certified life coach. Throughout the past 25 years, Susan has worked in hospice, in-patient, and home-based settings with teens and adults, and taught numerous courses to executive leaders and clinicians. Currently, Susan works for a measurement-based care organization, providing clinical coaching to therapists, psychologists, and psychiatrists countrywide to improve mental health outcomes for youth and adults. Susan's blog, www.susanecasey.com, chronicles her grieving process following the death of her younger brother. Her fiction has won numerous awards, including first place in the PEN/Nob Hill Literary Contest and Green Writer's National Literary Contest. *Rock On: Mining for Joy in the Deep River of Sibling Grief* is her first work of nonfiction. Both Susan's professional and creative work have been guided by her deep belief that every individual has purpose and inherent strengths and deserves the opportunity to reach their own unique potential. Susan lives in Maine with her husband Steve and golden retriever Indy.

Table of Content

Dedication

To my brother, Brian "Rocky" MacLeod Hathaway Jr. and to all the deceased siblings in this book. You will always be remembered and forever loved.

- ◆ *Joseph Belluccio:*   *5/10/60 - 7/7/15*
- ◆ *Keith Richard Brown:*   *7/25/51 - 11/10/81*
- ◆ *Jennifer Ren'ee Caffroy:*   *7/20/88 - 7/10/07*
- ◆ *Doron Cohen:*   *8/12/81 - 2/15/03*
- ◆ *William Clinton Davis:*   *7/1/86 - 5/24/10*
- ◆ *Alnah Doughty:*   *12/9/69 - 10/10/05*
- ◆ *Beall Dozier:*   *7/19/58 - 5/10/15*
- ◆ *Anne Jaye Ballen Gaynor:*   *1/24/63 - 10/18/00*
- ◆ *Ryan Gill:*   *7/25/79 - 3/30/13*
- ◆ *Steffani Anne Gordon:*   *12/14/70 - 7/6/86*
- ◆ *Brian "Rocky" MacLeod Hathaway Jr.:*   *11/24/70 - 2/14/14*
- ◆ *Mattijs Kerkdijk:*   *5/17/82 - 9/7/14*
- ◆ *Salonee Chintamani Kharkar:*   *7/20/85 - 8/16/12*
- ◆ *Paul McLaughlin:*   *8/3/73 - 6/24/14*
- ◆ *John Michael Rogers:*   *2/4/57 - 3/18/94*
- ◆ *Kay Sisto:*   *4/11/60 - 5/26/10*
- ◆ *Ben Steiman:*   *9/17/52 - 4/2/01*
- ◆ *Timothy James Stickney:*   *11/11/94 - 1/11/11*
- ◆ *James Whitten Walsh:*   *7/29/59 - 1/17/14*
- ◆ *Laurie Leigh Wile:*   *8/9/70 - 12/23/88*

CHAPTER 1
Secret Keepers

On a sub-zero winter night when I was sixteen years old, I snuck out of my bedroom window, climbed onto the garage roof, hung from the gutter, and jumped onto the picnic table piled high with snow. I scrambled over snow banks to meet my girlfriend who waited for me, headlights turned off at the end of my street. I slid into the passenger side, blew warm breaths into numb hands, and said, "I hope we don't get caught," as we zipped away like two delinquents to a party forty-five minutes away.

Several hours later, with Budweiser on my breath, I climbed back onto the garage roof and tucked fingers under the base of my bedroom window to shimmy it open. It was frozen shut. "I'm so screwed," was the only thought that came to mind at 1:00 a.m. Was the kiss from the cute boy I had a crush on for months worth it? It would depend on how badly the night would end. My teeth chattered as I exhaled white puffs of breath into the frigid air. I had no choice. My two older brothers' bedroom was on the other side of the house, and I had no way to get to their window, so I crawled over to my younger brothers' bedroom window and rapped loud enough to awaken one of them. I prayed it would be my twelve-year-old brother Rocky and not my seven-year-old brother Kevin.

I imagined Rocky and Kevin staring at a silhou-

1

ette outside their window and running into my parents'
room, wailing about a boogeyman. As I inhaled another
cold, teeth-chattering breath, I rapped again. "It's me,"
I said. "Susan." Rocky jumped out of bed, backed away
from the window, and rubbed tired eyes. I waved and
whispered again, "It's me. Your sister."

Rocky placed a hand on his chest, opened the window, and stepped back as I climbed through it.

"What are you doing?" he asked.

I hugged him. "I'm sorry. My window was stuck."
Even then, so young and lithe, he was beautiful with his
dark tousled hair, deep dimples, and eyes the color of
caramel. I slipped my pinky into his and said, "It's our
secret, right?"

He nodded. "I won't tell."

On that night, we became each other's secret keep-
ers. He kept mine, and I kept his.

*   *   *

Six years later, on an August Saturday afternoon,
Rocky blew through my parents' front door. His skin
was tanned, slick with coconut oil. He was eighteen and
preparing to begin his freshman year at Lyndon State
College in Vermont. I was twenty-two, still living at
home, and engaged to my future husband. I commuted
to the University of Southern Maine, pursuing a Bachelor of Arts degree in English.

"Nice day at the beach?" I asked.

"Awesome," he said. "Hey, come to my room when
you're done. I have to show you something."

My brother had a perpetual twinkle in his eyes like
he was up to something or would be soon. I hustled up
the stairs and knocked on Rocky's door.

"Sis?" he asked.

"Yeah, let me in."

He opened the door and said, "Swear you won't
tell Mom and Dad."

I grabbed his pinky. "Swear."

He hiked up the left side of his bathing suit shorts. Pegasus was etched into his bronze skin, wings stretched out wide, legs galloping through the sky. "What do you think?" he asked.

I stared at the beautiful winged creature on his muscled thigh, thinking how fitting he chose Pegasus. While many of us are comforted by curling inside a bubble of security where we have stable, steady jobs, in stable, steady neighborhoods with stable, steady friends, that bubble was too thin, too small, too confining for Rocky.

Whenever I stood in his presence, I always felt a tinge of envy. He made the daredevil, badass in me feel small and weak. As I matured, I played my life safer, but as Rocky aged, he nurtured a free, fearless soul, and sprinted through his life. Rocky was the wild one—the authentic, real-deal risk-taker. At nine months old, already tired of the slow pace of a crawl, he took his first step, ready and alert to begin his walk, then his run, and then his flight through his miraculous life. He was the natural athlete who at two years old, waddled around, kicking a soccer ball with his baby feet. In high school, as he ran across the field with agility and grace, the ball seemed an extension of his foot. He was the captain of his soccer and basketball teams. Rocky's magnetism drew people to his side with both admiration and fierce jealousy. He was "that guy." Girls flocked to him, guys wanted to be him. And Rocky didn't want any of it, tired of trying to live up to everyone's expectations of him. "One day," he said, "I want to go where nobody knows my name."

With a boundless spirit that stretched from one side of the world to the other, the universe was not too vast, frightening, or risky—it was his playground. Rocky embodied Pegasus' spirit—*the mythical immortal winged stallion, capable of everything.*

"It's beautiful," I said. "But you're so dead when Mom sees that."

"She won't," he said. "Not unless you tell her."

Rocky entrusted me with his secret, and it would stay with me until he had the courage to show my parents his tattoo a year later.

*　*　*

Through his freshman year in college, Rocky let his thick black hair grow below his shoulders. Home on summer break, after a shower, hair soaked, he said, "Hey, I need you to twirl my hair like this." He took a chunk of hair and twirled it into a tight tube.

"Why?" I asked.

"It will help make the dreadlocks."

"Dreadlocks," I said. "Are you kidding? Don't dread that beautiful hair."

"Yes," he said. "I want them. Come on, Sis, help me."

Rocky was a bona fide Deadhead and had the marching bears, one of the Grateful Dead's most beloved and iconic symbols, inked into the tender skin below his waistband. He and his college friends followed the psychedelic rock band around from city to city, believing in the members' message of peace, love, freedom, and mind expansion. Rocky was a devoted fan and with a head full of dreadlocks and tie-dyed T-shirts, he'd blend in with the cult-like community in Deadhead-land.

"OK," I said. "I'll help you."

I sat on my parents' bed, and Rocky sat on the carpet between my legs in front of their full-length mirror. He watched as I twirled and twirled, and I listened as he talked about college, his classes, and his blond-haired, blue-eyed girlfriend, Kristen.

"She's beautiful, Sis. Oh my God and she's soooo sweet."

I smiled. "So are you in love?"

Our eyes locked in the mirror. He laughed. "I think so. She wants to teach little kids. I can't wait for you to meet her. You're going to love her."

I finished twirling the last chunk of hair and sadness welled inside of me. I didn't want our little pocket of time to end. "I love you," I said.

Rocky turned around, wrapped his arms around me, and kissed the top of my head. "I love you too, Sis."

Two months later, in the fall, I was able to make a soccer game at Lyndon State, and I sat on the sidelines with Kristen. My brother was right; she was beautiful, kind, and smart. She leaned over and said, "I'm going to marry him one day." I fell silent as we both watched him soar across the field with Pegasus' wings peeking below his shorts, his dreadlocks flying behind him.

* * *

Though I grew to love Rocky's dreadlocks, my mother hated them. She begged him countless times to cut them off, but he felt they had become an extension of himself and a symbol of his free-spirited approach to life. When he finished up his junior year and returned home for the summer, I was newly married, living in an apartment in Portland, Maine, and working the 4:00 p.m. to midnight shift at L.L. Bean.

On a Friday morning in July, he called me. "You have to come over," he said. "I need you."

"What's wrong?" I asked.

"Nothing. I just need a favor. Can you come over right now?"

Twenty minutes later, I arrived at my parents' house. Rocky shot through the front door, jogged over to my car in khaki shorts and a white T-shirt, opened the passenger side door, slipped in, and said, "I need you to come with me to the hairdresser. I'm getting my dreads cut off as a birthday gift to Mom." There was zero enthusiasm as he delivered this news.

My mother's birthday was the following day, July 21. "Rocky, you don't have to do this. It's your head. It's your hair. Mom doesn't have to like it."

He looked at me and nodded. "I know. I just want

to do this for her."

"Do you have an appointment?" I asked as I backed out of the driveway.

"Yeah, in ten minutes." His cheeks flushed. "I didn't want to go alone."

Tears welled in my eyes. I never took his trust for granted. I never took my big-sister role lightly. I stopped the car, leaned over, and wrapped my arms around him. "I love you so much," I said.

"I love you too, Sis."

When we arrived at the hair salon, I asked him again, "Are you sure you want to do this?"

He nodded. Rocky sat in the chair, inhaled a fat breath, snapped his eyes shut, and scrunched his face as though he were in pain.

I laid a hand on his shoulder and squeezed it gently. "It will be OK."

The hairdresser opened the two silver blades of the scissors and snipped his dreads as they piled into a gnarly heap on the floor. When she snipped the last one, she trimmed his hair tight against his scalp. He ran his hands over his head, leaned into me, and sobbed. "I feel like I lost a part of me," he said.

I held him while he cried. "It's quite a gift you're giving to Mom."

"Are you going to be alright?" the hairdresser asked. "I feel bad."

Rocky sat up and wiped his tear-streaked face with the hem of his T-shirt. "Yeah. I'm fine," he said. "Let's go give Mom her gift."

When we arrived home, I went inside and said to Mom, "Close your eyes. Rocky has a surprise for you."

With red, swollen eyes, my brother came into the kitchen, went over to my mother, took her hands, and ran them over his head as he had done to himself earlier at the hair salon.

Mom opened her eyes and cupped his chin. "My handsome son," she said. As they embraced, he looked at me over Mom's shoulder and smiled.

*   *   *

Five years later when Kristen and Rocky were living in an apartment in New Hampshire, preparing for the birth of their son, Rocky called me. "Can we talk?"

Another secret. He would be asking Kristen for a divorce. He was no longer in love. They had been married for two years and together for ten.

"What about the baby?" I asked, rubbing my forehead. "She's giving birth in four months."

"I can still be a father, Sis."

I had received my master's degree in social work two years earlier in 1996, immersing myself in social justice issues, learning about oppressive "isms" (racism, ageism, sexism, etc.), enlightened about the marginalized, and how to serve without judgment. People had the right to live their lives, to make choices, to face consequences. As social workers, it was our duty to hold compassion for all human beings regardless of what those choices might be. In service, it was our calling to help individuals sift through the debris of their shattered lives and unveil the gems they could stuff into their pockets as a sign of hope for a brighter future. Though my heart ached during that conversation, I bit back words, swallowed grief, and pushed my judgments aside. *Just listen*, I thought, *just listen.*

"I can't stay, Sis. I will always love Kristen, but I'm not happy," he said. "But I won't leave until Michael is born."

"Have you thought about marriage counseling?" I asked. "It's worth a shot. You're having a baby, Rocky."

"Counseling isn't going to help me love her like a husband should love a wife," he said.

I understood. I, too, married at twenty-three years old and divorced my husband two and a half years later. Like my brother, I hadn't loved him the way a wife should love a husband. "I get it. I just wish you'd figured it out before you got Kristen pregnant." Our family adored Kristen, and she'd become more than a sister-in-law to me. I prayed once Michael arrived, Rocky would find his way back to his wife because I didn't want to imagine the depth of distress and heartache she'd endure if he left.

"She wanted a baby, and I wanted this to work, but I can't stay," he said. "Don't hate me for it, Sis."

I cried and said, "Hate you? There's nothing you could ever do to make me hate you. I love you so much. I do want you to be happy, and I want Michael to have a father."

"I'll be a good dad," he said through his own tears. "I will."

A few days later, I talked with Kristen and listened to her side of the story. She believed the baby would quench Rocky's insatiable thirst for adventure and curb his late-night drinking and partying with his racquetball friends. Kristen and I both prayed that he would make a 180-degree turnaround and become the father and husband we hoped he would be.

Through clenched teeth, I waited for a miracle, but I knew my brother. It was unlikely that even his newborn son would be enough to clip those wings. Shortly after Michael was born, Kristen moved out of their apartment and returned to Maine with her infant son. I was reminded again as lives were blowing apart and hearts were breaking, it was not my place to judge. I was dizzy, twirling in circles, confused as to who I should be consoling and how I went about consoling anyone, given the condition of my own heart. The line was short for those who wanted to offer compassion to my brother, so I started there. I wouldn't abandon him.

*   *   *

In 2000, two years after the birth of Rocky's son, he accepted a spa director position with the exclusive Ocean Reef Club in Key Largo, Florida. He was twenty-nine years old. Two years later, he made another career move as the spa director at Sea Island Resort in

Georgia. While he worked, catering to the wealthy and elite, I toiled about in my own bustling life, working as a clinical program director for the Salvation Army and beginning a new life with Steve, my second husband.

Late one night, the phone rang. It was Rocky. "Hey, bro! How are you?"

"I'm in trouble, Sis. I have to make a change."

We talked late into the night about his cocaine habit, which I had not known about prior to this call. I knew he had fooled around with it in college, but I didn't know he'd continued to use. He said it was the late-night parties with his colleagues at Sea Island when his recreational use turned into a full-blown addiction.

"You have to get help," I said. "Please go to re-hab before it's too late." I could feel the tremor begin at the base of my spine, neck hairs standing on end. I was his older sister—his secret keeper. His confidante. I couldn't hold this secret. I had to tell my parents. It was during this pivotal phone call that I began to understand that my brother, whom I loved and had always admired, lived a dichotomous life. An athlete. A spa director. An addict. The brother who flew through life with his feet barely touching the ground. A teacher of wellness. An adrenaline junky. And a thirst for cocaine, which had accelerated as he lived the high life with millionaires and billionaires.

"I don't need rehab. I know what I need to do," he said. "I've accepted a job on a cruise ship. I'm getting clean, Sis."

The gravity of his decision to leave Kristen and his son weighed on him, and the drugs numbed the emotional landslide he experienced in the aftermath. People have always said I wear my heart on my sleeve. If that was true, then my brother held his in the palm of his hand.

As Rocky traveled on the open seas as the spa director for nine months, he kicked his cocaine habit. But there was no cure, no suture for a bleeding heart. He fled as far as he possibly could from the life he left behind and accepted a position halfway around the world. On a whim, he traveled to Bali, Indonesia with his girlfriend, a massage therapist from England whom he worked with on the cruise ship. He fell in love with Bali, not the girl.

In late 2004, I received another call. Another secret. After Rocky finished his time on the cruise ship, he returned home to live with my parents while he contemplated his next career move. I prayed that he would find employment in the spa industry in Maine and stick around.

"Sis, I'm so excited," he said. "I was offered a spa director position at Four Seasons Hotels and Resorts in Jimbaran Bay and Sayan."

"In Bali?" I asked.

"Yeah. This is an incredible opportunity. Can you believe it?"

"No," I said. "I can't." I hadn't seen my brother for close to a year while he was on the ship. If he moved to Bali, when would I ever see him again? How could he leave us all? How was he going to tell our parents? What about this beautiful child he brought into the world?

"When?" I asked. "Why?"

"I can't stay here," he said. "Too many ghosts. I've just made too many mistakes."

My brother had become a conundrum to me. Fiercely independent, goal-driven, and persistent, Rocky didn't allow anything or anyone to block him from attaining his dream and desire to become the CEO of a four-star resort, but at the same time, he couldn't make peace with his decisions. He created the illusion of freedom but encased himself in his self-made prison, riddled with doubt and guilt.

"Come on, Rocky, we all make mistakes. It's called being human. You didn't kill anyone. You got divorced. Look at my life and what I've done," I said. "I'm no angel."

"It's not the same," he said. "You didn't abandon a child. My friends hate me."

"Nobody hates you, Rocky," I said. "Kristen is happy. She has a great husband, two beautiful daughters and a son she adores. She's made a new life in Texas. And it's never too late to make things right with Michael. And what about us? Your family?"

"Sue, this is a once-in-a-lifetime opportunity. It will be better for Kristen and Michael if I just disappear. I'm going."

I had the urge to bash the phone against the table, grind it into the floor, and scream, "Why are you so selfish?! What's wrong with you? What happened to you?" But instead, I said, "We'll never see you again."

"They'll fly me home twice a year. Please be happy for me."

I could hear the pleading tone in his voice, and I wanted to feel delighted, not dread for this second chance he'd been given, but a weight pressed on my chest. To see him, I'd have to book a thirty-three-hour plane trip and purchase a $3,000 airline ticket that I'd never be able to afford. I would get to see his sweet face two times a year when his company flew him home. I imagined the contorted face of my mother when she learned that her beloved son, the one that could do no wrong, was moving close to 10,000 miles away.

* * *

A few months after Rocky moved to Bali in 2005, I received another late-night call. Instead of the usual exhilaration I felt when I heard his voice, I was anxious, anticipating bad news. It was a pervasive feeling I couldn't shake. I lost sleep worrying about him. He was so far away and with a twelve-hour time difference, I rarely talked to him, which made it impossible to assuage my fears. Before I answered the call on this late night, I took several deep breaths and chanted a silent prayer.

My hands trembled as I spoke. "Hi, honey. I'm so psyched to hear from you," I said, hoping that would be the case. "How is the job going?"

"Sue," he said, barely audible through his tears.

Fear slithered around in my stomach. I clutched my glass of Chardonnay and took a long drink. "What's wrong?" I asked.

"Kristen asked..." That's all I heard. The sentence was garbled through my brother's hysterical meltdown.

I took another sip of wine, closed my eyes, and said, "Take a deep breath. I can't understand you."

"Kristen asked me to give up my parental rights so John can adopt Michael. Sue, how do I do that?"

My brother had a way of touching the deepest recesses of my heart. I could feel his heartache over making a decision that would last a lifetime, a decision that would come with another set of consequences, another demon that he would have to wrestle.

He said, "It's the right thing to do, right? I'm halfway around the world. I've not been a father to him."

I felt a range of emotions from sadness to rage. *Just come home and be a father. How can you give up your parental rights? He's your son! What is the matter with you?* But that's not what I said, and those thoughts were fleeting because I knew Rocky couldn't return home. I said, "Yes. It's the right thing to do. Michael deserves to have a father, Rocky. John is his father. He deserves all the rights that come with that title."

We both broke down throughout that call and many times following it. Rocky had made his choices and with all the judgments that flooded in from his friends and family, there was no one who punished him more than he punished himself.

I wanted to believe Bali would help to sweep out those ghosts that dwelled in Rocky's memory and haunted him during his waking hours. The wife he had failed. The son he had failed. But he never did or could forgive himself, even though the alternative, to resume a life with them, was not possible. My brother lived between worlds: the one he left and the one he couldn't quite rebuild.

Rocky didn't believe he deserved happiness after he abandoned his role as husband and father. People crucified him with harsh judgments. Friends clipped him out of their lives. My siblings and parents loved him, but they, too, had a difficult time understanding and supporting his decision to leave his son. When Rocky swung the final blow and relinquished his parental rights, it was as if he had slapped my parents across the face.

His decisions had many ripple effects and one of them acutely impacted our parents. They, too, suffered tremendous losses. They felt as though they lost Rocky, and they lost out on being grandparents to Michael. Kristen tried to keep my parents a part of Michael's life, but after they relocated to Texas, it became more challenging.

Thousands of miles away and a year after his move to Bali, Rocky began dating a young woman who also worked at the resort. A couple of months after they met in June 2006, we Skyped, and I got the chance to see my brother's tanned, beautiful, and radiant face. My body relaxed, my nerves calmed as I exhaled a slow breath and released pent-up tension.

I also had some news to share. I had just started an MFA program in July and was eager to tell him all about the program.

"Hey Sis, how's school going? Have you written the next great American novel yet?" Rocky joked.

We both laughed. "Not quite, but I'll let you know as soon as I do. I think I am going to love this program. I'm meeting the most talented writers."

"That's great," he said. "I'm really happy for you."

I cleared my throat, afraid to ask the question. "How are you, honey? How is every little thing?"

Rocky's whole face smiled. "That's why I'm calling. I've met someone. Her name is Setiawan." He paused. "The only thing is she's fourteen years younger than me, but she's so mature for her age. We've been spending a lot of time together. She's different, Sis. I really

13

can't wait to bring her to the States. She's never been," he said. "I want to show her everything. She wants to see New York City."

The lightness and joy I heard in my brother's voice and the exuberant expression on his face lifted the weight I had carried since he left his first family. "I'm thrilled for you," I said. "How long have you known her?"

"A couple of months but I feel like I've known her forever. She's Balinese. You're going to love her. She's beautiful and the sweetest person I've ever met."

"That's what you said about Kristen," I reminded him.

"I know. This is different. She saved me," he said. "She makes me so happy. I never thought I'd date anyone again."

A red flag popped up. Saved him. *Oh, God,* I wanted to scream into the computer, *do not feel indebted to this human being.* "You saved yourself, Rocky. I don't know this woman, but she didn't save you. No one can make us happy. That has to come from inside of us. You know this."

"She did, Sis. I've told her everything about me, and she accepts me for who I am."

I had no idea why, but I didn't have a good feeling about this new unfurling relationship, and I had nothing to base it on except instincts. My brother was vulnerable and felt unworthy of love and having a family again. I just wanted him to take his time before jumping headfirst into a relationship with a woman who he felt saved him.

"But do you?" I asked.

"Do I what?"

"Accept yourself for who you are and all that's happened in the past? Can you finally forgive yourself?"

A silence lingered between us where our secrets convened in the spoken and unspoken, in the trust and distrust, and in the fear that settled in the center of our two worlds. "Well," I asked, "Do you?"

"I don't want to think about the past. I just want to start over," he said. "That's all. I think I love her, Sis. I have a new life now."

Where nobody knows your name…that's what you wanted. "Are you bringing her with you when you come in December?"

"No," he said. "We can't afford it. If we get married, my company will pay for both of us."

Married? Though he told me many times that he'd never move back to the States, I believed it was always a possibility. If he married Setiawan, that chance would vanish. Bali was her home, and I couldn't imagine she'd leave her siblings and parents the way Rocky had left his.

"It's a little soon to be talking about marriage, don't you think?"

He laughed. "You only knew Steve for three months."

"True," I chuckled. "But that doesn't mean it was a good idea. Just give it a little time." Please give it time.

"I'm in no rush," he said. "I just wish I could bring her with me."

I, too, was eager to meet Setiawan, hoping my initial instincts were wrong about this woman. How could I possibly have doubts about someone I'd never met and had just heard her name for the first time? I was overreacting. My brother appeared happy, content, and at peace. He was going to be OK. "I'm excited for you, Rocky. I can't wait to meet her," I said. "And I am counting the days until you come home. Only four more months."

"Hey, don't tell anyone about Setiawan. I want to tell everyone when I come home."

Tears slid down my cheeks as I remembered our first secret on that cold frigid night. "I swear. It's your news to share."

"You're the best," he said. "I love you, Sis."

15

CHAPTER 2
The Stroke of Time

Rocky began to measure time by how many sleeps we had left before we'd see each other again. A week before he arrived in Maine in early December 2006, he instant messaged me on Skype and wrote, *only seven more sleeps, Sis; only six more sleeps, Sis*, until finally, it was only one more sleep till we'd see each other again. It would be his first trip home since his move to Bali in May 2005. None of us had seen him for a year and a half. Excitement buzzed in my family as we made plans and juggled our schedules as if royalty were flying in.

Mom and Dad picked up Rocky at the airport, while the rest of us wrapped up our day and convened at my parents' for a huge pasta feed. When I embraced my brother, I was beside myself with relief. He looked as he had when we Skyped: radiant, tanned, and happy. Maybe this woman he was dating had saved him. He was the brother I knew before the divorce, the cocaine, and the deep sadness. I rested my head against the soft cotton of his sky-blue Tommy Bahama shirt. He ran his hand down my back and said what he always said, "I love you, Sis."

I soaked the neck of his shirt, leaving black streaks of mascara. "It will come out," I said.

He smiled. "It's OK. I have three more just like it."

My Italian mother had all her chicks back in the nest, putting her heart in great danger of imploding with joy. She made Rocky's favorite meal. As we listened to him paint exotic pictures of Bali through his detailed stories, we twirled long strips of linguine around our forks, bit into hot Italian sausages and meatballs, sopping up the red sauce with thick, fat pieces of bread laced with garlic butter, and refilled thin-stemmed wine glasses with Cabernet Sauvignon.

Happiness oozed from the glint in Rocky's eyes,

and there was real passion in his voice as he shared stories about his girlfriend Setiawan, the color of the Indian Ocean, the monkeys, the paddies at the Tegallal and Rice Terraces in Ubud, the luxurious Four Seasons Resorts in Jimbaran Bay, nestled on the oceanfront, and the other in Sayan, Ubud, hidden in the lush paradise beside the Ayung River. Bali had become his home. We laughed, interrupted, and talked over each other as we had before marriages, before divorces, as we had when we were young, sharing space, time, and blood. I had the urge to pluck batteries from the ticking clocks, corral my family, and tuck them all inside a bubble to stop time and keep them safe.

"Tell us more about Setiawan," my mother said, as she heaped more meatballs onto Rocky's plate.

"I've never met anyone like her," he said. "I wish I could have brought her with me. She's gorgeous."

"Can you bring her to Kevin's wedding?" Mom asked.

"Yeah," I said. "That's a great idea." My youngest brother Kevin was getting married in September. Rocky was the Best Man, and I was going to officiate.

"We can't afford it," he said. "Maybe next year."

My mother and I looked at each other with a shared knowledge that he was planning for the future with this woman, a woman he had definitely fallen in love with.

* * *

Rocky's ten days home melted away like snow on a rooftop during a warm March day. Though we all begged him to switch his flights and stay through Christmas, he said, "I'd do anything to stay, but it's our busiest time of year at the resorts. Both sites are at capacity." He didn't mention it, but I knew he wanted to spend the holidays with Setiawan.

While my brother flew the 10,000 miles back to Bali on the seventeenth, my father called 911. My mother had slumped over in a chair. She suffered a massive stroke on the left side of her brain. It was possible she would not make it through the night.

Hours earlier, Mom called to discuss Christmas dinner and the tenderloin and lobster tails she ordered. She also talked about Rocky and how anxious she was to hear that he had landed safely, but I was too busy to listen. I was in the middle of critiquing my fellow students' manuscripts in my MFA program. I cut her off and said, "I'll call you later, Mom. I have to get these done."

My winter residency would begin in early January, but I wouldn't call Mom later nor would I attend my second semester. The day after Mom's stroke, I called the director of the MFA program, hysterical, as I told her that my mother was in the ICU, and I didn't know if she would survive. "I have to drop out," I said. "I hope I can come back in the summer." Even as I said the words, I watched my dream fly out of my life as quickly as it had flown in. I didn't know what the future held for my mother or me, but pursuing an MFA in fiction seemed frivolous and irrelevant. Still, an ache expanded in my chest.

Meanwhile, after Rocky landed in Indonesia and received the news, he jumped on another flight back to Maine without any of his luggage that somehow never made it on the connecting flight to Bali. When he landed thirty hours later, the only pieces of clothing he had with him were the jeans and gray sweater he flew home in and a suit he purchased at the airport, believing he'd be attending my mother's funeral. For ten days, he wore my father's clothes, which were at least two sizes too big.

Though Rocky was the second to the youngest in our family of five children, he had the ability to calm us all down with his humor and charm. He lightened the heaviness in the room by telling us stories about his adventures, making jokes, or devising a plan of who should do what. He was the perfect person to accompany me on a dreaded trip through Walmart two days after my mother's stroke.

We had to pick up several items Mom would need while she was in the hospital. The majority of my siblings and in-laws didn't think my mother would survive. Her brain continued to swell as she fought for her life in the ICU at Maine Medical Center. But I knew in my bones that she'd survive, and I told Rocky, "We have to buy her clothing for rehab."

Despite his lack of sleep and sixty hours of travel, he remained optimistic, reassuring me that whatever we had left of Mom post-stroke would be better than not having her at all. Ten years earlier, I worked as a medical social worker in an acute brain injury rehabilitation facility. I understood what a left-sided stroke stole: memory, language, partial vision, and the ability to cook. I was numb, in shock, and at a loss as to what my role in our family would now become.

Our mother was the nucleus of our family, the one who planned holidays, birthdays, and all other special events. She was a feisty, outgoing Italian who reveled in all those activities she'd no longer be able to do, like whipping up huge pasta feeds, calling her children every evening for long conversations, typing my father's surveys, and playing Family Feud on her computer. Yes, I thought, we'd be OK with what was left of our mother, but would she? And where will you be when we help Mom and Dad pick up the pieces of their life, Rocky? You'll be on the other side of the globe. I pushed these thoughts aside, relieved that he'd be with us through Christmas, my fortieth birthday, and New Year's.

As we made our way through the women's department in a daze, throwing sweatpants, T-shirts, and hoodies into the cart, Rocky spent his time choosing the tackiest clothing from the rack and asked, "Think Mom would like this?" And we both erupted into laughter. In the shampoo aisle, I dropped a bottle of Pearl on the floor and sobbed. "What if she doesn't make it?" I asked.

Rocky hugged me and said again, "It's going to be

OK, Sis."

My younger brother, ten inches taller, held me up. I felt the weight of the trauma between us as the future of our family crumbled, like an old decrepit chimney. For now, he was *home,* and I let myself collapse against his chest.

* * *

On December 20, the neurologist who treated Mom held up a black and white photo of the CT scan of her brain. "The dark places," he said, "are the damage caused by the stroke."

The dark places made up one-sixth of her brain. The doctor stressed the severity of the situation, preparing us for the possibility that Mom may die. "If she does survive," he warned, "she may never be able to do more than what she is doing now." (Which was little more than breathing, an occasional flutter of her eyes, and a subtle movement in her hand).

We prayed; we wept; we sat in a circle in hard-backed chairs in the conference room to make the decision as a family as to whether we wanted the neurosurgeon to take "life-saving measures" if her brain continued to swell. Life-saving measures meant removing the left side of her skull, which would allow her brain the room to expand beyond the confines of her cranium. We were cautioned that if we chose this route, the outcome would "not be good," and Mom would most likely spend the rest of her life in a nursing home with a feeding tube, being repositioned every hour to prevent bed sores. The air in the roomed thinned as our fears and the unknowns whirled around us.

"Wow," my sister-in-law said. "Do you think we should talk about donating her organs?"

I leapt out of my seat and spewed through clenched teeth, "Shut up! Mom is going to make it. I don't care what any of you say. If you can't be positive and believe she's going to live, go home. I don't want your negative energy around here."

I left them in their silence to get some air, and later, after I stopped fuming and calmed down, I rejoined my family. We arrived at a consensus that Mom would not want to live in a vegetative state and, no, we didn't want the surgeon to take "life-saving measures." There would not be another CT scan, regardless of whether her brain continued to swell.

The last words the neurologist said to our family prior to his vacation on December 23 were to prepare ourselves. We were directed to "watch" her. If she became more alert, the swelling was decreasing. If she became more despondent, the swelling was increasing, and if it didn't stop, it would press on her brain stem and kill her.

Two or three of us were at the hospital around the clock, waiting, watching, and praying for Mom to open her eyes. Dad leaned against the wall in the ICU, rubbing his forehead. He looked up and asked, "Do you think we should cancel the tenderloin?"

My father wore the look of defeat on his face better than any athletes who lost their chance at Olympic gold. "Yes, Dad. Cancel it. We will be here for Christmas," I said.

He nodded. "OK."

On Christmas Eve, my siblings and I went out for a quick dinner to one of the only pubs open in the Old Port. We drank beer and ate greasy food as I sank into reverent silence, pleading for a miracle. We paid our bill and hustled back to the hospital. When we got off the elevator, Christmas carolers were strolling down the corridors, singing *Amazing Grace*, lingering in front of sick patients' doors.

Please wake up, Mom. Please wake up, I chanted silently as we clamored down the hallway toward the ICU.

As we walked in, Mom rolled her head to the side and blinked at us. Thank you, God. We encircled her bed like a fortress, declaring my mother's "awakening" a true Christmas miracle. Our prayers had been heard by the celestial beings. She remained in the ICU for seven days and transitioned into a patient room for two days before being transferred to New England Rehabilitation Center for seven weeks.

Before Rocky's departure, he came to the rehabilitation center, walked into Mom's room, and said what he always said, "Your favorite son is home."

Mom nodded and smiled as she held out her frail hand. Rocky sat next to her on the right side, I sat on the left.

"Ready for a pedicure?" he asked.

Mom nodded and smiled again.

I sank my teeth into my bottom lip until the pain usurped the urge to cry as he lovingly massaged her feet with lotion. "I'll be back in a few months, Mom." His voice cracked. "I love you so much."

On December 29, my fortieth birthday, Rocky and my other siblings planned a party for me at the rehabilitation center. They cooked up Italian dishes, invited a few of my close friends, and hauled everything into the community room. Rocky wheeled Mom in, wearing my father's gray sweater and khaki pants he cinched tight with my father's leather belt. He lit the candles on my purple and white cake, and they sang *Happy Birthday*.

Due to the stroke on the left side of her brain where language ability is located, Mom could not talk, but many aspects of music and the melody of speech are located on the right side of the brain, which meant she could still sing. As she sang *Happy Birthday* to me, my heart swelled. Rocky was home, and my mother was alive. I promised God that I'd never ask for anything again. That evening, my friends, siblings, their spouses, and I went into the Old Port for the remainder of my birthday. We were not celebrating me. We danced in ceremonial gratitude that my mother survived and worked each day to reclaim tiny pieces of her functioning. As the night wound down, Rocky said he was going to stay at the pub and take a taxi home.

"Just come with us now," I said. "I don't want to

worry about you tonight."

"Sis, I'm a grown man," he said. "I'll be fine. I don't want to go home right now."

I left the pub and glanced back at Rocky with an uneasy feeling that another tragedy was about to happen to our family. I went back to the table and pleaded. "Come on. Please just come home now."

"Would you relax, Sis? Nothing is going to happen to me."

"Call me when you get home. I don't care what time it is," I said as I leaned over and kissed him on the forehead. "Don't get too drunk."

At midnight, the phone rang. It was Rocky. He was home. What had I been so worried about? Why was I always afraid something horrible was going to happen to him?

On January 1, I drove Rocky to the airport. We wept throughout the half-hour ride as we talked about our mother and the uphill journey my parents would be facing if she were able to return home. I didn't want him to leave Mom and me. As we stood outside Portland International Jetport in the frigid air, he pulled me against his chest and said, "I know you. You have to take care of yourself while you're taking care of Mom."

"I'll try," I said.

He let me go and witnessed both the will and sadness curled up in my eyes. He said, "I know you think that you're single-handedly going to rehabilitate Mom and help her learn how to talk again. Just take care of yourself. I'm sorry I can't stay longer. The wedding is not that far away."

"I wish you didn't have to go," I said, soaking the collar of his shirt again. "Maybe now you could move home."

"I'm sorry I won't be here for you, Sis," he said. "I love you so much."

We stood there in the cold, holding on to each other, quiet with our own thoughts about what the future held for our mother.

*   *   *

Over the stretch of nine agonizing months, awaiting Rocky's return, my mother had seizures, broke ribs, bumped into furniture, walls, and doors due to her right field cut, and endured endless hours of physical, speech, and occupational therapy. Mom and Dad were sinking into a depression, and we were all exhausted. I ran back and forth to their home, cooking dinners, doing laundry, and attempting to buoy their spirits. Gray, endless days bled into black, endless nights. When I spoke to Rocky on Skype, I traversed the days, trying to pluck glimmers of progress Mom had made to share with Rocky to keep the call upbeat. During the conversation and others, he would constantly say, "What? I can't hear you. Can you please talk louder?" He always told me my voice didn't travel, and he had to listen "really hard" to hear me. After I relayed the "glimmers of progress," he said, "You know why people have to listen so hard to hear you?"

"Why?"

"Because," he said, "you whisper to their souls, Sis."

If hearts could crack in two, mine would have. I felt a slight quiver in my chin. "I have to go," I said. "I love you. I can't wait for you to come home."

I disconnected the call, covered my face with my hands, and wept. If he believed I whispered to souls, how come his soul couldn't hear mine, begging him to move home? Why did he get to hop on a plane and fly away, leaving his broken family behind? I wanted to understand how, after this tragedy, he could return to Bali. I wanted to, but the truth was I didn't understand. The wedding couldn't come soon enough.

*   *   *

Finally, when it was time for Kevin's wedding,

Mom was strong enough to attend. We'd be staying in cabins for the weekend on Roach Pond in the Moosehead Lake region. My brother Jim and I headed up the Wednesday before so we could help set up the tent, tables, chairs, and decorations. Rocky would fly in on Thursday and drive up with my parents.

Aunts, uncles, friends, and family filled the rustic cabins for the weekend-long event. On Friday night, we cooked a smattering of food: chicken legs, melt-in-your-mouth spareribs, grilled potatoes, orzo salad with roasted vegetables and caramelized onion tossed with olive oil, sea salt, and lemon dressing. We licked sticky fingers, drank Harpoon IPA from a keg, blasted rock music, danced, and celebrated this joyous event, an event that would have been laced with sadness if Mom had not lived to witness her youngest son's marriage. Though she lost twenty pounds, making her look twenty years older, and she was so drugged-up she sat in a chair and drooled, she was alive.

The following day we disappeared into our cabins with flutes of champagne, showered, dressed, and primped for the wedding until it was time for the two to exchange vows. When Kevin and Jessica asked me if I'd marry them, I said it would be my deepest honor. Kevin is close to ten years younger than me. We shared a room when he was a newborn. He became my real-life baby doll, and I shared the mother role when he was an infant. With Mom's significant deficits post-stroke, the mother instinct resurfaced as I helped my brother, and soon-to-be sister-in-law, plan their wedding.

Like Rocky, Kevin was physically beautiful with the same deep dimples, lithe build, bright eyes, and a wide smile. Unlike Rocky and his carefree attitude toward life, Kevin was dependable, stable, responsible, and took calculated risks. I loved them both for their own unique qualities and gifts they brought to my world.

As I stood in front of Jessica and Kevin to officiate the ceremony, I glanced over at Rocky and Mom and felt the familiar quiver in my chin.

Kevin and Jessica had written their own vows. As Kevin read, "I envision our life to be a full life. Not one blurred by compromising pursuits but rather a joined life…that Sunday-kind-of-love we've always talked about," I filled with a depth of gratitude and boundless love I'd never experienced. It was as if God had descended from the heavens and encased us in a bubble of light.

After the ceremony, my Italian uncles (Mom's brothers) scurried to the kitchen of the main house. They were the appointed chefs for the event. They cooked up linguine and several types of sauces: Italian red, Alfredo, pesto, and a myriad of others. My next-to-oldest brother Paul and his wife Pam were not able to make the trip due to Paul's severe health issues. I wanted them to be there in spirit, so I wrote a song and asked Pam if she and her band could put music to it and record it as a surprise for Kevin and Jessica. As my uncles were setting up the feast, I played the song as Pam's angelic voice wafted into the room, singing, *The fairies and the dragonflies, the fairies and the dragonflies will lead you home.* For the remainder of the weekend, Rocky hummed that refrain.

Rocky stood up after the song to give his Best Man speech. In his white linen pants and sky-blue Tommy Bahama shirt, he attempted to deliver a reverential speech, imparting his admiration, love, and respect for Kevin, and his hope that he had been a supportive brother and friend. But his sensitivity, the heartache over our mother's stroke, and the emotionally charged event were all too much, and he wasn't able to regain his composure once he started to cry to give the powerful coherent speech he hoped to.

In an attempt to rescue the awkward moment, Kevin's best friend placed a hand on Rocky's back and delivered a moving tribute to the newly wedded couple.

I looked at Rocky, smiled, and mouthed, "It's OK."

For him, it wasn't OK. For him, he blew a vital opportunity to relay the depth of his love for his brother. He apologized throughout the weekend, not realizing that his emotion alone was more powerful than any words he could have strung together. Kevin and Rocky shared a bond that time and distance could never tarnish. The two were tied together by experiences that belonged only to them; they were tied together by blood. They were brothers.

*   *   *

Several months after Kevin's wedding, Rocky and I Skyped. He had news. Rocky and his girlfriend Setiawan were coming home in six months (September 2008) and we'd meet her for the first time. It would be almost a year from Kevin's wedding when Rocky would ask Setiawan to marry him during his trip home. He would propose in New York City. "Will you help me pick out the engagement ring?" he asked.

Rocky was thirty-eight years old and had his whole wondrous life ahead of him. A new beginning. A new wife. A new start. "This is incredible news," I said. "I can't wait to help you pick out a ring." Though I'd not met Setiawan, she offered my brother a second chance at love. The reservations I had about her and their relationship had dissipated over time. The excitement and pleasure in my brother's voice, on his face, in his eyes, and the wide arc of his lips sparked a kernel of hope inside of me. "I'm really happy for you, honey. You're too young and have too much to offer to go through this life alone."

"Thanks, Sis. I never thought it would happen for me again," he said. "But I really love her. She's not like anyone I've ever known."

I brushed a tear from my cheek. "This is going to be such beautiful news for Mom." Since my mother's stroke, I sought out tiny nuggets of joy I could infuse into her shrinking world to expand it in the slightest way. Though I had to hold Rocky's secret until he came home in September, the anticipation was enough to elevate my spirits beyond my mother's pain. Good things were coming her way.

"She wants to have a baby," he said, smiling into the video camera.

Words caught in my throat. Of course she did, she was fourteen years younger than my brother. A baby? What about the child he already had? "Oh," I said, stalling. "When? After you get married?"

"Yeah," he said.

"Do you want another child?" I asked.

"Well, I'm a lot older than she is," he said. "But I'd like to do it right this time."

Memories of his son Michael flooded the miles between us. I glanced at the picture on my desk of Michael at three years old, pushing his toy dump truck through the sand while Rocky sat next to him. This was the last picture taken of them together, the last time Rocky had seen his son five years ago. How would Michael feel when Rocky had another baby? Would he do it again? Would he leave his wife and child? Ashamed of these thoughts, I shoved them aside. "I think you'll be a great dad this time," I said. "You were young when you had Michael. It will be different." As I said the words, I wasn't sure if I made a statement or asked a question.

"It will be," he said.

I hope so. "This will make Mom's world," I said.

*   *   *

The day Rocky was due to arrive with his soon-to-be fiancé, I took a half-day off from work so I could be at my parents' house when they returned from the airport. A month earlier, I purchased a beautiful pink silk dress, as light as a whisper, by a famous European designer for a wedding in August, but it was a little too snug. I knew Setiawan was smaller than me, so I decided to keep the dress and give it to her as a "welcome to our family" gift.

Setiawan was Hindu. I knew very little about her

religion or the Balinese culture and hoped my offering would be accepted in the spirit it was intended. I didn't know if she might think it was a little weird for a future sister-in-law to be giving her a dress when we'd never met, and I had no idea about her sense of fashion.

When I heard my father's car pull in, I bolted to the driveway. My brother stepped out of the car and then Setiawan. She stood four feet eleven inches and weighed around ninety pounds. Black, shiny, thick hair hung to the middle of her back. She had a huge, beautiful smile, and dark, almond-shaped eyes. Though she was twenty-four years old, she could have passed for eighteen.

First, I hugged my brother, and then I embraced Setiawan. "Welcome to the U.S.," I said.

"I am glad to be here. It's pretty," she said, looking at the luscious jewel colors of the autumn leaves.

"I'm so happy you came," I said. "It's a perfect time of year. Let's go inside and put your stuff away."

We all grabbed pieces of luggage and brought them upstairs to Rocky and Kevin's old room. As they unpacked their clothes, they told us about their trip over and how tired they were. With a twelve-hour time difference, it's a brutal trip. "It will take you a few days to acclimate to the time change," I said.

She nodded. "Yes. We have to take a nap."

When we came back downstairs, I said, "I have a gift for you, and if you don't like it, I promise I won't be offended."

"A gift for me?" she said, placing a hand over her heart.

I opened the closet and took out the dress. "I thought this might fit you?"

My brother stood behind Setiawan, his hands on her shoulders, and mouthed, "Thank you."

"Oh my God," she said. "It's gorgeous. You treat me like a princess just like your brother."

The following day, Rocky, my dad, and I took a trip to Day's Jewelers and swooned over the scintillating diamond rings.

"I want to find the perfect one," Rocky said, as he searched row after row of gold-, platinum-, and silver-banded rings.

"They're all beautiful," I said. "What about this one?" I held up a traditional Tiffany-style ring. "It's yours for only 8,000 dollars."

My brother smiled. "I'd like to find one for 1,500 dollars."

Forty-five minutes later, Rocky settled on a 3/4 CT gold-banded ring with two small diamonds on either side.

"Do you have to propose in New York?" I asked, as I slipped the ring on my finger and held it at arm's length. "She'll love this."

"Yes," he said. "She's never been, and I have something special planned. We'll be staying at the Four Seasons."

"Oh, come on," I said, as I took the ring off and handed it back to Rocky. "We'll want to celebrate with you."

"Sorry, Sis."

"Come back next summer to get married," I said.

"I don't think I can wait that long," he said with that twinkle in his eye.

"Why? What's the rush?"

Rocky pulled out his credit card and gave it to the Day's representative.

"Would you like it wrapped?" she asked.

"No," I said and looked at my brother. "You have to show it to Mom."

While the representative completed the sale, Rocky said, "I told you, she wants to have a baby, Sue. I'm not getting any younger."

"OK," I said. "Then we'll just have to come celebrate with you in Bali."

He smirked. "Are you serious?" he said. "Would Steve go?"

"Yes," I said. I had talked to my oldest brother Jim,

my sister-in-law Gayle, and my husband Steve about taking a trip to Bali. "How does April sound? Jim and Gayle want to come too."

* * *

Two months later, on November 3, Rocky and Setiawan married in a temple in Ubud, Bali. Shortly after they wed, the four of us, and Gayle's mother, Janet, booked our two-week trip to Bali. Prior to the trip, I talked with Rocky and suggested we get our own hotel rooms.

"I think twelve days is too much to ask of Setiawan," I said. "There are five of us." I had only met Setiawan seven months earlier, but she and Rocky stayed with my parents, and the time we had together was in large group settings at dinners and cookouts with the family and extended family. Twelve days together under the same roof may be pushing it even for the most tolerant human being.

"Sue, you're coming all the way to Bali. You're staying with us," he said. "She's excited."

"Just ask her again. It seems like a lot to me."

"It's fine. I can't wait to see you guys," Rocky said. "Just leave it up to the bro. I've got the whole vacation planned."

* * *

When we arrived in Bali, we were all exhausted from the thirty-three hours of travel but thrilled to be in Indonesia.

"I can't believe you guys are really here," Rocky said as we piled into his car.

"I can't either," I said.

We chatted and laughed on our way to Rocky and Setiawan's home. As he pulled into the driveway, we all wanted to flop down on beds, curl under covers, and lay our heads on soft pillows, but we willed ourselves to stay up in an attempt to reduce jet lag. We talked on Rocky's balcony for hours, finally crawling toward our rooms in the wee hours of the morning.

The first few days Setiawan was gracious and welcoming. They lived in a rent-free home inside the gates of the Four Seasons Resort in Jimbaran Bay where my brother worked. It was spacious with a private pool in the backyard. Setiawan cooked fresh seafood for us and took my sister-in-law, her mother, and me shopping in Ubud. We went sightseeing, rode scooters, ate authentic Balinese cuisine, and drank Bintang beer. Rocky brought us to his favorite eateries where we soaked up the sun, sat at tables on the beach, and ate fresh fish and sticky rice with our hands.

As the days wore on, Setiawan became colder, irritable, and angry, spending more time away from the family. During our last few hours with Rocky, my husband and I treated everyone to pizza, my brother's favorite food, and we hung out at the house to savor the time we had left together. Setiawan took her pizza and ate it in her bedroom. When she finished, she joined us in the kitchen.

I still had about fifty U.S. dollars in Rupiahs, and I said to Rocky, "Can you exchange this for me? Do you have any U.S. dollars?"

Setiawan said, "Why you have to change it? Why can't you take it home for a souvenir?"

The tension had been building between us throughout the trip and her comment was the tipping point. I threw the Rupiahs at her and said, "Just keep it."

Everyone was stunned by my unusual and rude outburst. I didn't know if I liked Setiawan, which was a painful and disturbing admission because I adored my brother, and I wanted to love her too. After the money incident, she pulled Rocky out on the porch to talk over my contemptible behavior. Ten minutes later, Rocky came into the living room and sat with us.

He said, "I'm sorry, Sis. I asked her if she'd want to take fifty dollars home as a souvenir. And I told her I wasn't spending your last night here talking about this."

Embarrassed by my behavior, I said, "You're sorry? I'm sorry. I'm so ashamed of myself. I don't know why I did that. It's not about the money. I don't care about the money."

"Don't worry about it," Rocky said. "She'll get over it."

When we arrived at the airport, I opened my arms to Setiawan, hugged her, and apologized. "I think I'm just tired. It's not an excuse, but I have no idea why I did that to you."

"It's OK, Sue," she said. "I shouldn't have said 'keep as souvenir'."

As I boarded the flight, hours later, and sat down, I had that weird tingling in my left hand. I asked myself, *Who is Setiawan?* I couldn't articulate my reservations, but I knew something was off. I closed my eyes, lay my head on my husband's shoulder, and prayed that my newfound misgivings about Setiawan's unsettling behavior were skewed because I was tired. It had been a long trip, and we spent too much time together. I had to adjust my attitude because they were coming back to the States in two weeks. Rocky was taking Setiawan back to New York for their honeymoon. I pledged to make that trip a good one and remain open to the hope that Setiawan and I could build a loving and supportive relationship.

*   *   *

Throughout their visit to Maine, Rocky and Setiawan stayed at my parents' house, and we had no time alone before they continued on to New York. Their visit was enjoyable, and we talked about our trip to Bali and shared the photographs we'd taken. I felt good and more optimistic that Setiawan and I could build a healthy relationship.

Before they left for the airport, she confided in me and shared her urgency to conceive and was troubled that she'd not been able to.

We hugged and I said, "This will happen for you. You just have to keep the faith. You're going to be a wonderful mother."

"Thank, you, Sue," she said. "I love you."

"I love you too," I said.

Two and half years later, Setiawan gave birth to Anna on June 28, 2010. Rocky's new life with a family had begun. They would be flying home to the States in October when we'd meet three-month-old Anna for the first time. I imagined holding the gorgeous brown-skinned, dark-eyed infant, a blend of Rocky and Setiawan's physical characteristics, who would be giving him a second chance at fatherhood.

CHAPTER 3
Be Brave

On Wednesday, February 12, 2014, I was writing a script for my CEO for a leadership meeting I'd be attending in Tennessee the following week. There were several awards that would be given out. As the director of communications, I wrote the script for each recipient. I would also deliver a presentation on how to inspire leaders to create a passionate work culture. I was scheduled to fly out on Monday. When my phone pinged, I checked it and read a text from my brother Kevin. *Sue, I got an urgent email from Setiawan. I'm forwarding it to you now. Read it and call me ASAP.*

Even before I opened the email on my phone, sweat beaded on my upper lip. Something was wrong. I could feel it. Rocky had recently accepted a spa director position for the Rosewood Hotels. He'd be part of a team to grow the five-star hotels throughout Asia. A few days earlier, he flew to Kowloon, Hong Kong to meet his colleagues and decided to tack on a family vacation. He promised his daughter she would meet all the Disney princesses in Disneyland. After the trip, they'd return to Bali, pack up their home, and move to Beijing, China. Had something happened to Anna?

I screamed, "What?" into my kitchen as I read Setiawan's email. She explained that on their way over to Hong Kong, Rocky stopped in Bangkok to see an Ear, Nose & Throat specialist (ENT), hoping he'd get new information about the vertigo he continued to battle. The ENT doctor referred Rocky to a neurologist, who suspected he contracted a virus in Cairo, which he said could be cured with a week's worth of medication.

The doctor took him off Xanax cold turkey and replaced it with another medication. My sister-in-law wrote that during their flight to Hong Kong, Rocky began vomiting and was unable to take Xanax or any other medication. He couldn't even tolerate water. Early Wednesday morning Hong Kong time, Rocky had two seizures: the first one at 3:00 a.m. and the second one at 8:45 a.m. After the second seizure, Setiawan called rescue, and he was rushed to Queen Elizabeth Hospital. She wrote that he underwent numerous tests and had a brain scan. All the tests had come back normal. The doctors believed he was withdrawing from Xanax and would fully recover. To make a stressful situation more challenging, the hospital would only allow visits from 6:00-8:00 p.m. Children were prohibited, which meant Setiawan scrambled to locate an old colleague of Rocky's who still worked at the Four Seasons in Hong Kong to babysit Anna while Setiawan was with my brother for those two precious hours a day. She was terrified and begged us to pray that they would be able to fly back to Bali the following day.

After my brothers and I received the email, we jumped on my conference line to discuss the situation and determine how we could support my brother, Setiawan, and my little niece Anna, given the 8,000 miles between us.

"Do you think one of us should fly over there?" I asked.

"Don't be ridiculous," Jim said. "You're blowing this way out of proportion."

"I agree," Kevin said. "Let's plan on all of us taking a trip to Bali when he recovers."

"I'll call the American Embassy," Gayle said, "and get help for Setiawan." Gayle was the eligibility specialist for the Maine Department of Health and Human Services.

"Jessica," I said to Kevin's wife, an anesthesiologist, "Can you call the doctor tonight at Queen Elizabeth and find out what the hell is going on with Rocky?"

"I can't call the doctor for a few more hours," Jessica said. "It's the middle of the night over there."

I went to bed that night, praying for my brother as I had for my mother after her stroke. *God, I know I*

said I'd never ask for anything again if Mom lived, but please,
God, please don't take my brother away from me. I lay awake
thinking about a phone call Rocky and I had three years
earlier when I had fist-sized knots in my back and had
difficulty turning my head to the left and right. I had
hair and blood samples taken and learned that I had
toxic levels of copper in my system, along with adrenal
burnout. In short, it was a digestive issue, and I had to
stop eating gluten, pork, refined sugar, and fried foods.

I Skyped Rocky and explained my health issues,
and he urged me to take a week and go to a healing center. "I have something to tell you too," he said.

He suffered from vertigo for a year but didn't want
to alarm any of us, so he kept this information to himself. He said he first experienced vertigo in Cairo at the
airport. He lost his bearings, fell to the ground, and was
unable to walk. The illness took a tremendous toll on
his physical and psychological well-being.

"Why didn't you tell any of us?" I asked.

"I couldn't, Sis. I don't know why I have it, and I
didn't want to worry you guys."

Rocky said the doctor in Cairo couldn't pinpoint
the underlying cause of the vertigo. He prescribed Xanax as a temporary solution to help reduce the debilitating symptoms. From my work as a therapist, I knew
that Xanax was prescribed for depression and panic
attacks and can have dangerous side effects. It's not a
drug meant for long-term use.

"Rocky, you've been on Xanax for over a year?
That's way too long. You've got to get to the States and
see a specialist. Even the doctor in Cairo said it was a
short-term solution."

"There's nothing else that's helped, Sue. It's the
only thing that is managing the vertigo so I can work."
What my brother failed to tell me at the time was he
managed the psychological effects by numbing them
with heavy drinking.

I tossed and turned in my bed, reliving our conversation and subsequent conversations since the initial

call. I replayed the timeline in my head. Rocky had only worked in Egypt for the Cairo Four Seasons Resort for a few months before the Egyptian Revolution of 2011 forced him to evacuate. Again, our family feared for Rocky's safety. We were glued to the TV news reports, watching looters, and fires in the street. Rocky holed up in the hotel with other Americans, not sure when he'd get a flight out.

When they were able to get the Americans out safely, my brother flew back to Bali to rejoin his wife and daughter. Soon thereafter, he accepted a new position at the Mandarin Oriental Dhara Dhevi in Chiang Mai, Thailand. A year later, my brother's dream of becoming CEO came to pass when he was offered the CEO position at a hotel chain in Ubud, Bali. They were finally returning home, but he still suffered from vertigo.

A few months into his new position, Rocky was miserable, working seventeen-hour days. The long hours, stress, and exhaustion intensified his symptoms. He said the owner of the hotel was a dictator and emotionally abusive to staff. When Rocky informed the owner that he would be leaving to become the spa director of the Rosewood Hotels, the owner threatened my brother's life. Rocky went to the American Embassy and said he feared for his safety and the safety of his wife and child. Though Rocky was frightened, he quit his job two weeks prior to flying to Hong Kong to meet his colleagues. He was ecstatic and eager to leave his experience behind him and hopeful that he'd heal.

As I lay in bed thinking through how long he'd been taking Xanax and the stress he'd been under, I threaded my fingers in prayer, inhaled a breath, and thought, *I know he's going to be fine.* Rocky was vomiting and had a seizure because he was taken off Xanax too abruptly. It's a known side effect. That's all. Jessica talked to the doctor at the hospital, who confirmed Rocky was going through withdrawals and was expected to make a full recovery. Everything is going to be fine.

I imagined the trip we would all take together to

visit Rocky in Bali like we had in 2009. This time, we'd be able to bring Paul, Pam, Jessica, and Kevin to Rocky's favorite places, like Naughty Nuri's Warung and Grill in Ubud. The warung looked like a hole in the wall fronted by a smoking barbecue grill. I had no idea why Rocky loved the place until I bit into their charred, glistening pork ribs and had a sip of their mean martini as the locals whizzed by on their scooters. It became one of my favorite places in Bali, and I was eager to return and celebrate Rocky's recovery.

Still, as I lay there, staring out my bedroom window into the ink-black night, a cold fear coiled around my heart and burrowed there until the sun rose on Thursday, February 13. It was my fifteen-year wedding anniversary, and I scrambled out of bed when I heard my cell phone ringing. It was Kevin. He was in constant communication with Setiawan, either through phone calls or texting.

"Sue, Rocky started hallucinating. Setiawan said he's seeing ants and geckos crawling up the wall and across the ceiling."

"That's just the withdrawals, right?" I asked, thinking about how frightened Setiawan must have been. She told Kevin that he wanted to be released from the hospital, but staff refused because the doctor said he wasn't stable and needed to be checked out by a psychiatrist the following morning. Rocky physically fought with staff, injuring some of them. It took nine staff to hold him down, where they bound his hands and feet in restraints and left him in a crowded hallway for hours with ill patients until a room opened up on the psychiatric unit.

As Kevin relayed the horror of my brother's situation, I imagined myself standing next to his bed, holding his hand, stroking his cheek, cutting the bonds off, and whispering that it would be all right. "I'm here," I'd say. "You've got to hold on. I can't be in this world without you." I planted my head in my hands and wept. *You have to hang on...*

"This is a nightmare," I said. "Pray, Kevin."

"Yes, it is," he said. "I'll call you as soon as I know more."

I texted Setiawan, *Any news?* But I never received a response. The night stretched out, long, thin, and so tight, I thought it might snap. I went back to bed and said more prayers because there was nothing more I could do. As the minutes ticked by, my anxiety rose as I continued to imagine my brother withdrawing, hands and feet bound, as he lay alone in a hospital bed in a foreign country.

I should be with him. I need to take the next flight out. Screw the doctors. I won't leave his side, and they can't make me. Setiawan and Anna need my support. I threw the covers off and tiptoed downstairs, poured myself a glass of water, and sat there in the dark on my computer, searching for flights. The airlines, flights, and airfares blurred together. I'd be of no use to anyone if I didn't get a couple of hours of rest. I'd look at flights first thing in the morning.

Early Friday morning when I saw Kevin's number on my phone, I said another silent prayer before I picked up his call.

"Tell me some good news," I said.

"Sue, it's not good."

I wanted to slap my hands over my ears and scream, "Please stop talking."

"Setiawan left the hospital, and the doctor called her and told her to come back. His blood pressure dropped, and he wasn't breathing on his own," Kevin said. "They got his blood pressure under control, but he's still on a breathing tube."

"What?" I said. "What is going on?" I asked, panicked.

"I don't know."

After I hung up with Kevin, Setiawan emailed us with what she thought was good news. Our brother had been moved to the ICU. With her limited understanding, she believed it was a positive indicator because they moved him from the psychiatric ward to the ICU. I swallowed and called Kevin. "Good news?!" I yelled into the phone. "Are you kidding me? ICU is not an upgrade."

"I know," Kevin said. "I don't know what's going on, but Jessica said this doesn't sound like withdrawals."

It was as if an invisible hand ran the tip of an icicle down my back. "No," I said. "It doesn't. I really think I have to fly out there, Kev."

"Let's just wait to see how he's doing today."

It would take me over twenty hours to get to my brother if all flights stayed on schedule, which was unlikely given the back-to-back snowstorms. "OK," I said. "I'll give it a little more time. Call me the second you hear anything."

I checked my emails and texts incessantly for updates. The next three hours morphed into a stick of dynamite as I watched the wick burn, curling into itself, waiting for the explosion. Tick tock. Tick tock. When I couldn't stand the silence for a second longer, I called Kevin at 3:00 p.m. He had just spoken to Setiawan. The doctor had called her and told her his condition was critical. She took a cab back to the hospital and was able to see Rocky through the glass of the ICU. It was 3:00 in the morning in Hong Kong. Setiawan had to leave the hospital and bring Anna back to the hotel room and put her to bed; they both needed rest.

While Kevin and I were talking, he received an incoming call. "Hey, it's Setiawan. I'll call you right back."

I sat silent and still until my phone buzzed. "What is going on?"

"That was the doctor," Kevin said. "He asked her to go back to the hospital. His blood pressure has fallen again."

"What does that mean? They brought it up before." He didn't need to answer me because the deepest part of my soul whispered, *He's not going to make it.* I shook my head. *No. No. He will make it. He will.*

"I don't know, Sue."

"Do you think we could lose him?" I asked. My brother? Leave? No. My bigger-than-life brother with a hug that could melt a glacier and smile that could light up a midnight sky? The brother who received an award for being one the most influential spa leaders in Asia? The fearless brother who lived his life with zest and gusto?

"The thought has occurred to me," Kevin said.

"Kevin, I have to call Dad and let him know Rocky has taken a turn. I'll call you back. I love you."

"Love you too, Sis."

When he said that, it was Rocky's voice I heard. I questioned whether or not I should call my father. I didn't want to worry him, but my inner thoughts chant-ed, *He could die. His blood pressure dropped. It's all part of the withdrawals. He's going to be fine. Stop overreacting.*

I leaned over the kitchen sink and dry-heaved, as I slapped my hand against the porcelain until my palm reddened and swelled. It wasn't possible that this night-mare was happening to our family. We'd been through enough. My parents had been through enough.

I punched my parents' number into my phone. "Hey, Dad," I said.

"Any updates?" he asked.

"He's taken a turn, Dad," I said as my voice cracked. "He can't breathe on his own. It's not good."

My father remained silent until he let out some semblance of, "Oh, no."

"It's going to be OK, Dad," I said. "It has to be, right?" I don't remember what he said. It was brief, and I said I'd call him as soon as I heard from Setiawan. At 4:00 p.m., I texted Setiawan and asked her, *What is going on?*

Seconds later, my cell phone rang, and hell found me. "You have to be brave, Sue. Brian is gone."

A small voice rose up from inside of me. "Bri-an? What? Gone where?" Maybe she means someone else. We never called my brother by his birth name. No. Rocky was fine.

"He's free, Sue," Setiawan cried into the phone. "He's free. He's not in any more pain."

I closed my eyes and could see and feel her standing in a crowded hallway inside the hospital as her own shock held her body like a netted fish while pure, unrefined grief waited its turn, ready with outstretched claws to sink into skin and bone when shock released her.

"I don't understand," I said. My body trembled as I fell on hands and knees, asking the same futile question over and over again, *Why?*

"I have to go, Sue," Setiawan said. "I have to call my family."

I held the phone in my hand as it turned into a hand grenade. It was February 14, a day for lovers, a day when hearts were doled out in abundance. I stared at the phone, held my breath, knowing my news would blow up my family's valentine hearts into tiny pieces. Who do I call first? I rehearsed what I'd say to my father, but the words crowded in the back of my throat.

I coughed and dry-heaved again. Then there was my brother Paul, thirteen months older than me. He didn't even know Rocky was in the hospital. I never called him the night we all jumped on a conference call because I thought Rocky was going through normal withdrawals and would be discharged in a couple of days. I called my other two brothers because I wanted their wives to help with logistics. Jessica, the doctor, could call the hospital and Gayle, given her line of work for the state, could call the American Embassy. Setiawan had only reached out to Kevin. It was a massive oversight and one I would live to regret.

What I prayed for, begged for, before pressing numbers on the keypad, was "Please, please, God, don't let this kill my parents or trigger another stroke." As I made the first call to my father, I had one lucid thought: I'd rather be walking through flames than calling my parents and telling them their fourth-born child was dead. After I made the calls, one by one to my father, then to my brothers, and finally to my husband, I sank to the floor, my body trembling in a way I didn't know was possible.

* * *

My family gathered that night at my parents' as Mom and Dad sat huddled on the couch, wrapped in a blanket of shock and grief, their facial expressions haunting. This is going to kill them. How long will it take? Six months? A year? These questions played over in my mind as my brothers and sisters-in-law hugged and wept.

We sat in the living room where my four siblings and I had grown up and fought over TV shows, unwrapped Christmas gifts, ten-speed bikes, bean bag chairs, and soccer balls. The same space where we hunted for chocolate Easter eggs, spilled juice on the carpet, and had Backgammon tournaments. The space where I used to beg Rocky for a bite of his hotdog, breakfast sandwiches, pizza, French fries, or any other meal he had because he made his food look better than mine. It was the same space where my brother had been only seven short months before when he and his family made the long trek from Bali to visit us in June.

They coined their trip the "Asian Invasion." They brought scarves, wallets, handbags, and hand-painted umbrellas from Thailand. They packed a smattering of earrings, necklaces, and bracelets from Bali. They announced on Facebook when the items would be available to purchase. Over the weekend, they set up a long table in my parents' front yard, priced each Asian gem, and opened shop. A few days later, we celebrated Anna's third birthday. She closed her eyes and sent a wish out to the universe as she blew out three candles. I wonder now if whatever she had wished for has come true.

As we drowned in our own personal memories, we did all those things people do when that hammer whirls through the air and smashes life into shards of glass.

We hugged, we cried, and worked at the failing task of consoling each other. I made phone call after phone call to aunts, uncles, cousins, friends, and to his ex-wife, Kristen, hearing myself saying what couldn't possibly be true. Rocky. Is. Dead.

When I returned home that night, I was a foreigner to myself, having no idea what to do with the stranger who had taken up residence in my body. I opened my computer and worked until 3:30 in the morning, completing tasks for the leadership summit I was supposed to attend on Monday. I tugged, and yanked, and pulled as many loose ends as I could together for the summit as my ends were unraveling—my mind, my heart, and my nerves. I sent the materials off in a neat little email attachment while I numbly stumbled around in my shell of shock. I stared at the computer screen, got on Facebook, ran fingers over my dead brother's beautiful smile, and whipped myself raw as I scrolled through picture after picture, sure, so sure there had been a mistake of some kind.

"Where are you?" I asked my brother.

The hand on the clock moved around and around until it was morning. I still sat and stared at his face, read his posts, and over 200 condolences. One post that summed up Rocky's life and the impact he had on people he worked with read:

Brian, you knew you were very much loved and that keeps me sane right now. Thank goodness you were fabulous in sharing your genuine feelings. You expressed your love for your friends and your family and your life so freely, eloquently & passionately. Your positivity was truly spectacular. I am certainly and sincerely most grateful for your amazing kindness, generosity, honesty, and humility. It was an honor indeed to be your dear friend and to work with you and a privilege to get to know your earthly angels. I'm so very shocked that your last birthday was indeed your last here in this dimension and I'm so happy I was there with your wife and daughter to celebrate - and what's incredible is you didn't like or want or need a fuss; you gave & gave & gave & you'll continue to give us a chance to smile as we remember what a mag-

nificent human being you were. We're all proud of you! You were admired and respected for extremely good reasons. Thank you... for being YOU - for your character, your values, your help and your inspiration. You were rare & precious!

In those early hours, I reflected on a blog post I wrote after my mother's stroke titled "Glass in My Pocket." *As the days and weeks and months crawled by, Mom and I drilled down through heart and bone to find the courage to take our bags of glass out, the broken pieces of our lives, and show our pieces to each other. We moved them around like a thousand-piece jigsaw puzzle, changing the shape and form of our altered life, our relationship.*

Hadn't I already moved around the broken pieces of my life to create a new mosaic design? Is there truly no bottom to how much heartache a person, a family can endure in one lifetime?

*   *   *

My brother Jim and I were the only two with current passports. Within twenty-four hours of Rocky's death, we had to coordinate a three-week trip to Asia. My closest friends flew in like angels to help me make the trip possible. One friend, Taryn, arrived on my doorstep with a bag full of everything I would need: snacks for the plane, cold/flu medicine, diarrhea medicine, and Airborne to boost my weakened immune system. My other friends took care of other details. They brought food for my parents and reassured me they would be well taken care of. My other two brothers and sisters-in-law would not leave them alone. Another friend hired a cleaning crew because Mom and Dad were in the middle of a kitchen renovation to get the house ready to sell. My brother Paul took a sledgehammer and blew the wall out between the kitchen and dining room. A thin layer of sheetrock dust covered the floor and furniture. Lives are kind of like sheetrock, I thought, both crumble when they're hit too hard.

Bleary-eyed and numb, cloaked in a heavy weight

of grief, I tossed clothes into a suitcase with Taryn's help, disbelieving I was packing to go see my beautiful brother for the last time. If it were not for Taryn's guidance and directing me on what to pack, telling me, "You need more socks, two more shirts, another pair of pants," I would have taken an overnight bag with my passport. This can't be happening. He's on vacation. He's taking his daughter to Disneyland to dance with the princesses.

I massaged the knotted muscles in my neck, wincing in pain as I combed through one-way flights to Kowloon. Once we arrived in Hong Kong, we had to wait for Rocky's body to get released for cremation. Next, we'd fly his ashes back to Bali, but we had no idea when we would be leaving Hong Kong.

"Steve," I said to my husband, "flights are $3,300 apiece, plus the hotel. How are we going to pay for this?"

"Charge it," he said.

Though money couldn't keep me from seeing and honoring Rocky's life, and being there for Setiawan and Anna, I knew it would take a financial toll on us. I resumed my search for an airline ticket. With back-to-back snowstorms, hundreds of flights had been canceled, and there was nothing available for at least two to three days. I was exhausted and desperate to get to Setiawan and Anna but found comfort in knowing she was no longer alone. Jessica's brother had a good friend in Singapore who flew to Kowloon to support Setiawan through the nightmare. Setiawan's brother Farrell also flew over and planned to stay for the duration until we'd all fly back to Bali together.

As I stared at the flights with my splintered heart, my father called. "Susan, Crystal wants to book and pay for your flights."

"What? She's never even met me," I said, astounded.

Crystal was the second wife of my cousin Russ who I had not seen in over thirty years.

After they married, Crystal reached out to our family, determined to reunite us all. They visited my family in the summer of 2012 while I was away on a writing retreat. How could I possibly accept a gift of this magnitude from a stranger—at least to me?

"She doesn't want you and Jim to worry about anything," Dad said.

I hung up the phone; my heart was replete with overwhelming gratitude as I asked God, *Why would this stranger do something like this for me?*

Crystal's assistant made our travel arrangements, including our hotel reservations where my brother, Setiawan, and Anna had been staying on their vacation, the same hotel chain that Rocky was going to work for in Beijing.

"Once you know when you'll be flying to Bali and back to the States," Crystal wrote in an email, "let me know and I'll take care of it."

Six days after Rocky's death, Jim and I boarded our flight to Hong Kong.

CHAPTER 4
A Trip Through Hong Kong Hell

I stumbled my way down the aisle of the plane, wincing as the strap of my computer bag dug into my shoulder. Jim walked in front of me in search of our seats. I laid a hand on top of each seat, chanting, *twenty-three D, twenty-three D*, so I wouldn't forget. I hadn't slept more than two hours a night since I received the call from Setiawan that Rocky had died.

From Portland International Jetport, we will take an hour-and-a-half flight to New Jersey, I tell myself, and then we'll take a sixteen-hour direct flight to Hong Kong International Airport, where we will meet Setiawan and Anna. Maybe Rocky will be there. We had a poor cell connection. Maybe I didn't hear her right.

My nerves sizzled inside a body that had become a holding tank for shock. *Twenty-one, twenty-two.* Jim stored his carry-on in the overhead compartment of seat twenty-three. "Give me your computer," he said.

"My computer?" I clutched the strap. "No. No. I'll put it under my seat." I needed it close. Snacks and every imaginable medicine were stuffed inside my computer bag. I needed them. In case. I didn't trust myself. My memory. If I couldn't see my bag and touch it, I might forget it. I brought my computer along to send updates to my friends, brothers, extended family, and to my inconsolable parents. Two parents who had lost a child and who were terrified they were going to lose two more in a fiery plane crash as we headed overseas to cremate my brother. To cremate my brother. I shoved my computer under the seat, clicked my seatbelt, yanked the strap tight, and stared out the window.

If Jim spoke to me, I didn't hear him. I was trapped inside my mind, reliving the call from Setiawan, her words playing over and over again. *You have to be brave, Sue. Brian is gone.*

"Brian? What? Gone where?" It was odd to hear

my brother's birth name. Formal. Out of place. He was and always would be Rocky to his friends and family. I thought again that maybe Setiawan was talking about someone else. Brian died. Not Rocky.

As the plane ascended from Portland, I turned and looked at Jim with an urge to pinch his arm, to hear him yelp, or squeal, or make any sounds at all to tell me this was real, and that it was happening in real time. I turned away from him as my thoughts drifted back to the calls I had made to my family. I don't recall what I said, what my father said, or my brothers, or my husband. I only knew that I boarded a flight that would take me to see him One. More. Time.

Throughout the longest twenty-three hours of my life, or what I thought were the longest before I arrived in Hong Kong hell, I talked to Rocky silently as if he sat between Jim and me. I cannot sleep on flights, and with little to no sleep over the past six days, I had no idea how I'd remain healthy. My nervous system was shot. Our bodies go into shock for a reason. It allows the time for a slow absorption of the truth to soak through skin and bone until it finally reaches the heart. If the truth, the finality, was absorbed too quickly, I think the heart would drown in a tsunami of grief.

Still and quiet in my seat, I replayed the last conversation I had with Setiawan about the circumstances surrounding Rocky's death. Technically, my brother's heart stopped beating, but that was not the cause of death. When a person dies without a definitive cause, the Hong Kong police get involved and order an autopsy. Setiawan was Hindu, and autopsies were not permitted in her religion. Hindus believe the purpose of life is to exit the physical realm here on earth and enter a state of extinction of all desires and passions. They believe souls live on after death and reincarnate, returning to earth to continue their soul's purpose. Setiawan feared an autopsy would disturb my brother's soul and its departure from his body.

I attempted to reason with Setiawan and said an autopsy was vital to help us understand what caused his death. I asked her questions, like, *What if it was genetic?* I wanted her to understand that knowing his health information was important because of Anna and his son Michael. Setiawan didn't have the power to stop the autopsy from happening, but I wanted her to feel peace, not fear, around a decision that was being made for her. At the end of our conversation, she said, "OK. I understand."

* * *

Twenty-four hours later, we landed on Hong Kong soil. Every muscle in my body ached, and my heart felt shriveled, drying up, and dying. I no longer felt connected to my body. I could feel myself breathing, walking, and talking to my brother as we deplaned, but nothing felt connected in any tangible way. We searched the faces in the airport as we stumbled around in a grief-infused haze, looking for my sister-in-law and niece. We couldn't use our phones because we didn't have an international plan. I thought I had a SIM card, but it turned out to be a memory card.

Blood rushed through my ears, pounding, whooshing. I couldn't think clearly. Where was Setiawan? About thirty minutes later, we spotted her. I embraced her and my niece, peeking over her shoulder, hoping to see Rocky, the smile, the dimples, the jet-black hair, and almond-shaped brown eyes. My younger brother, the one who came to me when he needed his sister. The one who would hug me in a tight squeeze and say, *Thanks for making the trip, Sis. I love you.* I lifted my niece, stared into eyes she inherited from my brother, and pleaded with Rocky, with God, to help me find my way.

On our drive over to the Rosewood Hotel in Kowloon, Setiawan reviewed the harrowing details of Rocky's final hours and what we'd be undertaking over the next several days in Hong Kong. She informed my brother and me that Rocky would be cremated in five days, on February twenty-fourth on Cheung Chau Island, named the dumbbell island due to its shape. How beautiful, I thought, my brother would be cremated on a peaceful, secluded island. Cheung Chau Island, as it turned out, had a population of over 24,500 people and was a major tourist attraction in Hong Kong. The island was only two kilometers long and composed of two granite hills linked by a narrow central causeway—no more than 200 meters wide at points. It's been a major fishing port for centuries and still has a large fishing fleet.

We also learned that no one ever, other than the locals who lived on the island, have been cremated there. They made an exception for Rocky because they were backed up for weeks with scheduled cremations, and he was an American citizen. Setiawan fought to get Rocky cremated closer to where we were staying in Kowloon, but it would have required a much lengthier stay, which was not feasible emotionally or financially. We planned to take the five-hour flight back to Bali to release his ashes at his favorite beach.

We had such little time to complete what felt like an endless list of to-dos. We had to drive thirty minutes to the hospital to get my brother's body released, drive another hour to the ferry, and take a forty-five-minute boat ride to the island where we would say our last goodbyes. The day after my brother's cremation, we'd take my niece to Disneyland to follow through with Rocky's promise to introduce Anna to Elsa, the princess in the Disney Movie *Frozen*. The following day we'd take the trip back to the island and retrieve my brother's ashes. Two days later, we'd fly to Bali and wait three days to get the approval to drive an hour to Pantai Karang Sanur Beach, where we'd release Rocky's ashes in the Indian Ocean.

With the twelve-hour time difference, it can take a week to fully acclimate. There was no time to acclimate to anything. Every day I went to bed at 4:00 or 4:30 a.m. and woke up at 7:00 a.m. The days and nights leaked into each other. In the evenings, I wrote in detail the tasks we completed and places we traveled to, ensuring I chronicled every event because I knew I wouldn't be able to rely on my memory when I returned home. The emails I sent off to my family and friends helped me to feel closer to them as if we were walking through this nightmare together. Before my brother's death, I was a positive, optimistic person, believing there is a blessing in every tragedy. I coached myself through the days, asking Rocky each morning to show me the blessing of the day.

On the first night in my hotel, I went to Setiawan and Rocky's hotel room and saw his clothes hanging in the closet, his silky sky-blue Tommy Bahama shirts, white linen pants, and his leather slip-on shoes at the bedside. This can't be happening. I ran a hand down his shirt as Kevin's wedding flashed through my mind. Rocky had worn this same outfit as he wept his way through his speech. I bit my bottom lip. Please don't let me cry. Not now.

In the silence of his hotel room, I could almost hear him, humming that refrain of the song we had played for Kevin and Jessica, singing those words, *The fairies and the dragonflies, the fairies and the dragonflies, the fairies and the dragonflies will lead you home.*

"Thank you, brother," I said, "for my blessing today."

Mining each day for the blessings helped me to contain my own grief, which gave me the strength and fortitude to support Setiawan and Anna. I cried myself to sleep in the wee hours, but during the day, I searched for the gifts like sea glass on the beach, and every day, I found one. Some were smaller than others, but it didn't matter. When they showed up for me, I thanked God and my brother and tucked them into the pockets of my heart.

The day arrived when it was time for Rocky's cremation, another Hindu tradition. Sleeping had become an activity of the past. Exhausted didn't come close to describing the depth of my fatigue. My muscles and bones felt as though they were melting under the weight of my physical and emotional duress. I had pulled a back muscle earlier in the day, and my niece wanted to be carried at all times, which made breathing painful.

Before leaving for the hospital, we had breakfast in the hotel restaurant. My sister-in-law had several items to place in my brother's casket: pink carnations from my niece, white roses from her, a letter, and several photos. She placed the bag of "offerings," as she called them, on a chair behind me. As soon as our breakfast arrived, the smell alone made me queasy. I breathed through my mouth until everyone finished, slid my chair away from the table, hitting the chair behind me, which knocked over a tall lamp that smashed to the ground and broke in two.

Setiawan said, "What are you doing, Sue?"

Everyone in the restaurant stared at me. The manager rushed over and said something inaudible as he picked up the lamp.

"I'm so sorry," I said. "It was an accident." But the manager didn't seem to care and charged me $175 for the lamp. I thought, *I hope this is not an indicator as to how this day is going to go.*

On our drive to the hospital, questions tramped through my mind. Did I want to see my brother one more time in physical form? How do I face the unimaginable? How do I console my niece and sister-in-law? How do I witness my brother's cremation? How will I survive any of this? The ache in my heart left me feeling that this life was too hard for me. The edges too sharp. I didn't believe I was strong or brave enough to see my brother's still, lifeless body. And yet, there I was an hour later, staring at a body, a face that had no resemblance to my beautiful brother.

They had not taken care of him. His mouth was sewn in a crooked line. His right eye was half open. A nightmare. I moved toward him, leaned over, and pressed my lips against his forehead. Ice cold. I jumped back, startled. My brother had lain in a freezer for days. Bile rose from my stomach, burned my tongue as I bolted from the room. I was dizzy and breathless as I left the hospital and ran full sprint down to the water, my brother behind me. Tears streamed down my skin. I grabbed the railing, leaned over, and stared at the ocean. Without looking at my brother, I said, "They didn't take care of him."

Jim put his arm around me, crying too. "No, they didn't."

We stood there together, plagued by the images of our brother, by his crooked mouth, and half-open eye, haunted by imagining the person who didn't take the time and care to prepare his body for cremation. We were plagued by the finality of his life. As I held onto the railing, which will be branded into my memory until I take my last breath, I was never more grateful that my parents didn't have to see their son. For them, their memories will remain untarnished. When they close their eyes, they'll remember his stunning smile and deep dimples. They'll hear his voice and see the sparkle in his brown eyes. They'll hear him say, "Your favorite son is home." For my brother and me, it will be impossible to think about Rocky without remembering the last time we saw him, lying frozen on the bed.

We followed the hearse to the ferry. An hour later, six men tied ropes around the casket, slid bamboo poles under the rope, and hoisted my brother's casket onto the ferry. Two social workers that helped us throughout this process were both present on the ferry, along with a woman from the funeral home. This offered me some measure of comfort.

Forty-five minutes later, we arrived at Cheung Chau Island. We climbed off the ferry and waited for the men to carry my brother's casket off the boat. I glanced around and understood why it was such a popular tourist attraction. The main street was lined with shops and restaurants. The smell of cooked seafood filled the air. We were overwhelmed by the clusters of locals and tourists, ambling around us. I'd learn later that vehicles were not permitted on the Island, but there were small trucks that carried building supplies and other items. They zipped along the walkways and startled me when they whizzed by.

The men placed my brother's casket on a metal

plank with four wheels and began to push it through the streets. Masses of people walked by us without glancing at the casket as though it were an everyday occurrence. The road to the crematorium was long and narrow, littered with fake money. The locals believed their loved ones would be wealthy in heaven if they left a trail of paper bills. I leaned over and picked one up, thinking I would have given up everything I owned, every cent in my bank account, to bring my brother back.

The road climbed toward the clouds, steeply winding past small houses, bushes with bright red flowers, and an elementary school with a playground. My niece demanded to be carried. We passed her around like a doll until we finally made it to the top of the mountain, to the cemetery and crematorium, sweat-soaked and parched.

I braced myself as I walked into the crematorium. It was small with a few scattered seats and barren walls. I imagined filling the space with his favorite flowers, red roses, and mine, sunflowers. I kneeled at my brother's casket and said my own silent prayers and goodbyes. I laid a hand on his coffin, ran my fingers over his name, written in Magic Marker on a gold plate. Under his name, someone had scrawled *U.S. Citizen.* I filled with a rage that was foreign to me. Suddenly, I hated everything: Hong Kong, the people who didn't take care of my brother's body to prepare it for cremation, the people who wrote his name with a Magic Marker, and the fact that we had to climb the mountain twice. We would have to make the same trip back in three days to collect what would be left of my brother, a bag full of ashes.

I felt a welling sadness that frightened me. My brother had died. He would not be able to raise his daughter, and Anna would never know the depth of her father's love. Setiawan had lost her life partner and would forge ahead as a single mother without employment. What were they going to do? Light-headed, the room began to spin. I listened to Setiawan recite a Hindu prayer, Anna beside her with her tiny hands clasped, head bent in prayer. When we finished with our prayers and letters, all of us too exhausted and numb to cry, we watched as the casket moved on a conveyor belt through a red curtain.

In the Hindu religion, from what I've read, cremation is one of the most important rituals after death because the fire is associated with purity and has the power to scare away harmful ghosts, spirits, and demons. Cremation releases the soul from the body so it can be reborn. There are exceptions. Children under the age of two are innocent and do not require purification. Holy men, lepers, and people with smallpox are typically buried. It was confusing because Rocky was not Hindu. Though I believed in reincarnation, I also believed Rocky's sweet soul passed over to the other side the moment his heart stopped beating.

As his casket disappeared behind the curtain, like the final act in a Broadway play, I thought, *This is too much. I can't do this. I can't.* I went outside to breathe. I wanted to be anywhere other than at the crematorium in Hong Kong. I walked through the cemetery and looked out over the water. The views were breathtaking, and I felt Rocky's presence. I said, "We're taking Anna to Disneyland tomorrow like you promised. The day after, we'll come back for your ashes and release them at your favorite beach. Just two more sleeps, honey. I love you."

Thanks for making the trip, Sis. I love you too.

I hoisted Anna on my hip and said, "Want to go to the playground on our way back to the ferry?"

She nodded and snuggled her head under my chin.

"I love you, Anna." I wrapped my arms around her, held on to her like an anchor, to ground me, to keep me from tumbling off the edge of my tilted world, and began the trek back down the mountain. Anna's heart beat against my own, which triggered another stream of tears because it occurred to me that Michael was the same age as Anna when Rocky left his son and moved halfway across the world.

When we got to the playground, Anna transformed into a normal three-and-a-half-year-old child, spinning on the merry-go-round, swinging, giggling, and playing as a child should, not walking down a mountain after witnessing her father's cremation. How was I going to leave her behind? When would I see my brother's daughter again? Why does love have to hurt so deeply?

Before we boarded the ferry to go back to the hotel, I stopped at a jewelry vendor and bought a silver bracelet, its links were x's, like kisses. I said to Rocky, "I'll never take it off." Then I bought seven identical bracelets: one for my mother, one for each of my four sisters-in-law, one for the social worker who had helped us, and one for me.

*　　*　　*

Another night without sleep and without sustenance. The days were gray, cold, and loud. Construction on every corner assaulted my senses. My legs moved. I walked. I talked. I picked at rice noodles and fish cakes without savoring the authentic Asian spices. The Susan I once knew had retreated someplace where I could no longer find her. If it were not for Anna, I would have pleaded with God to take my soul in the night as he had done to my brother.

As I lay awake in the hotel room bed, waiting for morning to nudge me out of my stupor, I ran my fingers over the bracelet and replayed the video Setiawan had made around Christmastime of my brother and Anna. Rocky smiled as he held her tiny hand and twirled her around the living room, dancing to theme song, *Let it Go* from the Disney movie *Frozen*. They talked about the princesses she'd meet in Disneyland.

My right eye twitched from fatigue and incessant crying throughout the nights. The knots between my shoulder blades were hard as rocks. I couldn't imagine going to Disneyland the day after my brother's cremation but that was exactly where we were going to spend the day. We'd ride the Mass Transit Railway (MTR) from Kowloon to Lantau Island, which would take us less than an hour. "I'm doing this for you, Rocky, and for

Anna. Please help me hold it together."

After breakfast, we walked to the Kowloon subway station and feigned excitement as we rambled on to
Anna about the famous characters she'd meet: Goofy,
Mickey Mouse, Donald Duck, and the princesses: Belle,
her favorite, Elsa, Cinderella, and Snow White. Anna
was somber throughout the subway ride. In Sunny Bay,
we switched subways and rode the Disney MTR for the
remainder of our commute. We sat on plush cobalt seats
and looked out windows designed in a Mickey-Mouse
silhouette. For those who chose to stand, they clutched
Mickey Mouse rungs that hung from rods fastened to
the ceiling.

When we arrived at Disneyland, we walked to the
booth to buy day passes. As soon as we strolled through
the gate, Setiawan had a full-blown meltdown. "I can't
go, Sue," she said, crying. "You take Anna. I'll meet you
at the gate later."

I stared at her with both compassion and disbelief.
I, too, didn't want to be in Disneyland. Between my exhaustion and grief, and the jubilant characters dressed
in bright, vibrant colors, screeching children, and the
overwhelming joy people exuded, I teetered on the
brink of insanity. This is wrong. All wrong. My external
world was in complete opposition to my internal world.
They were en route for a head-on collision. "Maybe we
should just leave," I said.

"No," Setiawan said. "It was on Brian's bucket list."

I imagined reaching out, placing my hands on her
shoulders, shaking her, and saying, "Please stop calling
him Brian." My brother was only Brian to Setiawan and
his colleagues. "I think Rocky would understand if we
left."

I held Anna in my arms, subdued and listless as she
rested her head against my shoulder.

"He promised Anna," Setiawan said.

I nodded and said, "OK." I glanced at the map in
my hand of the Disney Park, which was an overwhelming maze. "We'll get lunch over there," I said, point-
ing to the first restaurant I saw not far from where we

stood. "If you change your mind, meet us there."

Jim and Setiawan's brother Farrell followed Anna and me to the restaurant.

"Is Mommy coming?" Anna asked.

I rubbed her back. "Mommy is sad. She's taking a little break. Do you want a cheeseburger, some French fries, and a soda?" I asked, as I silently prayed that Setiawan would be able to regain composure and rejoin us.

Anna nodded. I cuddled her on my lap while Jim and Farrell ordered the food. "You're going to meet your favorite princess today," I said.

"I miss my daddy," she whispered.

"I know, angel," I said, stroking her fine curly black hair. "Remember, Daddy lives here." I tapped a finger over her heart. "He's always with you."

I stretched lunch out for as long as possible with a toddler who was antsy and wanted to meet Belle. As I stood to throw out the trash, Setiawan blessedly walked over to our table and said, "I'm coming with you."

Thank God, I thought as I put my arm around her shoulder. "You sure you're going to be able to handle this?" I asked, afraid she'd change her mind, turn, and march away.

"Brian would want me to," she said.

Another blessing. Thank you, brother.

There were people and chairs lined along a magical brick road, waiting for the *Fantasy of Flight* Parade to begin. I pointed and said, "The parade is going to start soon. You'll get to see the princesses."

Anna slipped her hand into mine as we walked toward the parade. We passed a store that sparkled with princess dresses. Anna stared, mesmerized.

Setiawan said, "You like? You want one?"

Anna nodded. I looked over at my brother and Farrell. "This could take a while. Don't go too far. I don't want to lose you guys."

Inside, little girls tried on Snow White, Belle, Sleeping Beauty, and Cinderella dresses, piling them in a heap on the floor. It was mayhem. A headache inched across my right temple and settled behind my eye. Anna tried on a few, lacking the enthusiasm she'd have if her father were present. When Setiawan helped her into the buttercup-yellow gown that Princess Belle wore in *Beauty and the Beast*, she refused to take it off.

"That's the one," I said. My petite niece was stunning in the dress with her almond skin, hair as black as ebony, tiny chiseled nose, and a mouth like my brother's. I pulled a box from the shelf that held both a jewel-studded crown and a gold sparkling wand. "You can't be a princess," I said, "without a crown and a wand." I opened the box, took the crown, and placed it on her head.

When I handed her the wand, Anna smiled. "I'm a real princess now."

After we paid for the princess costume, we went outside where Jim and Farrell waited for us. As Setiawan snapped pictures with her iPad, I swallowed the ball of sadness in my throat. She's beautiful, Rocky. Please show me a sign that you are here. I want to feel your presence. I miss you so much. I imagined him holding Anna's hand, twirling her around like he did in the video, asking, "Who loves you most?" Beads of sweat rolled down my back. My body, my cells, all of me wept for this child's loss, for mine, for my brothers', for my parents', for Setiawan's. For all of us.

Jim put his arm around my shoulder. "How are you holding up?"

"I'm so very tired," I said.

He ran a hand down my back. No words were necessary. Jim was tired too, and what promised to be a long day had only begun.

Music drifted through the air. "The parade is starting," I said. "We should go."

Scores of people lined the brick road. I nudged my way through the crowd, tugging Anna along behind me, hoping to get her a front row view. A marching band kicked off the parade. Band members were dressed in stark white pants and red vests, as they blared horns and beat drums. My headache mushroomed into a full-blown migraine. I sank my hand into my jeans pocket and pulled out two Excedrin tablets, popped them into my mouth, and washed them down with what little water I had left in my bottle.

The band moved on, giving way to lavish floats. Dumbo, ears flapping, hovered over the title float. Mickey Mouse drove a giant airship named "Flights of Friendship." The next float featured Winnie the Pooh next to his pals Eeyore and Tigger. Four performers dressed as Tigger bounced around on pogo sticks while bungee-jumping bees rose into the air, performing tricks. On a swan-shaped airboat, adorned with giant fuchsia and pastel-pink roses and green petals, Snow White, Cinderella, Sleeping Beauty, and Belle waved at the crowd.

I kneeled next to Anna. "Oh look," I said. "There's Belle."

Anna was mesmerized when Belle picked her out of a gaggle of little girls, flashed a smile, and waved.

"Oh my gosh, Anna. She's waving at you." Thank you, Rocky. I don't know if you're really here, but I have to believe you are behind these small blessings. It's the only thing I have to hang onto.

Anna held up her tiny hand and waved back. I tucked her against me, kissed her cheek, and said, "You're the most beautiful princess here today."

She laid her head on my shoulder. "I wish Daddy was here."

"Me too, baby girl. Me too." I would have swapped hearts with my brother if it could have brought him home to Anna.

As one float after another passed by, I searched for my brother's face in the swarm of people. Where are you? You can't possibly be gone. But he was, and soon, Jim and I would be leaving Setiawan and Anna a half a world away.

When the last float, "To Infinity and Beyond," based on *Toy Story*, came toward us, I wished I could have used Anna's wand to magically transport us home. Buzz Lightyear and the Green Paratroopers finished the parade with parachute bungee jumping, delighting both children and adults. They cheered and clapped. I was struck again at how they could possibly be happy and joyful given what had just happened to our family.

For the remainder of the day, we stood in line after line for Anna to get her picture taken with Disney characters, and of course, Belle. She had no interest in going on any of the rides. Even at her tender age, she was courageous and brave as she followed through with Rocky's wishes. He had described the Disney characters she'd meet and how they'd get their picture taken.

"Where's Goofy?" she asked.

Rocky promised they would get a special picture of Goofy for Grandpa, his favorite Disney character. We combed Disneyland, searching for the anthropomorphic dog with a Southern drawl. When we found him dressed in his orange shirt and black vest, I exhaled a grateful breath. My migraine had turned low-grade thanks to the Excedrin. One more picture and we could check this off my brother's bucket list. Everyone was "over" Disneyland, including Anna. Tomorrow, we'd make the long hike back up the mountain to retrieve my brother's ashes. I only had to hang on for two more days before we boarded a five-hour flight to Bali to bring our brother home.

CHAPTER 5
Ashes to Ashes

On the flight to Bali, Setiawan carried the sack that held Rocky's ashes. I couldn't touch or look at the bag that was chock-full of what was left of my brother. I had been a seeker of higher spiritual truths, committed to walking a path toward enlightenment for twenty years. I read book after book on the afterlife and immersed myself in the teachings of spiritual leaders, like Moo-ji, Eckhart Tolle, Deepak Chopra, Wayne Dyer, Neale Donald Walsch, and Marianne Williamson. They taught me that we are consciousness itself. Our body dies, but our soul lives on. Though my beliefs and convictions offered me comfort, and I had deep faith in God, I wasn't going to see my brother in physical form again in this lifetime.

Did I believe I'd see him when it was my time to pass over? Yes, but I had never lost someone so close or so young. It was unimaginable to me that I was capable of feeling that depth of pain. Rocky was never going say, "Only two more sleeps, Sis." He was never going to wrap his arms around me, hold me in a tight embrace, and say, "I love you, Sis." I was never going to have the privilege of holding his secrets or laugh until my stomach hurt as he shared stories of his adventures. There were never going to be any more visits back to the States. It was over. I clenched my fist and screamed silently, *Why, God?*

"You okay?" Jim asked.

"I'm pissed," I said. "Pissed that he's gone."

"I know, Sues," he said. Jim was the only person who called me "Sues" and it softened the jagged edges of my anger.

Jim is a special human being. At seventeen years old, a car struck him as he crossed a busy street during a torrential downpour, throwing him thirty-five feet. When he reached the hospital, he was pronounced dead on arrival. Though I came close to losing my oldest brother, my parents protected my siblings and me from the severity of his accident. I was only twelve years old and had no idea Jim arrived at the hospital without a heartbeat. The doctors were able to resuscitate him, and he emerged ten days later from a coma. He had to relearn how to do simple tasks: how to hold a fork, button his shirt, walk, and talk. He spent weeks in a rehabilitation facility. The near-death experience changed him. There is a quiet tranquility about my brother and an unwavering optimistic attitude toward life regardless of the circumstances.

On a camping trip we took years ago, a week of relentless rain "dampened" our spirits and left our tents and sleeping bags a soggy wet mess. While we all hung out under a tarp, contemplating whether or not we should abandon the trip, Jim sat in his canoe, casting a fishing line into the lake, yelling, "The sun is going to come out anytime now." And the sun did show its face on our last day after we packed up our drenched camping gear and headed home.

"You were right," I said. "The sun came out."

I looked over at my oldest brother with a deep gratitude for his presence. Setiawan and Anna sat several rows behind us. "Do you really think she'll move to Maine?" I asked.

"I don't know," he said. "It won't be easy."

Setiawan and I had talked ceaselessly in Hong Kong about the possibility of selling her house and moving to Maine. Neither one of us knew what a move would entail. Anna had dual citizenship, but Setiawan's five-year visa would run out in December, only nine months away. Without my brother, we didn't know if she would be able to get her visa renewed to move to the States permanently. She asked numerous questions about living in Maine. What would she do for work? How much would it cost? How much was daycare? Where would she live? The more we discussed the possibility, the more disheartened we became by the minutia.

I learned later that Setiawan would be denied a renewed visa because Anna had dual citizenship. If she came into the country with Anna, Setiawan would be able to become a U.S. resident, but that would not be permitted because Indonesia was considered a terrorist country. If Setiawan had family in the U.S. that met the Family-Based Immigration criteria, she may have been able to secure a visa. Setiawan had to have a parent, spouse, son, daughter, brother, or sister who lived in the U.S. Without Rocky, there would be no reason for her to visit the United States. I couldn't imagine leaving them in Bali with all the memories she'd be facing when she returned to their home, but I understood that Setiawan's life was in Ubud with her parents, siblings, nieces, and nephews. It would be painful to say goodbye because I knew that it would be years before I'd be able to visit them again.

* * *

When we entered the home my brother had built, the one he'd been so proud of and given me a tour of on Skype, he was present in every room. I searched for him in his closet and ran my hand down his silky ocean blue Tommy Bahama shirts and crisp white linen pants that hung there, just as they had in his hotel room, waiting for him. Slip-on loafers were lined in a neat row, and pictures of his wide smile and deep dimples sat on tables in neat little frames. "Where are you?" I asked, crushing his favorite T-shirt into my face as I inhaled his scent.

In the evening, I tiptoed outside and sat on his porch swing, ready to hear the crunch of dried Balinese grass under his footsteps. My sister-in-law came outside too, where she fell to her knees, pounded the earth, and begged to understand what she'd done so wrong to deserve this heartbreak. She looked around in the darkness, searching for God, for any celestial being who could answer the one question that burned on her tongue, *Why did this happen to her? To Anna? To Brian? Why?*

I gripped the swing, hung my head, and wept for all their unrealized dreams. I wept for Anna and what she would do in the future without her daddy to take away her pain. I wept for my brother who would never experience his daughter's high school graduation, her college tours, and maybe a wedding. I wept for the possible grandbabies he would never hold and the stories he would never share with her. How would she ever know how magical he was, how he adored every inch of her, and how much he wanted her?

I walked toward Setiawan as she continued to pound the earth with a white-knuckled fist, screaming, "What did we do so wrong, God?" My heart ached for her too, my brother's wife, his love, the one who held his dreams as if they were her own. The one Rocky imagined sitting next to while they rocked in their porch swing, holding each other's wrinkled-skinned hands as their grandchildren splashed around in the pool they had planned to install.

Did my loss compare to hers? Both of our lives had been turned upside down. Mine by grief over losing a sibling I had known since his birth, a sibling who played a role in shaping the person I had become. Setiawan lost her husband and her daughter's father. She lost her only source of income. I would return to my life in the States while she would have to rebuild her life without Rocky. We were both hurting and though a knife straight through the heart would have been a comfort in comparison, I believed I had to remain strong and support Setiawan. When I returned to Maine, I would have to be available to support my parents. I was both surprised and infinitely grateful that their hearts continued to beat. When would it be my turn to grieve openly?

A deeper compassion took root as I kneeled down beside Setiawan and laid a hand on her back. "You didn't do anything to deserve this. It's nothing you did. I know it feels like it, but you aren't being punished."

Setiawan looked up at me with dark rings under her eyes. She said, "Why this happen to us, Sue? What we do that was so wrong? Maybe *your* family is cursed."

Goose pimples rose on my skin, and a chill rippled up my spine despite the 80-degree temperature. "Cursed?" I whispered. "You think my family is cursed?"

She nodded. "Lots of bad things have happened to you guys. Maybe your family is cursed."

A hush fell over the night. I stared into the eyes of the woman my brother had married, the one I flew 10,000 miles to support through this harrowing, horrific ordeal, and I saw a stranger staring back with dark, penetrating eyes. "Tragedies happen in every family. Mine is not cursed. Please don't say that again," I said and left her on her knees, whimpering in the silence of the night.

As I walked into the house, memories of the bad things flashed through my mind: the death of my biological father when I was ten months old, Jim getting hit by a car, Kevin losing his house in a flood, Paul struggling with his life-threatening health issues, my mother's stroke, and Rocky's death. In my objective, analytical mind, I knew that everyone faced multiple traumatic events, but in my unrelenting sorrow, Setiawan's comments invited another chill that made me shudder as I asked myself, *What if my family is cursed?*

* * *

Three days after arriving in Bali, we had another long list of tasks. First, we went to the U.S. Embassy to complete a stack of paperwork so Setiawan could receive Social Security. They were nine months behind on applications. My sister-in-law had no other source of income. She had minimal credit card debt and no savings. Rocky and Setiawan had poured my brother's income into building their home in Ubud and owned it outright. Prior to my departure to Hong Kong, one of my best friends started a GoFundMe page, raising several thousand dollars for Setiawan and Anna. She'd be able to pay off her credit card and live on the remainder of the money until she began receiving the Social

Security checks. Now that they would not be moving to China with my brother, Setiawan would also need to buy a car because driving Anna to and from school on the scooter was not safe.

By the end of the meeting at the Embassy, we were all relieved. They guesstimated Setiawan would receive $1,200 a month. Rocky had told me that people could live a good life on $200 a month in Bali. When Setiawan began receiving the monthly check, she'd be wealthy, I thought. If she were allowed to move to Maine, she'd have a difficult time securing housing for that amount.

After we returned home from the Embassy, Setiawan received approval to release Rocky's ashes at his favorite beach, Pantai Karang Sanur, an hour away by car. Our plan was to arrive at sunrise the following morning because it was Rocky's most treasured time of day. Each new morning promised another dreaded, depleting series of events. I couldn't remember what it felt like to awaken energized. After an early dinner, we retired to bed, and I knew it would be another sleepless night.

Since my arrival in Bali, I slept in Setiawan and Rocky's bed because she didn't want to sleep alone. For me, I felt closer to my brother tucked under his covers with his daughter between his wife and me. I lay awake at 4:00 a.m. with Anna's almond-skinned legs and arms curled around me while she slept. I listened to her soft breaths and could feel her chest rising and falling. I wanted to hold her there in the safe, quiet space of sleep where she could dream beautiful dreams. When the alarm sounded at 5:00 a.m., I swept her dark curly hair from her eyes, snuggled her close, kissed her cheek, and said, "It's time to get up, baby girl."

Anna cooed and placed her tiny hand on my cheek. Her long lashes fluttered as she struggled to open her eyes.

"I will wake her up after I take a shower," Setiawan said.

I relished in the few stolen minutes when it was just the two of us. I closed my eyes, wishing I could bring her father back. Instead, she would watch her daddy's ashes float away from her as the sun rose.

When Setiawan returned, she said, "You have to get up, Sue. We can't be late."

I gave Anna another kiss and pried myself away from her. "I'll take a quick shower."

Under the hot stream of the shower, I tipped my head, hoping the water would rinse away the hopeless feeling in my heart. Five minutes later, I stepped out of the shower and caught a glimpse of myself in the mirror. With red and swollen eyes, I looked ready for my own casket. I massaged cream into my skin and slipped into a beautiful blue and white sleeveless dress, speckled with tiny crystal stones, the one Anna helped me to pick out during their last trip to Maine in June 2013, eight short months before Rocky's death.

We walked out of the house into the dark and piled into the rental car, subdued and alone with our thoughts. Setiawan's brother and his family would meet us at the beach. On the drive to Pantai Karang Sanur, saliva filled my mouth. I was going to throw up. I swallowed, rubbed my stomach, and inhaled a few breaths. I wasn't ready to let him go. There were too many dreams to share, conversations to have about Anna, and places to travel to together. Would I ever see my niece again?

When we arrived at our destination, Setiawan, her brother Farrell, his three children, and Anna entered *Pura Blangjong* (a Hindu temple) for prayer. Diann, Farrell's wife, was menstruating and therefore prohibited from entering the temple while she was bleeding. Jim, Diann, and I sat at a picnic table and waited until they emerged from the temple. Together, we all walked down to the beach where I thought we were going to release his ashes.

Setiawan pointed in the distance—about 200 feet away—to a stone platform with a cottage (a small structure with a roof where people sat to watch the sunset). "We have to go there," she said.

I blinked and said, "You're kidding, right?"

"No, Sue. Come on," she said as she walked across

the sand toward the ocean. She carried a silver bowl that held the sack of ashes, flowers, and photographs. Her sister-in-law balanced a bright yellow and pink woven basket on her head, filled with five or six smaller bamboo baskets (known as keben) that Setiawan would use as receptacles for offerings to the gods.

As Setiawan walked ahead of me, I looked at my beautiful dress and suede sandals. If I knew we were going to wade through water, I would have worn a bathing suit. I slung my purse over my shoulder, kicked off my sandals, and held them as we walked through mudflats and hip-high sea to a point overlooking the Indian Ocean. In awe, we gazed at the highest mountain in Bali, Mount Agung, its peak reaching through the clouds. The beauty vanished as we each felt the first and second sting. Jellyfish shot venom through our feet with each step we took as we went deeper and deeper into the water. The pain, for the moment, distracted me from the ache in my heart.

With bleeding, burning toes, I clambered up slick rocks to the stone landing. We paused while Setiawan unpacked the pink and yellow basket. She placed gold, purple, pink, and yellow flower petals into the five smaller baskets. When she finished, we followed her as she carried the offerings and silver bowl down the other side until we reached a spot that sparkled as the sun rose.

We stood on the rocks while Setiawan and Anna waded into the ankle-high water, kneeled down, and opened the bag that held my brother's pale-gray ashes. Jim clicked photographs, capturing the last of Rocky's remains as Setiawan and Anna each held a corner of the sack and tilted it toward the ocean. The ashes spilled into the water, mushrooming into a gray mass, swirling around Setiawan and Anna, clinging to their kebayas (traditional blouse-dress combination), which triggered another wave of nausea. I massaged my stomach, watching as his ashes glinted under the Balinese sun. Setiawan set flowers, pictures, and the baskets afloat. Tears blurred my vision. I placed a hand over my heart and asked, *What now, Rocky?*

When we returned to my brother and Setiawan's home, there would be no time for much-needed rest. We had to prepare for another Hindu ceremony that would release his spirit to a higher realm. The ceremony was supposed to take place in the backyard, but Setiawan moved it inside the house because of a light rain shower.

Elders from the village came to prepare for the ritual, dressed in white tops, white sarongs, and undengs (headcloths). They created an assembly line from the sliding back door all the way out to the gardens. An elder held a hose, while another began picking up square concrete garden stones. One by one, the elder rinsed mud and ants off the stones and passed them down the assembly line. Another elder placed the stones on my brother's living room floor. Together, they lay the stones in a large square, and then stacked the stones two high, leaving a twenty-by- twenty-inch hollow square in the center.

"What are they doing?" I asked Jim.

"Looks like they're making a fire pit," he said, stroking his beard. "Probably just for show. They're not going to light a fire in the house."

"Hope you're right," I said.

While the men made a makeshift fire pit, the women opened boxes full of bright jewel-colored fruit: mango steen, rambutan, ambarella, pomelo, coconuts, pineapples, and bananas. They pulled out heads of crisp lettuce, corn on the cob, several varieties of beans and rice, blazing orange and yellow flowers, candles, and sacred cloths. They dressed the three pineapples in the orange cloths and placed leis around the stems.

"They look like people," I said.

"This is wild," Jim said.

My brother and I watched in awe as they transformed the living room into a holy grail. They created an altar and decorated it with a smattering of fruits and vegetables. Then they repeated the process with the fire pit, placing bamboo baskets of beans, rice, flowers, and vegetables on each stone. Two other men carried in armfuls of kindling and piled it into the fire pit. An hour and a half later, we were ready to begin the ceremony.

Before entering the circle, we were required to wear sarongs to cover our legs below the knees and sashes around our waists. The Balinese women wore kebayas and leis around their necks. Setiawan wore a translucent cobalt silk kebaya with striking embroidered maroon flowers stitched around the neck and along the hemline. She lent me a black and white sarong that she tied for me in authentic Balinese style. My brother Jim looked out of character, wearing a brown and white sarong cinched with a red sash and orange lei around his neck.

The Elders hung long pieces of string from one end of the ceiling to the other and attached braided palm leaves. As the leader or holy man began to chant, they lit the logs and threw rice and flowers on the fire. Flames shot high into the air and licked the string, singeing it. Though the sliding glass doors were wide open, plumes of gray smoke filled the room, which triggered the fire alarm. I hustled Anna out of the room and led her into the bedroom. I shoved towels under the door to prevent the smoke from seeping in. I opened another door that led to the backyard to let the fresh air circulate.

Jim came into the room and whispered, "They're going to burn the house down. Can you believe this?"

"No. I can't," I said as I imagined Rocky walking into his living room and dousing the flames with a bucket of water. "I'm going to talk to Setiawan." I opened the bedroom door and motioned to her. Setiawan got up from the circle and walked into the bedroom. I closed the door behind her and said, "I don't think this is safe."

Setiawan was offended and angry that we had left the ceremony. "It's fine, Sue," she said and stormed out of the room.

Jim said, "She's going to have smoke damage all

over these walls."

"Well, there's nothing we can do about it. It's like they don't even hear the fire alarm going off," I said. "It's crazy."

Jim stepped outside into the humid air to smoke a cigar and drink a can of Bintang beer. I stayed with Anna, tucked her into bed, and read her a story. She seemed unfazed by the fire in the living room as though it were life as usual. The ceremony lasted for more than two hours. When it ended, the holy men put the fire out while the women disassembled the altar. They all helped to clean up the debris from the fire, brought the stones outside, and finally left. Farrell, Setiawan's brother, cleaned the tile floor that was miraculously undamaged. I walked past him and ran my hand over the soot-covered walls, remembering how proud Rocky had been of his home. What would he think about what happened tonight?

The scent of smoke lingered as Jim and I joined Setiawan and her family for dinner. It was after 9:00 p.m., and we were all famished. As we ate sticky rice with our fingers, fresh fish and chicken kabobs, I said to Setiawan's family, her brother, sister-in-law, and their three kids, "We'd like to take you to dinner tomorrow on our way to the airport." Our flight didn't take off until 10:00 p.m., and Farrell was driving us to Ngurah Rai International Airport, an hour away. We'd have several hours of "wait" time at the airport.

"Matur Suksma," Farrell said.

Farrell and his family spoke very little English, and Jim and I spoke zero Bahasa with the exception of a few polite phrases, like hello, thank you, good morning, and goodbye. Farrell had said, "Thank you very much."

"Our pleasure," I said. We planned to bring them to another one of Rocky's favorite eateries. We took them to Naughty Nuri's on Monday. It had been our plan, my brother's and mine, to go to the same restaurants where Rocky took us when we visited in 2009 so we could honor his spirit and share our fondest memories of that trip.

After dinner, we cleaned the dishes, packed the food away, and said goodbye to Setiawan's family. It was finally time for bed, and I prayed for sleep. The following day would be a long travel day. We would leave Thursday night and land in Maine late Friday afternoon. I needed a restful night.

Before we headed into the bedroom, Setiawan said, "I have to talk to you, Sue."

"Now?" I asked. The heat rose in my body, and my left hand tingled. Those two sensations were my intuitive guides, alerting me that the conversation would not be a pleasant one. "What do you want to talk about? It's late. We should really get some sleep." I stretched my arms over my head and yawned to punctuate my point. Jim had already gone to bed, and I wished he stood next to me as a pillar to hang on to.

"Why did you abandon your brother?" she asked with her arms crossed.

Not again. Not tonight. I can't do this. We've been over this. The last time Rocky came to Maine in June 2013, he wasn't himself. The Xanax he took for the vertigo mixed with his drinking altered his personality and warped his perceptions of reality. The day they were flying home, I brought everyone chicken bomb subs from our pub because Setiawan had requested them. Rocky took the sandwich without looking at me or saying, "Thanks." I couldn't think of anything I had done to upset him.

"Can I talk to you alone?" I had asked him.

"Yup."

We went outside and sat on my parents' front steps. I looked at him and asked, "Are you mad at me?"

"You don't care about me," he said. "You abandoned me."

"Abandoned you? What are you talking about?" I searched his eyes and the expression on his stoic face for more information about this ludicrous statement. He chose to move a twelve-hour-time-zone away and I abandoned him? He wasn't the one who had to drop out of graduate school and drive forty-five minutes to the New England Rehabilitation center every day for seven weeks straight after Mom had her stroke. He hadn't given up every Saturday for the past seven years to spend time with Mom, trim her nails, shave her legs, help her bathe, take her to lunch, and take her shopping to give Dad a little respite and to give Mom a social outlet. Sadness and anger melded together, and I held them both at the same time.

"You haven't asked me anything about my life since I've been here," he said.

Stunned, I said, "I don't know what you're talking about. We sat for hours the other night, and you told me all about your new position as the CEO. Not to mention, Rocky, since you've been home, we've had one cookout after another. It's not like we've had scads of alone time." Tears welled. "And I've come over here every single day since you've been home, and you're always asleep in the middle of the afternoon."

"Never mind," he said. "This is my last trip home."

"I love you and you know I love you." I placed a hand on his back. "I'm not sure where this is coming from, Rocky, but it's not true."

I believe that Rocky was depressed by the vertigo and the way it impacted his life. I also know he missed us, his family. After Anna was born, he wanted us to be more a part of her life. When he returned to Bali, he had long conversations with my father. Rocky made amends and apologized for the way he left. He ended up writing a post on Facebook about what a wonderful time he had with us, and I choose to believe this is true.

When he flew home that evening after our unresolved conversation, I waited, week after week, for Rocky to contact me directly and apologize, but he never did. I think he waited for the same thing, a call from me. We finally talked on Christmas Eve, as we did every year, but my whole family was in the room, and we never had an opportunity for a one-to-one chat before his death in February.

"I didn't abandon Rocky," I said. "We already had this conversation in Hong Kong."

"He said you did. You not there for him. You say you were, but you were not."

She may as well have taken a can of gasoline, doused me down, and tossed a match. Setiawan and I had a complicated relationship. It was during their last visit to the States the previous June that I thought we had made a breakthrough. She apologized for being mean to me and said she was immature and had grown up since becoming a mother. Rocky and Setiawan had made several visits to the States since they married in November 2008. She confused me. There were times when she was sweet and kind, expressing her adoration and love and then, without warning, she would turn on me. I struggled with my attempts to understand her. I asked myself, *Was it cultural? Was it immaturity? Was it a mental health issue? Was it some combination of the three and now compounded by grief?* I understood she had earned the right to be angry—it was a stage of the grieving process—but I didn't have the emotional reserves to remain balanced, calm, and clear-headed.

I slapped the kitchen table with my hand, startling both Setiawan and Anna. "I'm not doing this with you tonight. I don't understand you. One minute you love me and the next you hate me," I said. "It's exhausting. I know you're hurting. I'm hurting too, but please stop telling me I abandoned my brother. I think it's best if I sleep on the couch tonight."

"I not going to the airport with you tomorrow," she said as she marched off to her bedroom and closed the door behind her. Two minutes later, she returned with a blanket and a pillow and said, "You can sleep in the bedroom if you want."

I didn't want to, but I couldn't let our last night end on a bad note. Regardless of how complex our relationship had become, my brother loved her and his daughter. I loved my brother and my niece. I would do whatever I had to do to maintain a relationship with Setiawan so I'd be able to have an ongoing relationship with Anna.

"OK," I said. "I'm sorry."

"Me too," she said.

I lay on my brother's bed that night, replaying the first trip I took to Bali and how poorly it had ended when I threw rupiahs at her. I rolled over, my last and final time in his home, and rested a hand on Anna's back as it rose and fell in rhythm with her breaths, her heartbeat. I stared at Setiawan sleeping soundly, asking myself the same question I had in the past. *What is it?* And it hit me. I couldn't trust her words, her emotions, or her behavior. If she said she loved me, I couldn't trust that to be true because her love felt conditional based on whether I agreed with her as her mood shifted.

The morning was awkward due to the tension in the air between Setiawan and me. I tiptoed around on shards of glass, holding words in my mouth, terrified I'd say something that would trigger an outburst, either on her end or mine. We were both emotionally tapped and raw. We ate breakfast together and focused our attention on Anna, conversing with her rather than with each other. Shortly after breakfast, she drove Anna to school, returned home, and said, "I'm very tired. I'm going to take a nap."

Setiawan slept for most of the day, succumbing to exhaustion. I was relieved. My anxiety had risen when she took Anna to school because I didn't know how we were going to get through the day together.

While she rested, Jim and I strolled into town in ninety-degree weather and eighty percent humidity. Thirsty and drenched in sweat, we bought some Bintang—the same beer we drank with Rocky when we visited him in 2009. Earlier, Jim had discovered a path in the jungle-like woods in the back of Rocky's house. We took our beer and walked down the path to a man-made muddy canal where the locals bathed. We drank the beer, reminisced about our trip, our brother, and our experiences that felt no more real to me than the Disney characters that had danced in our faces in Hong Kong. I talked to him about Setiawan and our conversation the previous night.

"She's young and hurting, Sues," he said. "You need to cut her some slack."

"Yeah. I know. Maybe you're right." We managed to eat up several hours by the stream, polishing off the six-pack. "To you, Rocky," we said and clinked our cans.

With a slight buzz, we headed back to the house to shower, finish packing, and prepare for our long trip home. Farrell and his family would pick us up early; we'd treat them to dinner, and then he'd drop us off at the airport several hours before our flight. I couldn't wait to wake up in my own bed.

I sat in the backseat with Anna on our way to the restaurant. Setiawan changed her mind in the morning and decided she would like to accompany us during our last few hours in Bali. I'm not sure what changed her mind, and I didn't ask. I had more time with Anna, and I was grateful to Setiawan for not taking that away from me. I wiggled Anna's toes, reciting the nursery rhyme "This little piggy went to the market. This little piggy stayed home. This little piggy ate roast beef. This little piggy had none. And this little piggy went wee, wee, wee all the way home." When I wiggled her pinky toe and said the last line, I ran my fingers up her belly and tickled her under the chin.

Anna inherited the perfect combination of her mother and father. She looked neither Balinese nor American. She had my brother's smile, his mouth, chiseled nose, and dark hair. She had her mother's roasted-almond skin tone, dark eyes, and petite build. Rocky told me story after story of the way people were drawn to her. I witnessed this firsthand at Disneyland. Five different strangers walked up to Setiawan and asked her permission to take Anna's picture with their daughters.

Anna giggled and said, "Again."

We played the game for the entire hour ride to the Cendana Cafe on Muaya Beach Jimbaran. Memories of Rocky assaulted me as I stepped out of the car and smelled the scent of grilled fish in the air. This was the first restaurant he brought us to when we visited him in 2009. It felt right to end our trip here. We walked into Cendana and strolled by large tanks that held live lobsters, crabs, Barracuda, Jackfish, Yellow Crazy fish, Red and White Snapper, Grouper, Barramundi, Tiger Prawns, and squid. Patrons chose their seafood, and it was grilled fresh in bamboo leaves.

We ordered a feast: fish soup, chicken sate, Tiger Prawns, Grouper, squid, crab, sweet sticky rice, vegetables, and sauces. We walked through the open restaurant and chose to sit outside at a table on the sandy beach under a smoke-filled sky. We cracked open coconuts and sipped the sweet juice from our straws as children ran breathlessly into the waves.

I imagined Rocky sitting across from me, teary that we were leaving. I tipped my head to the sun, closed my eyes, and made a silent vow to my brother. *I promise I'll make my relationship work with Setiawan. I'll try harder. I know you loved her. I won't abandon Anna, Rocky.* A tear slid down my cheek. I excused myself and hurried to the bathroom. I looked at my reflection in the mirror and said, "I won't let you down, Rocky." I bowed my head, thinking about a line from Kahlil Gibran's poem on pain: *Even as the stone of the fruit must break, that its heart may stand in the sun, so must you know pain.* Yes, I knew pain, but how would my heart heal and stand in the sun again? *How do I live in this world without you, Rocky?*

CHAPTER 6
Lifeline

The minutes on the flight ticked by as though an angel had reached down and hit the slow-motion button on the world. Setiawan refused to let us take any of Rocky's ashes home to our parents, so Jim and I flew home empty-handed. I was weighted down by my images of Rocky and by all that was left undone and unsaid between us. As a therapist, I had the intellectual understanding of the grieving process, but that knowledge did not provide a roadmap to lead me out of the emotional landmine where I found myself after Rocky's early departure from our lives.

I knew the five stages of grief, rehearsed them in my mind—denial, anger, depression, bargaining, and acceptance. The stages are nonlinear and take time, I said to myself. They take time. How much time? Questions that I didn't have the answers to crowded around in my head. How would I return to work? How would I stay strong for my parents? How was I going to write Rocky's obituary when I still couldn't believe he was gone? How was I going to plan his memorial service? When the plane hit the tarmac in Portland, Maine, the most pressing question on my mind was, *How will I survive his death when I have no desire to go on living?*

As soon as I returned from Asia, Kevin and I began planning the details for Rocky's Celebration of Life, and everyone pitched in. Kevin chose the venue while Jim and I were in Asia. We reserved the Portland Ocean Gateway, a structure that reached out into Casco Bay and was designed to resemble the prow of a ship. Gorgeous, massive glass windows offered a panoramic view of the ocean. It was the perfect spot to celebrate Rocky's life given his deep appreciation and love for the water.

Kevin had several black and white photos blown

up and framed, marking time throughout Rocky's life. We chose a caterer, rented video equipment, and Kevin's wife, Jessica, made centerpieces for the tables. My brother Paul and sister-in-law Pam helped with other details. They bought the guest book, special parchment paper for his obituary to be printed on, and smooth river stones for the guests. They would choose two stones each, one to throw in the ocean and say a prayer, the other to take home as a keepsake. We planned to have two jars, one for Anna and one for Michael. We were going to ask the guests to write a wish for each of Rocky's children and place it in their jars.

One night, as I lay in bed at 3:00 a.m. thinking about the remaining details, I decided it was time to watch a slideshow a dear friend of mine had spent hours creating for the memorial. A slideshow I'd been dreading for weeks. I got my numbed self out of bed, tiptoed to my office, and sat there in the pitch-black by the glow of my computer. I tasted the salt on my tongue from my own tears as I hit "play."

Forty-three years of my brother's life were captured in frozen moments, strung together as he grew up in front me. A newborn tucked against our mother's chest. A one-year-old, enamored with toes he discovered on his baby feet. A toddler in a highchair, smearing chocolate cake on the tray. A five-year-old, clutching an orange Popsicle, Kevin nuzzled beside him, licking his own. At six, he walked along a beach on a winter day, dressed in a snowsuit. In the next shot, he blew out ten birthday candles. In his teens and twenties, he gazed up at stars, dribbled a basketball, headed a soccer ball, slung arms around college pals, and kissed the cheek of his newborn son. In his late thirties and early forties, there were photos of a Balinese wedding, family trips to Egypt, Thailand, and Hong Kong. Then there were pictures that marked beginnings before endings. My mother smiling at her son before her stroke, a wedding before a divorce, five siblings, arms around each other, before there were only four. I reached out a hand (as I often did) to touch his face, to touch an instant of his life that had passed at the same time the camera clicked. Then it struck me. I'd been given the gift to have Rocky as my brother—not ONLY for forty-three years—but FOR forty-three years.

I hit "play" on the slideshow. This time I looked into it, rather than at it. Listened into the music rather than simply to it. Something new emerged in the pictures. I heard the lyrics to his favorite songs. I shifted my attention and awareness on the joy he brought into my life and everyone else's life he touched rather than on the grief his death left behind. Grief and joy are wedded; they are one. Where there is joy, there is grief. Where there is grief, there is joy. One is more predominant than the other at any given time, depending on which one we shine our light on.

Even after my newfound epiphany, I still didn't have the energy to complete simple daily tasks. Disrobing, showering, and dressing were daunting and took energy I didn't have to give. When the sun set, I Face-Timed with Setiawan in attempt to mend our relationship, and to support my brother's widowed wife, and include her in the ongoing planning of his memorial service. Though she would not be attending, I wanted her to feel a part of the process and planning. Each call, I felt the intensity of her pain across the thousands of miles. My words to her slipped through my fingers and lay between us, motionless, useless. Nothing brought her relief except the thought that one day she'd rejoin him.

I let go of my bitterness toward her for the hurtful, biting comments, and for the mood swings. I began to trust her, forgive her, and love her, which felt like the greatest way to honor my brother. I rationalized her earlier behavior and chalked it up to deep grief. I had never lost a spouse and she had never lost a brother. We didn't understand the depth of each other's pain, but we did share an everlasting love for Rocky, and we could meet in that sacred space. At least that's what I hoped for until we FaceTimed in late March about Rocky's ex-wife, Kristen, and his son, Michael, a story I had already listened to, in great detail, in Hong Kong.

Setiawan had knocked on my hotel room door, walked in, and said she needed to talk to me. She told me she had contacted Kristen through Facebook and set up a FaceTime call with her, requesting contact between Anna and Michael. She wanted them to have a relationship, given they were half-siblings. Setiawan told Kristen that Rocky had drafted several emails to apologize for leaving his son but never had the courage to send them. Rocky held tight to the belief that Kristen and Michael would never forgive him.

Kristen thanked Setiawan for contacting her and said that maybe Anna and Michael could have a relationship in a couple of years. What would a fifteen-year-old teenager and three-and-a-half-year-old toddler talk about now? Setiawan became enraged as she spouted her rendition of the story, blaming Kristen and Michael for causing Rocky such heartache. Setiawan couldn't reconcile with the fact that Rocky had, at one time, loved another woman who gave birth to his son. Though Rocky relinquished his parental rights, he never stopped loving Michael.

On our FaceTime call, Setiawan's face looked strained and petulant as she rehashed the story. "Why you like her, Sue? I know you talk to her. How can you be friends with her?"

I inhaled a deep breath, released it slowly as I thought about my response. *Keep cool, Sue. Just lie and tell her you don't have a relationship with her. No, I can't do that because she sees the Facebook posts.* "Calm down, Setiawan. My relationship with Kristen has no bearing on our relationship. She was an important part of our family for ten years, and we love her. And she's my nephew's mother. I can love you both at the same time."

The conversation continued to slide downhill, and I ended the call before it ended our relationship for good. "I love you and Anna so much. Let's talk again soon," I said.

After I hung up, I checked my phone and saw a message from Kristen. She wrote, *Why is she doing this?* Then she forwarded me a text conversation she and Setiawan had over Messenger on Facebook.

I cried as I read the messages, again digging deep to understand Setiawan, her grief, and her hurtful words. Kristen, too, sat in a cloud of confusion and crafted a message back, explaining that she and Rocky shared a long relationship and had been best friends for many years. They brought a child into the world together. She wrote, *We had many wonderful memories. Those are never going away.* Kristen adored her son, and she and Rocky created a remarkable young man as a result of their bond.

When Setiawan sent her response to Kristen, she wrote that she loved Rocky more than anyone in the world and would fight anyone who tried to harm him. She acknowledged that Rocky knew he had made a mistake when he left his son and wanted to make amends. But, Setiawan wrote, *Many people in his life couldn't let go of the past and accept the truth.* She ended her message to Kristen, writing, *No one in this world is perfect.*

I shook my head as I read the back and forth conversations until Kristen requested that they cease contact. Rocky would have loathed the hurt unfurling in the wake of his death. Kristen had not asked to be dragged into the family drama that ensued. I knew he loved Kristen when they married. I knew he loved Michael and tortured himself over the years for leaving. We discussed his apprehension in contacting Michael during my visit to Bali. He didn't feel he had the right to have a relationship with him. Yes, he sent a few Facebook messages and signed them Uncle Rocky because he didn't know what to call himself after he gave up his right to be Michael's father. Confusion and pain clouded his judgment.

In Setiawan's grief and longing for my brother, she had to twist the truth into a morphed version she could live with. She held on to her belief that Kristen and

Michael could not forgive Rocky. Michael had a father who raised him, a father he loved and looked up to. He didn't hold a grudge against Rocky, a man he didn't know. Kristen had let go of the past years ago. She, too, didn't need or want an apology. But for Setiawan, she felt she had to "fight" for Rocky after his death, but what she was fighting for remains a mystery. Someone had to be blamed for his death. Someone eventually became most of us.

As the days rolled on from one heartbreaking call and email to the next, I arrived at the conclusion that there were no winners in the game of loss. I don't recall the order of events that followed, cracking my relationship with Setiawan until it was almost irreparable. I only remember how each one felt like sandpaper being dragged over an open wound as I grieved the loss of my brother. First, it was the obituary I wrote when I returned from Asia. Under surviving relatives, I included Kristen and Michael. Setiawan demanded they be removed. I compromised and deleted Kristen's name but kept Michael's.

Secondly, arguments erupted over money. In addition to the funds raised through the GoFundMe site for Setiawan and Anna to help them rebuild their lives, my uncle gifted thousands of dollars to set up a college trust fund for Anna. Kevin sent an email to Setiawan, explaining our family's goal to manage the college fund in the U.S., so we could continue to contribute to it over time and invest in its growth. Anna would have a healthy college fund by the time she graduated from high school.

Instead of responding to Kevin, she sent me an email, stating that she was capable of managing the money, as she was Anna's mother. As the email exchanges became heated and nonproductive, our family relinquished our college-fund goals and wired the money to Setiawan. Maintaining a relationship with Setiawan continued to be more important than squabbling over money, and I hoped we could begin anew.

* * *

Once the busyness ended three months after Rocky's death, I was terrified. Without external distractions, I had too much idle time to think, to be with myself when I wanted to be anywhere but alone with my pain. I wasn't sleeping. I was barely eating. I decided to return to a blog I created a few short months before my brother died. Initially, I created it with the intention of writing inspirational pieces to help motivate readers to take their lives to the next level, to take risks and chances to live a fuller, more impassioned and abundant life. I couldn't have known that my brother's death would show me what living a courageous and fierce life was all about. I transformed the blog into a platform to shine a light into the grieving process. With raw honesty, I shared what it felt like to lose so deeply.

The writing was a therapeutic outlet that offered me a venue to discharge my internal pain, to get it out of me and onto the page until I hit the four-month mark of my brother's passing. I felt like I had driven a truck a hundred miles an hour over a cliff, slamming headfirst into an ocean of pure unadulterated grief. Between the trip to Asia, planning Rocky's memorial service, supporting my parents, and the stressful, strained relationship between Setiawan and me, I slowly came unglued. I retreated from my support system and disengaged from the world.

I took a three-month leave of absence from my position as the director of communications at an international behavioral health organization, where I had worked for fourteen years, because I couldn't focus. I was not going to get through the grief alone and realized I needed outside help, as I curled into the black, vacant space of his death.

On a desperate afternoon, jeans sagging off my shrinking body, a friend said to me, "Have you called Lindsey yet?"

I forgot that she gave me her name and number two months earlier. Lindsey was an Intuit energy worker and grief therapist. I made the call and scheduled my first appointment for the following day. As soon as Lindsey opened the door, goose bumps rose on my skin. She had worked on my body fifteen years earlier. When she smiled and said, "It's nice to see you again. Come in," I knew I'd find my way home.

Lindsey explained she would help me to release the intense sadness in my body. "First," she said, "we need to ground you. You keep leaving your body, trying to reach your brother. He lives inside of you, not out there. You have to come back to your body. You're drifting."

And I was. Hours would go by and I'd "awaken," not remembering where I drifted off to as though I lived outside of myself. After weeks of therapy, she encouraged me to attend a thirty-five-hour facilitator training at the Center for Grieving Children in Portland, Maine. At the end of each subsequent session I had with Lindsey, she'd ask, "Did you call the center yet? Have you signed up for the training?"

I'd shake my head. "No, not yet. I don't think I'm ready to help anyone with their grief."

Then one day in September, after a session, Lindsey said, "Call them. They need you, and you need them."

I hugged her and said, "OK. I will."

When I called the director at the center and inquired about the training, she said there was one opening left in the fall session. She invited me to attend the orientation to make certain I understood the commitment I'd be making prior to the training. After the orientation, I signed up for the facilitator training. The training sessions were designed for participants to do their own grief work to ensure they could be present and hold the space for people in the bereavement groups. Once I completed the thirty-five hours, I'd be eligible to be a substitute for facilitators when they were not able to be in their assigned groups. Bereavement groups were held on Tuesday, Wednesday, and Thursday nights for the littles (ages three to six), middles (ages seven to nine), tweens (ages ten to thirteen), teens (ages fourteen to eighteen), young adults (ages nineteen to thirty), and adults. All the facilitator slots were filled. I would have to wait until there was an opening before I could have my own group.

A week before I began my training, I scheduled an appointment with a tattoo artist in Portland to get a Dragonfly memorial tattoo. I walked in with a friend, nervous and scared that it was going to be a painful two hours. The tattoo artist, David, lined up ten miniature plastic cups filled with SkinCandy© ink. The colors were so vibrant and exquisite, I was tempted to dip my pinky finger into the Candy Apple green, lick it off, and hold it on my tongue. Next, I'd try Red Berry Cherry, Raspberry Jam, Candy Corn Yellow, Tangerine, and Tastywaves. I liked the idea of sweet ink soaking through my skin, one droplet at a time, becoming a permanent glaze of hardened sugar.

"Will this hurt?" I asked.

"It's different for everyone," he said. "Women usually do better than men."

The artist poured liquid green soap on a cloth, ran it over my ankle to cleanse it and prepare the delicate skin for something permanent. He turned on the tattoo machine that mimicked the sound of a dental drill, but there was no Novocain. I closed my eyes and imagined Rocky standing next to me, flashing that glacier-melting smile, saying, "It's no big deal, Sis. It'll be over before you know it."

"This is for you," I said. "I was going to get Pegasus on my thigh, just like yours."

I like the Dragonfly better, Rocky said. *Remember the song?*

I blinked back tears from the memory of my brother's wedding when we played the song, not the pain from the needle, biting into my skin, moving up and down fifty to 3,000 times per minute. I wanted to feel the sharp, biting pinpricks to share my brother's experience, etch it into my memory like our tattoos, like his: the dolphins, marching bears, and Pegasus. Though he described the sensation to me anytime I asked, now that he was gone, it helped me to feel closer to him. I shut my eyes. My breathing moved in rhythm with the humming of the machine, the stop and go of the needle piercing skin and making wings.

I had Rocky's name etched into the wing. "Perfect," I said. "Can you add a tiny red heart in the center of the Dragonfly?"

David smiled. "Absolutely."

I left with my brother's name on my skin and felt ready to begin my training.

A week later, I attended the first training session. We were asked to close our eyes and remember the last time we were with the person we lost. The smell of their skin: *Dove soap*. Their clothing: *White button-down shirt and khaki shorts*. The expression on their face: *Pained*. The last words spoken: *You abandoned me, Sue*. There, in the circle of hurting people who were no longer present in the group but somewhere else, remembering the last time they touched the face and smelled the skin of the one they lost, I held out my arms, embraced my brother and said, *I didn't abandon you. I'm right here. I'm right here.* I wept until I couldn't breathe.

After I completed the first weekend of training, I lay in bed with a violent head cold, questioning whether or not I could facilitate a bereavement group because I had plenty of my own grief work to do. How could I be present for others who were going through this dark, hopeless process? I hadn't kissed the bottom of the well yet and emerged someone new.

I threw the covers off, turned on the bedside lamp, and ran my fingers over the dragonfly. *I can do this, right, Rocky?* I lay back down, shut the light off, and made the decision that I'd finish the training, and trust that when a facilitator position opened up, I would be ready. The tattoo and volunteering at the center were two tangible ways I could honor my brother's life. The center would become my saving grace.

The following day I sent Setiawan an email to check in with her. We were going through a good patch, sending loving emails to each other, and I believed we were growing closer. I attached a picture of the tattoo, unaware of the underlying sarcasm in her response to me when she wrote, *Nice tattoo, Sue.* Shortly after that exchange, she spoke to my sister-in-law, Gayle, on Face-Time. Setiawan communicated her disgust over my tattoo and couldn't understand how I could have my brother's name etched into my skin but not my other three brothers and my husband. She became obsessed with the tattoo and wasn't able to let her anger go. She didn't understand that it was common for people in the States to get memorial tattoos as a way to hold on to the memory of their loved ones while moving forward at the same time. I sat at my computer, reading another email about her disdain, and cried for the relationship I wished we could have together.

As our relationship continued to deteriorate, it became more difficult to read her Facebook posts. In the last post I read, before blocking her, she wrote that when Rocky returns to earth through reincarnation, he would only search for her and Anna because his story was done with everyone else.

My heart broke for my parents, and I hoped my father hadn't read it. I understood blocking her would be the final blow to whatever semblance of a relationship we had left with each other, but I came to the realization that even if her behavior was due to deep grief, I couldn't continue to open myself up for ongoing hurt. Once I blocked her, she blocked me from her page and from Rocky's page. I no longer had access to the heartfelt, meaningful messages his friends, colleagues, and family left, both before and after his passing. My brother's daughter was also no longer accessible to me, and I had to find a way to live with the choices I'd made. I asked myself, *Was it really worth it?* My petulance toward Setiawan had won. I blew it. No one ever explained to me how death could impact family ties. I cut my brother's wife off, and I'm the one who lost.

CHAPTER 7
Healing Through Story

Five months after Rocky's death, I woke up in the early morning, the sky still drenched in ink, whispering, *Rock On: Mining for Joy in the Deep River of Sibling Grief.* Its meaning was elusive, living somewhere in the future. As the days and months crawled along under a cloud of despair, I awakened again at that same thinly veiled hour, repeating, *Rock On: Mining for Joy in the Deep River of Sibling Grief* until it struck me; it was a book title.

A week after I had this second flash of inspiration, it was my turn to submit work to my writing group, but I had nothing other than a title and a loose idea about a book where I'd weave together my story with stories of others whose siblings had died. I sat down and wrote an introduction about people I interviewed, who at the time only existed in my imagination. When I submitted the piece and arrived for my critique, my writing group asked, "How did you get all these people for the interview?"

I laughed and said, "I haven't interviewed anyone. I don't even have anyone to interview. I just made it up to give you an idea of where I'd like to go with this project."

"Where will you find these people?" they asked.

Answer: I have no idea. I left the writing group, thinking, *How am I going to do this?*

I had nothing more than a desire, a soul-need, to write a book about sibling loss in the hopes of making sense of my brother's death. I also wanted to toss a lifeline to others who were coping with the loss of their siblings.

I imagined the improbability of rounding up at least twenty-five people who would be willing to entrust me with their most painfully intimate, raw, and true stories. Crazy, stupid idea. I took these thoughts to bed with me that night, deciding the project was too big, too hard, and too overwhelming. In the morning, as most mornings, I talked to Rocky, always feeling his spirit around me.

I heard, *Call Mini.* Mini was my brother's college friend, who had become my friend after Rocky's death. I punched her number into my phone and shared my vision for the book with her. She knew seven or eight people who had lost a sibling.

"I'll reach out to all of them and ask them if they'll do it," she said.

Forty-eight hours later, I had seventeen people who not only agreed to be interviewed but also were grateful to have the opportunity to talk about their siblings. Two weeks later, I had a total of twenty. Emails flooded my inbox from people who knew people who had lost a sibling. If I had known then how emotionally grueling the process would be and the years of work ahead of me, I'm not sure I would have had the courage to write this book.

Throughout 2015, I interviewed a total of twenty-seven people from Maine to Israel. The phone interviews ran from one-and-a-half to three hours in length. I thought I'd facilitate these interviews, transcribe them, and use excerpts in the book to offer a glimmer of hope to others, but they are the ones who offered hope to me.

I thought about what I would like to be asked about my own grieving process, so I asked questions like, *How did the death shift the course of your life, if at all? Did your experience change your perspective on life? Did you harbor any guilt? Did you feel you received communication from your sibling since the death? Did you reach out for help during the grieving process? What would you say to your sibling given one more chance?*

When I began the interviews fourteen months after Rocky's death, I thought I was further along in the grieving process. I soon learned that I was in the heart of it. I read and reread the emails from Setiawan to ensure the details of Rocky's death were accurate, which sent me back into the past, back to Hong Kong, back to his body on the table. I pounded my desktop, sobbed day after day, and asked myself how I ever thought I could undertake this project.

My sadness intensified as I carried their traumatic stories around with me. There were times when images of the deceased siblings, and the way in which they died, crushed my heart.

As I listened to people's responses, their tragic stories, I wept with the person on the other end of the line, triggering memories of my brother. When their voices cracked, I felt my own break. I did not anticipate how honored I would feel to bear witness to the participants' pain, and to feel the love they had, and have, for the brothers and sisters they lost to murder, suicide, cancer, overdoses, and accidents. I listened with a whole heart as they shared their sacred thousand-mile swim through their agony and sorrow.

The interviews reaffirmed my experience and beliefs about sibling loss. Some of the surviving siblings made comments about feeling like "the forgotten ones," and their need to bear their grief alone, squelch it, and hide it when they were in the presence of their parents, and the surviving spouse and children. Most held on to the limiting belief that they needed to be the strong ones because they "had only" lost a brother or sister, not a child or a soul mate. Our siblings have a critical impact on shaping who we become, regardless if the relationships are close, strained, or estranged. One interviewee said that many widowed spouses have the opportunity to find new love and rebuild their lives, but siblings lose a piece of themselves forever.

I sat with these thoughts as I transcribed the interviews, hearing the same themes again and again. When I finished the transcriptions, I had hundreds of pages of material. After I sent the interviews out to each interviewee to read and sign a release form to use their stories, three people pulled out.

Next, I scoured the Internet, researching each deceased sibling to read their obituaries and any articles I could find on their accidents or murders. I collected more and more information and became overwhelmed by the size of the project, the emotions it elicited, and the lack of clarity on how to structure the book.

Seeking guidance, I scheduled an appointment with a medium named Debbie, who was respected for her authenticity and ability to communicate with spirits.

I walked into Debbie's meeting space, and before I sat down, she said, "Your brother wants to write a book with you."

The hairs on the back of my neck rose. "I know," I said. "I'm already writing it." I believed in mediums and had seen four since Rocky's passing, but this was the first time anyone had ever been so specific.

"He doesn't like how it ends," Debbie said. "He says it's not about his sad story."

I cried and said, "He doesn't know how it ends because I haven't written it yet."

Debbie laughed. "He said you can be stubborn when you've made up your mind."

I walked out of the session pissed at my brother because it was a *sad* story. All the stories were heartbreaking, and yet, I couldn't get those words, *it's not about his sad story*, out of my head. I needed more time and distance from the material, which prompted me to take a hiatus from the book, possibly forever.

Nine months later, and three years after Rocky's passing, finally I had renewed energy for "playing" with the material, the stories, and the structure—all the elements I loved about the writing process. "Oh my God," I said aloud. "It isn't about Rocky's sad story."

The material was heavy, the stories were sad, but the messages, transformations, and resiliency of each individual were light and hopeful. I enjoyed the challenge of mining for joy in each story, including Rocky's. The people who shared the intimate details of their sibling's death showed me the beauty and blessings that can arise in the wake of tragedy. Though I still had periods of time when I wrote into the heart of my grief and the tears flowed, I noticed they didn't flow as frequently or for as long. Halfway through the manuscript, I woke up one morning and decided to create a new first chapter. I wanted to capture my brother and our bond while he was alive. The first chapter turned into seven chapters that were pure memoir, which led to a new problem. How would I honor my brother's story with those of the other siblings?

On March 30, 2017, I sat in front of my computer, closed my eyes, and asked Rocky for some inspiring guidance. *Show me how to do this? There has to be a way.*

I sat quietly and listened for an answer. Ten to fifteen minutes later, a scene flashed through my mind. I saw Ryan, one of the deceased siblings, in a bar getting stabbed as if I were sitting on a barstool, witnessing his murder. I had my answer. I would begin the stories with each sibling alive on the page before they died and then segue into the interview. I started with Ryan's story and looked at the date of his death—March 30, 2013. I gained this insight on the fourth anniversary of Ryan's death. I have no doubt that he reached out from the other side and handed me this gift.

As I continued to heal during this project, the beauty of the stories rose to the surface. One of my favorite quotes by Wayne Dyer reads, "If you change the way you look at things, the things you look at change." When I began this venture, I could only see the tragedies and the injustices. When I gained distance from my story and theirs as I mined for joy in my own life, I was able to view them from a different perspective. I noticed how most of the interviewees had also reclaimed joy in their lives, and how their hope and mine rose from the wellspring of despair.

The stories people shared with a vulnerable and open heart were life changing. As I wrote, a deeper healing took place, anchoring my belief that loving and losing far outweigh never loving at all. As I walked through the darkness, I found the courage to say *yes* to life with heart and arms wide open. Hope, joy, and a renewed perspective on the fragility and beauty of life lives in the spirit and memories of those we loved and who have passed on to the other side. The stories to follow helped to nudge me, step by step, out of my shadows of deep grief.

Note: I took creative license to imagine the thoughts and feelings of the deceased siblings prior to their death to bring them more alive on the page.

CHAPTER 8
Losing Anger

Jeneen Gallagher: interviewed in June 2015, Florida
Ryan Gill: 7/25/79-3/30/13
Cause of death: Murder

On a sun-drenched Saturday in Boynton Beach, Florida, thirty-three-year-old Ryan—a redheaded, blue-eyed 'gentle giant'—had a bounce in his step as he finished his shift at a local restaurant. He popped into his apartment for a quick shower and a change of clothes and headed to the bar across the street to meet his co-worker for a bachelorette party.

The bar was packed, and the crowd of people laughed, swapped jokes, and told stories. It was a light, easy night as Ryan and his friends sat around a table, fooling around, clinking drinks as the bride-to-be talked about the upcoming wedding.

When a round of shots arrived for the women, sent over by two dark-haired brothers at the bar, the women said, "No thanks." They were not interested in accepting drinks from drunken strangers.

One of the two brothers—offended by the decline—became enraged and screamed profanities at the women.

Ryan, who stood six feet four inches tall, believed women deserved to be treated with respect. He wasn't going to be a bystander, watching, as his female friends were harassed. He walked over to his friend, advised her and the others to move to another table, and to ignore the two men. Then, Ryan asked the brothers to *take it easy*.

According to police reports, the enraged, intoxicated brother, Alexandre Magradze, approached Ryan and argued with him. The other brother, Vakhtang Magradze, who stood five feet three inches, jumped on Ryan's back and jammed a knife in and out of his neck. Though Ryan was larger and more athletic than the brothers, he lost the use of his arms from the stab wounds. A bar manager tried to break up the fight and was stabbed several times in the back by Magradze. Another staffer who tried to help was stabbed in the nose area.

The police were on patrol at the Backyard Boynton Beach bar that Saturday night, but they couldn't get a clean shot.

An officer yelled, "Drop the knife!" as he stunned Vakhtang with his taser.

The stun gun couldn't penetrate through the heavy jacket Vakhtang wore that warm Floridian evening. He swung the knife at the officer in an attempt to stab him, but the officer kicked it out of his hand and cuffed him, while Ryan lay still on the barroom floor. He later died in the hospital. http://articles.sun-sentinel.com/2013-04-01/news/fl-boynton-beach-stabbing-folo-20130401_1_fatal-stabbing-ryan-gill-knife

"Fuck you. Fuck you. Fuck you!" Jeneen, Ryan's younger sister, wailed into her bedroom when she received the news of her brother's death.

I didn't have to close my eyes and imagine the screams. I could hear them as if I were there, hovering in the dark shadows of Jeneen's bedroom, gripping the bedposts, listening as her mother delivered the life-altering news. "Jeneen, something happened. Ryan went to Delray Medical, and he didn't make it."

Jeneen repeated *fuck you* over and over, smacking herself, willing herself to awaken from a night terror. It was 3:30 in the morning, and her son, asleep in his bed, did not hear his mother's screams. "This is not real," she said, until she noticed Ryan's best friend, Joe, standing in the doorway. His contorted face told her the unimaginable had happened to her brother and the truth soaked through bone. *This is real. It's real.*

Jeneen and I cried as she shared the horrifying details of her brother's death. Her sadness turned to rage when she talked about the brothers who murdered her only sibling, the brothers who stole Ryan and Jeneen's future, their dreams, and the memories they had yet to make together.

As I imagined Ryan, lying on the floor, and Rocky, lying frozen on the bed in the basement of Queen Elizabeth Hospital, swaddled in blankets, I felt Jeneen's rage. Her stolen future. I felt as though I were sitting with her in her home in Florida, as I sat in my office in Maine.

"Why, why, why?" she asked.

After Rocky's death, I swore off saying, "I'm sorry for your loss." The words are trite and meaningless in the wake of heartache. There were no sentiments to offer this woman who had lost her brother two years ago at the time of the interview in such a senseless act of violence. I knew anger. I punched pillows, screamed at God, and wanted to die too, but that unhealthy energy became so toxic, I had to find a way to let it go, rise up out of me, and feel it drift away.

"Are you still angry?" I asked.

"I've gone through the grieving process but not in order. I had a lot of denial," Jeneen said. "I was really angry for a very long time. I was in the shower one day, where I do my best and worst thinking. I was crying, but I was crunching my fingers and grinding my teeth, thinking, *Why is this crackhead alive and why is my brother dead? Why do those brothers still get to talk to their parents and each other?* This sense of peace came over me. I heard Ryan say to me, *Don't let them destroy you. They've taken enough. Don't let them have any more.*

Jeneen's sense of peace reminded me of a day soon after I returned from Asia when the Maine ground was a blanket of hard-crusted snow. I put on my down jacket, gloves, L.L. Bean boots, and a red-knitted hat with sky-blue flowers. I stuffed a small notebook and pen in my pocket and headed out with my two golden retrievers to get some air, to get away from myself. We trekked down a snow-packed trail that led to an open field. As the dogs chased each other through the snow, I sat on a rock, pulled out my notebook, and wrote until my fingers grew numb. *I felt the crunch under my boots, searching for clues, something tangible to give hope shape. As I sank through the hard crust of snow to the softer underbelly, I had this thought: grief can wrap its hands around your heart and imprison you in the past, turn your heart cold and hard, pulling the shade on light, slamming the door on beauty, on love, on all that's good, and real, and worth living for. Grief can do that; it can. But here's something else I'm learning about grief. If it has the power to harden the heart, it also has the power to soften it, like that underbelly of the snow.*

With each tragedy, every loss, space is left behind, leaving room for hope, for new love to bloom, for deeper roots of gratitude and appreciation for the good, the joy, the laughter, and beauty in our lives. For me, I've prayed for my brother's passing to soften my heart and to make those moments of joy that much sweeter than they were before.

I closed my notebook that day, tilted my head to the sun, and blinked in the wide-open space. I felt that same sense of calm come over me as if Rocky's spirit kneeled beside me, whispering, *It will take time, Sis, but I promise you, you're going to be OK. I love you.*

"What happened to you after you heard Ryan's words?" I asked Jeneen.

Her voice cracked as she wept. "I know what he'd want for me, and he wouldn't want me to be this angry person."

Ryan's essence and the words Jeneen heard transformed the anger she had been holding onto. She made the conscious decision to let go of the toxicity that no longer served her along her grief journey. She said, "They don't get any more from me. That was a difficult change that was necessary and positive. I'm not an angry person. I don't want to be, and my brother wouldn't want me to be."

Since the day her brother was murdered, Jeneen's life has changed in every conceivable way. Two years before Ryan was killed, he made significant life changes. He quit smoking, joined a gym, recommitted to fitness, and returned to school. Then, in a moment, his life was taken from him.

"I think about all the things that used to matter so much and it's stupid shit," Jeneen said. "If one of my friends upsets me, how important is it? They might not be here tomorrow. Life is too short. I have to look at this experience as a blessing."

Jeneen remained in a job that she loathed for a year and a half. One day as she sat at her office desk, she asked herself, *Is this it for me?*

"I'm not going to do that," she said. "Life is precious and it's really short. I'm not going to sit in a place and be miserable to collect a paycheck. God doesn't want that for me, and my brother doesn't want that for me. I never viewed life like that before. His life was cut very short, and now I ask myself, *What would he have loved to do?* He didn't make a mistake, but he still died. Let me learn from that and live every day like it's my last."

* * *

Kim Sisto-Robinson: interviewed in June 2015, Minnesota
Kay Sisto: 4/11/60-5/26/10
Cause of death: Murder

Kay, with her silky brown hair pulled up into a ponytail, lips painted red, packed books and pictures into boxes. She had finally mustered the courage to leave her thirty-year marriage. Her husband, Mike, was abusive and psychologically controlling. She was indignant as she thought about the last year and his stalking behavior when he hacked into her Facebook page. Kay had to change her cell phone number. Though they were separated, soon to be divorced, he refused to move out of their home.

She had yearned to leave for years but chose to remain in the marriage, frightened Mike would kill himself if she left. Her three boys, Michael, Aaron, and Jordan, were grown and knew how abusive their father had been to their mother and to them.

Kay had a conversation with her beloved sister, Kim, where she talked about her need to leave, but fear paralyzed her. "What if he kills himself? I could never forgive myself," Kay said.

"That's not your problem," Kim said. "You have to get away from him."

"Everyone will hate me," she said. "They'll blame me."

Kim looked at her beautiful sister. Kay completed Kim's world. It was never just Kim or just Kay. It was always Kim and Kay. Kim felt her sister was too kind-hearted and, metaphorically, collected wounded birds and tucked them under her wing. Kim couldn't stand the sight of Mike. The first time she met him thirty years earlier, she thought he looked like a monster.

"So what? Who cares what anyone thinks," Kim said. "You've got to get out. He probably already has a grave dug for you." Though this was Kim's greatest fear, she didn't believe Mike would actually kill Kay.

Kay shook her head, dismissing her thoughts about Mike dying by suicide and traumatizing her three sons. She no longer had a choice because she was withering inside. Kay had to escape no matter how painful it might be for her sons.

Mike watched as she continued to pack, knowing there was no chance to save the marriage. "Please don't go," he said. "Don't do this to our family. I promise I'll change this time."

"No," she said. "You've made that promise a million times. I'm leaving, Mike."

Mike left the room and Kay sighed with resolve. How had she stayed with him all these years, believing love could change him, transform him into a kind and loving partner? She'd been so naive, but a new future awaited her, a future of freedom.

Just a few months ago she'd told Kim, "I feel a

burst of joy just knowing I will not need to be with him anymore." Kay embraced that feeling as she placed a few more personal items in the box. She grabbed her cell phone and tucked it in her pocket. Kay had plans. She would get her own apartment, and with her sister's help, they'd decorate it any way they wanted to. It would become Kay's sanctuary. Mike could keep the house. She didn't care anymore. It was just a house, not a home.

Kay was a prayer warrior and asked God for two signs on her walk she'd taken earlier. She asked to see an eagle and a butterfly as an affirmation that everything would be OK. God had shown her both that day. Everything was going to be alright.

With a renewed sense of hope, Kay headed toward the door while Mike retrieved a gun. He snuck up behind her, lifted the barrel to the back of her head, and pulled the trigger three times. Kay dropped to the floor. Blood pooled around her head, a red halo on the tiled floor. Satisfied, Mike lifted the gun, pressed it against his temple, and pulled the trigger.

When Kay's son Jordan returned home from his college class, he tried to open the front door, but it wouldn't budge. He walked around the house and peered into the window. Chills ran up and down his spine when he saw his father lying on the floor. Jordan called 911 and went into the house through the back door. His blood curdled when he saw his mother. He ran over to his father, grabbed the gun from his father's hand, kicked him in the gut, and screamed, "What did you do to my mother?" His father didn't respond. Mike was dead.

Sirens blared in the distance. When the cops arrived, they took the gun from Jordan, initially believing he was the one who murdered his parents. They escorted him to the cruiser, brought him to the station, and interrogated him for hours until they were convinced Jordan had not been the one who killed his parents.

While Kay fought for her life in an ambulance, Kim was home mowing the lawn, listening to *Pillars of the Earth,* a novel by Ken Follett. It was a gorgeous May day, and Kim couldn't wait for the evening. She and Kay had movie tickets to *Sex and the City.* The much-needed night out was planned. Chicken cooked in the oven to feed her husband and two sons. After a shower, she'd get all dolled up, meet her sister to have a nice dinner, and then go to the movie.

In the previous six months, Kim refused to step foot inside her sister's house. The sight of Mike made her queasy. Kim was elated Kay was on her way to freedom, and they'd celebrate in true Kim and Kay style. She smiled as she thought about going on a shopping spree, buying new outfits, getting their hair done, and painting the town red. Kim turned the lawn mower off and went into the house to check the chicken when the phone rang. The aroma of roasted chicken wafted through the air. She picked it up and said, "Hello."

"Mom, one of my friends just called me and told me there are police cars in front of Aunt Kay's," her son said.

Kim, her bond with her sister—more like a twin connection—knew intuitively something unspeakable had happened. She dropped to the floor and remained there until her son came home, helped Kim to her feet, and steadied her, as they walked out of the house, leaving doors open and chicken burning in the oven. She stumbled toward the car in a black, inky haze, without the ability to imagine the unimaginable.

"It was the darkest day of my life," Kim said, remembering her sister and best friend. "After many hours in the hospital, we were told she was brain dead. They kept her heart beating until they could harvest her organs. I don't remember the first three years. I think I went crazy. I remember thinking, *What am I going to do now?* We were a part of each other. Almost like twins. That's kind of what we were. It's amazing that anyone can move forward."

"How did you manage to move forward?" I asked, feeling her heartache as she sobbed throughout the interview.

"I couldn't do anything. I couldn't drive for months. I actually tried to start drinking every day and couldn't. But what I could do was write. Two weeks after her death, I started writing about Kay's story and mourning. Someone came to me and said, 'I know someone who will set up a blog for you.'"

For her own self-preservation, Kim began to write about her anger, her screaming and yelling, and it became a safe platform to release her intense emotions. After Rocky's death, I slammed fingers on the keyboard as I stared at a photograph of me and my four brothers with arms slung over each other. I cried and scribed my way through the ache in my bones. At the nine-month mark, I wrote: *The past nine months have crawled by in a blurry, non-linear haze. I'd attach wheels to the next three, hitch them together like freight train cars, and shove them over a cliff if it would speed up time, whiz me past the four-season mark a little more quickly. Many who've lost deeply have offered me this wisp of advice, "Give yourself four seasons. It will get better." What no one told me was all that happens while you're waiting around for those seasons to hurry up and come, to hurry up and go.*

The more Kim wrote poetic prose with raw honesty, the blog grew until she had hundreds of followers who left comments, writing, *That's how I feel.* She began receiving letters, cards, and books from all over the world. A letter she received from a woman in Paris stated, *I want you to know Kay is my angel and that's why I left my abusive marriage.*

As Kim continued on her journey toward healing six months after her sister's death, she and her family started The Kay Marie Sisto Memorial Walk to End Domestic Violence. The walk became a part of their healing process. After her death, Kay's organs were donated, and one of Kim's deepest desires was to meet the man who breathed through Kay's lungs. The man arrived with his family and completed the walk.

"Two weeks ago, I got a letter from the woman who has Kay's liver."

The letter arrived on the fifth anniversary of Kay's death. The woman listed twenty things she could now do as a result of the transplant.

"That's one way that Kay is giving back. I don't know how you can go forward if you don't give back," Kim said. "I have a Facebook page, and everything is about domestic violence. If I find an article, I'll post it."

Nine months after Kay's death, Kim wrote a blog post, *Letter to Kay's Murderer*, and published it on her blog, Myinnerchick.com, on February 25, 2011: In one excerpt, she wrote:

Why couldn't you have left Kay alone?
Found somebody else to save you?
Found somebody else to make you feel whole?
Kay's love, love, love overflowed into the universe like oxygen.
You tried to take it all.
Absorb it all. Make it your own.
But her love wasn't enough for you.
I told Dad 15 years ago — "He's Going To Hurt Her One Day."
And you did—Didn't you?
You son-of-a-bitch. You evil son-of-a-bitch.
She was the best thing that ever happened to you...the best part of you.
And she was Everything to me.
Connected to my veins, my heart, my soul, my blood, the root of my roots.

"Where are you now with your anger toward Mike?" I asked.

"I've released it. I just feel sorry for him. He could have been so much more. It's taken five years for the veil to lift, but now I'm seeing the light with bringing awareness to others who are abused and bringing awareness to organ donation. I get letters from people saying they left their relationship after they read my blog. Those things have been very healing. Even talking about that day, everything turns black. I incorporate that pain into my life because she was so beautiful, and she made me beautiful."

*   *   *

Michal Gonzalez: interviewed in June 2015, Israel
Doron Cohen: 8/12/1981-2/15/2003
Cause of death: Bombing on the Gaza Strip

Doron, tall, handsome, athletic, ambitious, and a rule follower, didn't consider himself a hero, though his sister, Miki, and his parents did. His sister said he fit all the characteristics of a hero, which is why they were all terrified when he entered the service for a three-year term as an Israel Defense Forces soldier and Staff Sergeant.

At twenty-one years old, he was proud to serve his country and fulfill his lifelong dream of becoming a Tank Commander. Now, with three months remaining, he felt a measure of relief that he'd survived because he couldn't imagine the pain it would have caused his parents and sister if he'd been injured or killed. He was one of the lucky ones, and now he was in the clear. When he told his parents he only had to guard borders for the remaining three months, his family was finally able to exhale, knowing he was safe and would be returning home soon. Both he and his sister had grown and matured into adults. I imagined that he was looking forward to moving out of younger-sibling mode and moving into friendship mode. Three easy months and he would be home.

Doron smiled as he thought about life after the service while he and three other soldiers rumbled along the Gaza Strip in their tank, headed south. As their tank neared the Israeli settlement of Dugit in the Gaza Strip at 8:30 a.m., it ran over a hundred-kilogram explosive device. The tank burst into flames. Doron and the other soldiers were killed instantly, as thick, gray plumes of smoke billowed into the blue sky.

In a news report I read, it stated, "Major General Doron Almog told journalists Saturday evening (February 15, 2003) that the Palestinian militant group Hamas planted the bomb. Hamas had earlier said its Izzedine al-Qassam military wing planted the explosives that destroyed the tank.

A statement faxed to news agencies said the attack was carried out to avenge the death of two of Hamas' militants killed by Israeli forces in a clash near the Gaza town of Beit Lahia earlier this week.

Palestinian witnesses said Israeli helicopters hovered over the scene as rescuers tried to approach the tank which burned fiercely following the explosion. They said a number of bodies were retrieved from the tank and carried away on stretchers after the blaze was extinguished over an hour later." (http://www.haaretz. com/news/funerals-held-for-4-troops-killed-in-gaza-tank-blast-1.18985)

When Doron's family was informed of his death, Miki said, "The perfect family by the books explodes because some part was missing."

Miki had been a flight attendant and made the decision to quit her job and "ground" herself. Following the traumatic death of her brother, she felt it was her duty to live her life as her brother had. She wanted to be a good student, a good daughter, an ambitious person, and be kind to people. She said, "That creates a big change in me because I was not a rebel anymore. I became the good girl like he was the good boy."

Like so many siblings who try to fill the shoes of their deceased sister or brother, believing it will help to alleviate some of their parents' pain and loss, there comes a turning point when the surviving siblings must reclaim their own lives. For Miki, she felt lost for the first year-and-a-half to two years and had no idea how to maneuver through her upturned world.

"After those two years, I actually fulfilled for my parents and me everything they expected from him. I made a very good career. I was the best employee of the decade. I was high ranked in the positions in the company. One day I got tired of that. I got tired of being the good girl, the one to satisfy my bosses and my parents."

To help Miki in her healing process, she went to see a spiritual healer in the center of Tel Aviv. When she entered the healer's home, she said something magical happened to her. They met for an hour and twenty minutes a week. They talked for forty minutes and meditated for another forty minutes.

"It was amazing. I allowed myself to connect with my spiritual parts with her," Miki said.

"I lived with her until I moved here. She helped me to be at peace with the death of my brother."

The energy worker helped Miki to understand that Doron's destiny was not her destiny. She asked herself, *How am I going to make it good and not get stuck in the pain and the hurt?* Miki said before she could heal from the therapy, she had to feel the pain and anger first and allow herself the time to grieve.

I could hear my own energy worker, Lindsey, say to me, "The anger will come. In time, it will come, and you'll have to deal with it. You'll have to feel it so you don't get stuck in it."

Though I had experienced flashes of anger in Hong Kong, they didn't last long. I realize now that I was still reeling from shock and denial during the duration of that trip. When I returned home, I thought, *Piece of cake. I'm not an angry person.* As Lindsey professed, the day arrived when rage consumed me over Rocky's death. A more palpable rage arrived later and smoldered, like hot embers in a wood stove, when my widowed sister-in-law, imprisoned by her own pain, began to project her profound grief, and subsequent bitterness, onto our family. I was ill prepared to deal with the ugliness of anger. I'd awaken each morning soaked in sweat, as I lay in bed and thought about Setiawan. I worked with Lindsey for close to a year, and during each session, she'd remind me to let myself feel my way through, at times, the debilitating emotions. I'd weep on the table as the pain and anger sliced through my heart like a million tiny knives.

"You have to feel it," she said. "So in the end, you can be free."

Nine years after the loss of her brother, Miki traveled to Thailand to contemplate her life with an open heart. She fell in love with her future husband, who was from Chile. She uprooted her life, left Israel, her parents, her friends, and her apartment behind to begin anew in Sweden.

"I said *hasta la vista*. Everybody was shocked. *How can I do this? I grew up in Israel.* I moved to Sweden when I was thirty-five years old," Miki said. "I was brave enough to leave everything behind and to create a good life and to live the life I wanted because if I didn't lose my brother, I wouldn't have been brave enough to do it. But I did it, and now I've lived here for three years, and my husband and I have two kids."

I'm moving to Bali, Sis, I could hear Rocky say as Miki shared her story of how she mustered the courage to leave and how happy her parents were for her despite how far away she'd be from them. Where had my deep sense of responsibility come from that it was my role to remain in Maine and be there for my parents long before Rocky's death? After his death, I felt anchored to my parents, responsible for taking care of them as they aged and as they grieved. What would it feel like to dream about having that kind of courage?

"I have to explain," Miki said. "The people losing their son, daughter, and sibling in the army in Israel is like a cult, and you live it all the time. If you're home, outside you're tagged as the person who lost her brother in the army. I don't want to be tagged like that. I am a person of my own. And now I'm living here very peacefully."

Though Miki has come to terms with her brother's death, she said, "I think he died for a stupid reason for a stupid war that doesn't relate to us and doesn't belong to us, but I've learned to live in peace with myself and my sorrow. Not the whole country's sorrow, not my parents' sorrow, but with my sorrow. Every year I go to Israel for Memorial Day. I have reached this peaceful place with his death and released the anger, released many things the moment I was alone without the impact of the people around me."

* * *

At a time when I was grappling with my anger over my brother's death, I felt detached from my family and myself. I remember thinking during one of our family gatherings, which no one ever told me, that each and every time we were in the same room, we'd walk along the sharp and fragile edges of those cracks in the foundation of our family. We were like high-wire acrobats without a balancing pole or a safety net, teetering so close to the edge, as memories crowded around us like ghosts on the haunt. I asked myself, Do I whisper my brother's name, "Rocky?" Do I stand in the center of my family and scream "ROCKY" as if I were on a mountaintop, hollering to God, the angels, and the spirit guides? Or was I to hold his name in my mouth, like a bitter slice of apple? I didn't know what to do, what to say, or how to act around my family. I didn't know how to console my parents. I felt unanchored and vulnerable.

When I was in graduate school, I wrote my dissertation on the healing benefits of writing. After Rocky's death, writing became my oxygen mask and offered me that sacred, safe place to bleed my heartache and wrath onto the page. Through that process, I came to know for certain that our siblings want us to live joyful, thriving lives. I've found fully re-engaging in my life has been the most powerful way to honor Rocky and release the anger over his passing.

After I was able to let go of my anger over Rocky's

death, I still had to deal with intense and unsettling emotions around Setiawan. As I worked with my grief therapist, I came to the realization that it was a choice to cling to or liberate myself from my rage, sadness, and regret. It took three years of deep emotional and spiritual work for me to release the remaining kernels of anger over what transpired between Setiawan and me. Through meditation and prayer, I was able to forgive her and myself. I wish only peace for Setiawan and pray she finds new love again. I was also able to surrender and accept that I could not have any contact with Anna. I hope one day when she's older, I will be able to talk to her and tell her about her father. For now, I hold her in my heart and hope that we'll see each other again before I pass on and reunite with my brother.

When anger comes, as it will for the majority of us who have experienced a profound and untimely death, the question becomes, "How do I let go of my anger?" As Jeneen, Kim, and Miki moved through their grieving process, they were able to release their rage over the unjust and barbaric murders of their siblings. Anger is a toxic energy that can get stuck in the body and wreak havoc on our nervous and immune systems over time. Rage detaches us from our true essence, our soul. It steals our joy and sense of peace. It blinds us to the beauty in our lives. But, as most of the surviving siblings noted, first we must feel it fully so the energy can move through our bodies and rise up and out of us, offering space for new and peaceful energy to take its place.

CHAPTER 9
Letting Go of Guilt

Darra Gordon: interviewed in July 2015, New York
Steffani Anne Gordon: 12/14/70-7/6/86
Cause of death: Struck by a train

On Labor Day weekend, Darra's mother had slipped away for a beach weekend with her boyfriend. Darra's grandparents were babysitting, even though Darra was fourteen years old and her sister Steffani, the one she looked up to, was close to sixteen years old.

Friday night, Darra was over-the-moon-excited to be given the privilege of hanging out with her sister. It was the first time her older sister ever confided in her about her boy troubles; they were becoming friends.

Steffani said, "I can't believe he went away with his friends and didn't invite me."

"That sucks," Darra said, feeling as though she and her sister had reached a new level in their relationship. Darra didn't want the night to end.

On Saturday night, Steffani knocked on her sister's door.

Darra said, "Come in."

"Listen," Steffani said, "I'm meeting some friends tonight, and I need you to cover for me. Just tell Nana and Grandpa it's OK if I go out with these people. Don't tell them they're on the list."

Again, thrilled that her sister trusted her, Darra would have done anything for her hero, hoping one day her sister would include her in her plans. "OK," she said. "I'll lie."

Steffani was one of those souls who was more sensitive to the vibrations of the world. Things hit her harder, which is why Darra believed she used drugs to numb the emotional pain. Darra loved everything about her sister except the drug use. Steffani was sweet, bright, and athletic. She was a gifted skater and almost trained for the Olympics. Darra admired her sister's sense of fashion and all of her friends who wore cool clothes.

Darra heard her sister come home and later that evening, she heard her sister sneak back out to meet people who were on the list of individuals she wasn't supposed to be hanging around with because they were a bad influence.

Out in the night air, Steffani was finally free, and by the time she got home, her grandparents would be tucked under the covers fast asleep.

Steffani met up with her friends in the city. When she arrived, her friend passed her a joint laced with PCP. She exhaled a plume of smoke, feeling high and blissful. As the hours ticked by, she had trouble maintaining her balance. When they all had to leave and get home, Steffani was slumped over, barely conscious. Her friends didn't know what to do with her and left her by the train tracks.

As the train headed toward her, Steffani stumbled on the tracks. The conductor couldn't stop in time before striking her, killing her on impact.

Darra was in a deep sleep when she was awakened at 2:00 in the morning by a loud banging on the door. She threw the covers off and got out of bed when she heard her grandmother answer the door and let out a glass-shattering scream.

Darra ran to the stairs, sat down, and listened as two police officers relayed the horrible details of Steffani's tragic death. "We need someone to come and identify the body," one of the officers said.

Darra's grandparents made the dreaded call to her mother, who returned home after she identified her daughter's body.

"I just remember my grandmother giving me a nudge to go out the door, telling me to greet my mother and give her a hug. My parents were going through a divorce at the time, so Dad was not living with us," Darra said. "It was the first time in my entire life I saw my father cry and the last time until the end of his life when he once again spoke of my sister."

After the death of her sister, Darra's world tilted. Her home went into foreclosure, and she bounced around to different friends' homes, changed schools, and had no friends to provide her with comfort. Darra had never felt that depth of loneliness.

Her mother, a psychologist, was drowning in a sea of grief and turned to pot and booze to ease the crushing ache in her heart. It would take a year before she'd return fully to her daughter, who now saw the world through a different lens.

"I had a sense of how big the world was and how many people were in the world, but at the same time, I could see just how tiny we were in the universe itself," Darra said. "It created a feeling of spirituality for me. It was nothing I had learned, just something I experienced."

Though she was a teenager, she believed it was her duty to be responsible so nothing would ever happen to her that would cause her mother more pain.

"I didn't think my parents would ever survive anything ever happening to me. I was very cautious. I really felt that the load of the world fell on me. I had to become my sister for my mother. Mom loved shopping [like my sister]. I grew up very fast, and I understood that I needed to be really careful with myself."

I shared that same feeling after Rocky died. The pain it caused our family, my parents, was almost too much to bear at times. I prayed to God every night to please keep my brothers and me safe. *Please,* I'd beg, *take my parents before you take any of us.*

"I know what you mean," I said to Darra. "As a young teen, did you ever feel any guilt that you had lied for your sister?"

"I spent years of feeling guilty that it was my fault, and I was responsible for everything. It was one of the heaviest loads and impacted me a huge amount," she said.

Darra went through her life, rewinding the events of that night, imagining if she could have done one thing differently, if she had spoken up, her sister would still be alive. They would have become best friends, raised their kids together, and celebrated holidays and birthdays.

"That was the most difficult thing to overcome. It took me becoming an adult and looking at a fourteen-year-old to understand it wasn't my role, and it wasn't my job to keep my sister safe. Again, I think a lot of the work I did with the therapist helped me to see the world was not on my shoulders."

As a result of Steffani's death, Darra chose a vocation to honor her sister's life by giving back to young people who are going through hard times. "My whole trajectory has been totally different since her death. I believe that's why I got into the nonprofit world. I always wanted to do something to create meaning for my life," Darra said. "Why am I here and she's not? I'm working with young people who are at risk. I hope that providing kindness honors her."

* * *

Maryann Garcia: interviewed in March 2016, Connecticut
Joseph Belluccio: 5/10/60-7/7/15
Cause of death: Cause unknown

Joseph's younger sister, Maryann, always told him he beat to his own drum, and he was fine with that, he thought, as he lay in the hospital bed, grateful the surgery had gone well even though he was still in a lot of pain. At fifty-five years old, he had enjoyed his life, his neighbors, and the stray friends he picked up along the way. He was a city guy, and though he never had a wife and kids of his own, Joseph adored his nephews and niece. It didn't matter what they did together, he made sure it was fun, whether he went on their class trips or took them to the zoo. Joseph had a tight bond with his older sister Debbie and younger sister Maryann, but it was his mother who he'd committed his life to after his father died the previous year. They didn't live under the same roof, but Joseph embraced the role as her primary caregiver and visited her every day, where they chatted over a cup of coffee. He thought, *What would Mom do if anything happened to me?*

Joseph didn't have a bucket list of what he wanted to do before he died; he wasn't that kind of guy. Life was simple by design. Traveling around the globe didn't interest him. He got pleasure from being surrounded by the people who mattered to him, people who loved him.

Since last May, Joseph had grown to appreciate his life even more than he had before. His health issues began with a pain in his stomach. After numerous tests, the doctor thought he had a blockage of some kind and prescribed medications. The pain worsened and became debilitating until Joe couldn't tolerate it anymore, and he was admitted to the hospital. It was like that for a while—in and out of the hospital. It had worn on him. Finally, he had a colonoscopy, and the results nearly crushed his spirit. He was diagnosed with colon cancer but required more tests and surgery to identify what stage he was in.

A week later, Joseph was discharged. Maryann and Debbie helped their brother down the hospital hallway when they bumped into the doctor.

"We got the test results," the doctor said. "It's good news, Joseph. You are in stage one. It's very treatable."

They were all relieved, and when they got to the car, Joseph said he wanted to stop by their mother's house to tell her the good news. After he returned home with his sisters, Joseph took a shower and changed into clean clothes. He would make a full recovery. It wasn't his time to die. As Maryann and Debbie were getting ready to leave, he thanked them and said, "I'm going to take a little walk and get some fresh air."

We can do this, Maryann thought. *This is going to be*

OK.

A week later, Joseph called Maryann and told her he was still suffering from intense pain. Maryann said he needed to go back to the doctor, though she wasn't overly concerned because her brother never did well with pain and was somewhat of a hypochondriac. She promised him she would visit the following week to check in on him. Two days later, on Monday, Joseph called her at work, reiterating how much pain he was feeling. Maryann told him to push through it and assured him he'd feel better soon.

Later that day, Maryann called her mother and said she planned to travel to the Bronx to check on Joe, but her mother said it wasn't a good time because Joe still wasn't feeling well. The following day, Maryann was at her son's basketball game when her mother called. Maryann picked up the phone and said, "I'm at the game, Ma. Can I call you back?"

"I'm worried about Joe," her mother said. "I didn't see him today. He didn't come over for coffee."

"That's strange," Maryann said. "I called him on his cell phone, and I called him on his house phone. He didn't answer me and didn't call me back." Still, Maryann wasn't alarmed because if Joe wasn't feeling well, he didn't want to be bothered.

A half hour later, her mother called again and said she was going to have Joe's neighbor, Fran, go and check on him. As Maryann, her husband Luis, and son Mark were leaving the game, her mother called again—this time hysterical.

"Ma, what's the matter? What's the matter?"

Fran got on the phone and said, "He was cold."

"What do you mean?" Maryann asked. "What do you mean he is cold? Are you trying to tell me my brother's dead?" Luis looked at her, and she said to Fran, "I'm coming. I'm coming."

Frantic and in shock, Maryann said to her husband, "You have to get me to the Bronx as quick as possible. I think Joe's dead." But even as she said the words, she

120

couldn't comprehend it could possibly be true. She was in Connecticut, and it would take her an hour to get to the Bronx. Maryann couldn't get a hold of her sister, and her mother was alone. She had to remain calm. Maybe Fran was wrong or confused.

When her sister finally called her back, Debbie said, "I'm here. I'm here."

Maryann said, "OK. I'm coming." She disconnected the call and said, "Luis, please hurry up."

At that time, she didn't cry because she simply didn't believe her brother died. He couldn't be dead. It's a mistake.

When they arrived at her brother's apartment, it was crawling with ambulances and bystanders. *Oh my God. It's true,* she thought. When Maryann saw her mother, clinging to her walker, screaming and crying in the middle of the sidewalk, she jumped out of the car and ran to her mother's side, while her sister was bent over, hysterical and vomiting. The EMT worker asked Maryann if he could examine Debbie.

"Yes," she said, feeling like she was trapped in a bad episode of *Cops. This can't be happening.*

As they took Debbie's blood pressure, Maryann tried to calm down her seventy-nine-year-old mother, terrified she was going to have a heart attack. She was desperate to see her brother, but she wasn't allowed to go into his apartment until the police arrived.

Extended family members began to show up, in-laws, kids, cousins, aunts, and friends.

"We were all there," Maryann said. "When the police arrived, they told me we could go in, me, my mother, my sister, my husband, and my older sons. My brother was seated at his desk like he just fell asleep as peaceful as can be."

When her mother started screaming her son's name, Maryann was frantic to soothe her. "All my concern was for my mother," Maryann said. "I didn't think about myself. I didn't even know how I felt."

As the nightmare stretched into midnight, Maryann, frazzled and dazed, held her brother's cat close to her chest as she combed the streets, looking for a neighbor who would adopt her brother's beloved pet. At 3:00 in the morning, the medical examiner finally arrived and asked Maryann and Debbie a few questions.

"Do you want an autopsy?" she asked.

"We both said, no. Not that we didn't want to know what happened, I just didn't want to put my mother through any of it. It was about 4:00 in the morning and it was just me, my mother, my sister, and one of my brother's neighbors who watched as they carried my brother out of his apartment in a black body bag. Then my mother and I walked back to her apartment alone in the night. I still could not believe this was happening."

There were numerous tasks that needed to be accomplished. Maryann had to get paperwork from her brother's apartment so her mother could make arrangements, but the police refused to give her the key because her mother was next of kin. Maryann had no other choice but to break into her brother's apartment. Her mother's fragile health couldn't withstand going through the court proceedings to gain access to Joseph's apartment.

"At that point, I just put a smile on my face. I took the paperwork, said thank you, and left [the police station] with my girlfriend. We did what we had to do, and now I have his paperwork and his safe. I was not going to have my seventy-nine-year-old mother, who just lost her son, jump though anybody's hoops. Me and my sister went and we made his arrangements at the funeral parlor of his choice."

To spare her mother further pain, she and her sister arranged a viewing and a short service all in one day. Four days later, Maryann left her mother briefly to return to her home in Connecticut, pack some clothes, and take a shower. Maryann had a close-knit group of girlfriends who descended on her with food, support, and an abundance of love.

"Every day new friends came and went. And it

helps you get to the next day, the next moment. A call or a text, it carries you through."

We talked about the last phone call with her brother when he told her he wasn't feeling well. It triggered a memory of when Rocky and I talked about his vertigo. I told him I had a friend who suffered from vertigo, forcing her to take a six-month leave of absence from her job. I said I'd ask her what caused it and how she healed. I'd let him know as soon as I found out anything. I followed through with only part of my promise. I sent her an email, and she explained the vertigo was the result of the flu. She said she required balancing activities to regain her equilibrium. I never passed the information onto my brother because I kept forgetting. He, too, never followed up with me, but I still hung onto guilt for a long time because of it. I asked Maryann if she carried any guilt.

"Oh yeah. I carry guilt. Yes. When it came to my brother, the last few days, I was working, and I took off work for his surgery and took another day off to pick him up from the hospital. I tried not to take any more days off."

Maryann lived an hour away from her brother and was unclear what Joseph's aftercare would entail with chemotherapy, radiation, and follow-up doctor's appointments. She had limited personal days she could use at her place of employment and needed to save them so she'd be available to support her brother.

"I was thinking rationally, but of course I have guilt over not going down there. The last time I spoke to him, I feel guilty because he wasn't feeling good, and I was trying to be positive, and I told him everything would be all right. Obviously, hindsight is 20/20. That guilt helps me to make different choices today."

At the time of the interview, Maryann was in the early stages of grieving. She had lost her brother eight months prior to our conversation. She said, "Every day I cry. I feel like there is a part of me that's gone that I'm never going to get back. I'm not the same person I was before he died. I don't care about a lot of the stuff I used to care about."

As with most siblings in the early stages of grief, Maryann had difficulty concentrating and retaining information. Her brain felt scrambled as though she were walking through a fog. As the days and months passed, Maryann knew she needed help to deal with the pain and guilt over her brother's death.

Though she had good friends who had lost their parents, she said, "Until I went through it, I didn't get it. I will be the first to say I was naïve, stupid, whatever you want to call it. There are certain things in life that you don't know what it's like until you've walked in those shoes. And this is one of them."

Maryann and a dear friend, who was grieving the loss of her mother, decided they'd support each other by going to a grief group together.

"It was hard, but we went together, so it made it a little bit easier," Maryann said. "I'm not going to say it solved all my problems, but it did make me realize that I'm not the only one that cries every day and is in a fog. The group meets once a month and we are going to go again."

*   *   *

Jill Williams: interviewed in June 2015, Northern Utah
Jennifer Ren'ee Caffroy: 7/20/1988-7/10/2007
Cause of death: Undetermined - Gunshot wound to the head

Eighteen-year-old Jennifer's heart pumped with a new level of excitement and hope that she hadn't felt since she lived in Las Vegas, where she was nicknamed *Vegas* by her friends. It suited her at the time because she had an electric energy about her and could ignite a room with her smile alone. If friends had a problem they had to sort through, it was Jennifer's ear they wanted and her advice on how to resolve it. With a tender heart, it was her goal to leave people better off than how she found them. If she could stop a friend's tears and make them smile instead, she felt she had accomplished an important task. Her life had been good. It was a time when she had been passionate about cheering, swimming, and drawing.

Two years ago, when she was sixteen years old, her parents worried about the drugs, violence, and fast pace of the city. It was no place to raise a young teenage girl, they said, so they up and moved the family to a small Wisconsin town, which was close to Jennifer's maternal grandfather's home. Jennifer was excited about the change even though she was going to miss her friends. Her brother, Jeremy, who she adored, was moving to Wisconsin, too.

Jennifer glanced in the mirror, ran a hand down her long sandy brown hair with golden highlights, and admired the rhinestone stud in her right nostril. She'd been miserable lately and was still upset with her older stepsister, Jill, from a call they had two weeks ago. Jennifer hung up on her and hadn't spoken to her since. But she loved Jill and knew they would make amends soon.

Life was about to get better because she was moving to California with her brother Jeremy and his fiancé. Though she loved her parents and had met some new friends, most of the kids bullied her because of the way she dressed, styled her hair, and the jewelry she chose to wear. Jennifer wasn't afraid to be a little different and to be herself. She had her own unique fashion sense and didn't care about the latest trends. She wouldn't mold herself into someone she wasn't just to get the kids off her back. It was time to leave.

Jennifer was ready to spread her young-adult wings and abandon the small Wisconsin town. Maybe she'd come back and maybe she wouldn't, but she was definitely leaving and had dreams of going to college for a nursing degree. She was tired of feeling depressed and started smoking more weed to numb emotions that bubbled up. It had been bearable when Jeremy moved back to Wisconsin. He lived in a cool apartment with his friend Adam. Jennifer spent most of her free time there, hanging out and partying.

When Jeremy's fiancé conceived, he made the decision to relocate to California to be in close proximity to his biological father. Jennifer begged him to take her with them, and he agreed. They were driving to California the following day. It would be a dream come true.

Her parents weren't psyched about it, but she was a legal adult, and they couldn't stop her. Besides, she would turn nineteen in eleven short days. They just asked her to promise them that she would finish high school. Jennifer made the promise and was more than ready to make a fresh start and meet her tribe the way she had in Vegas.

The following day, after Jeremy packed his car, he had to inform Jennifer there wasn't enough room for her. He was sorry, but she wouldn't be able to drive with them.

The hopes she held shattered into a million glinting pieces, but she told him she understood, she'd be fine, and not worry about it because she didn't want to make her brother feel bad. Maybe she could move out to California later and pursue an RN degree.

The following evening, she went to her brother's old apartment to chill out with Adam. After all, misery loves company, and Adam fit the Webster's dictionary of MISERABLE since his breakup, and lately, she did too. Maybe things turned out the way they were meant to. It was clear Adam needed her support. She committed to staying with him throughout the night to ensure he didn't do anything stupid. Jennifer had already collected the guns in the apartment and gave them to her mother to hang on to. Jennifer hated guns, couldn't stand the sight of them. Their power frightened her. Guns killed and she was terrified Adam might try to end his life if he was under the influence of drugs and alcohol.

As Adam got high, I imagined him droning on about his life, how much he missed his girlfriend and daughter, asking over and over, Why did she leave? How could she do that to me? How could she take my daughter away? Jennifer did what she always did; she tried to cheer him up. She thought about how she could make the elderly smile in the convalescent home where she worked. She corralled the clients to the common area, played rap music, and inspired them to dance with her. Jennifer would do anything to infuse sunshine into their drab, dreary days. But her cheering-up tactics were not working with Adam. He was a mess. It had been a long, disheartening day, and her mood was anything but light. When Adam pulled a .357 revolver with a six-inch barrel from a desk, she inhaled a breath. *Where had the gun come from?* A few minutes later, a shot rang out and echoed in the night.

While Adam wandered outside the apartment saying, "I can't believe you did it. I can't believe you did it," Jeremy and his fiancé had just made it to Colorado. Her sister Jill and her boyfriend were on their way home from a ten-day visit in Utah. They decided to make a pit stop at a bar in Palm Springs, California, to have a cocktail and a bite to eat. The two were relaxed, excited, as they discussed the possibility of a permanent move to Utah when Jill's cell phone rang. It was Jeremy's biological father, who Jill had known since she was a toddler. When she answered the call, he asked, "Have you talked to your brother?"

"No," she said. "The last I heard they were in Colorado." Her phone beeped, alerting her to another incoming call. It was her step-cousin, Billy. She said, "I have to get this. I'll be right back." Jill clicked over to her cousin and said, "Hey what's up?"

"What are you doing?" Billy asked.

"I'm at a bar having a drink," she said, the sun warm on her face.

"Oh my God, Jill," he said, "you don't know."

"Know what?" she asked.

127

"Jill, Jennifer's dead. She shot herself."

The color drained from Jill's face. "I have to go," she said to her cousin.

She clicked over to Jeremy's dad, who was still on hold and said, "I just found out. I have to call Dad." A tremble rippled through Jill as she stumbled outside, sat on a curb, and called her father over and over until he finally answered. "Please tell me not Jennifer."

"I'm sorry, Sis," her father said.

"Please, Daddy," Jill begged, "not Jennifer."

"We're waiting for the police," he said.

Jill asked, "How is Mom?"

"She's not doing well. We are looking at going to the hospital."

"Please call me. Please let me know." Jill didn't know how her stepmother, who suffered from chronic health issues, would survive the traumatic death of her daughter. As soon as she hung up with her father, unable to process Jill's death, Jeremy's fiancé called and said, "I don't know how to calm him down. I can't calm him down."

"Put him on the phone," Jill said. When Jeremy got on the line, Jill said, "You have to come to California so we know you're safe."

"This is my fault," he said, overwrought with emotion. "This is my fault. I should never have left her. I'm going to go after him. Why didn't he take care of her?! This is my fault."

As I listened to Jill talk about her brother and his guilt over his sister's death, I asked her what she did when she got off the phone with Jeremy.

"I just remember knowing that I had to take care of things," she said, tearful. "My dad had my stepmom to worry about. I was the one who called all of my family. I called my older sister, my bio mom, aunts, uncles, and friends. My dad was so strong. He's very religious and he said, 'It's going to be OK. There is a bigger plan.'"

For twenty-three-year old Jill, the nightmare had

just begun. As rumors began to spread about whether or not Jennifer's death was a suicide or homicide, the town's people cobbled together their own rendition of what transpired in the apartment that night. *They were playing a game of Russian roulette. There was, after all, only one bullet in the chamber. They were secretly in love, a story of Romeo and Juliet. They conspired to kill themselves, but Adam chickened out. Adam did it; it was a clear case of homicide.*

The small-town police had never dealt with such a horrific, complex scenario. They weren't equipped to investigate the evidence. Neither Adam nor Jennifer's hands were tested for gunshot residue. Those who knew Jennifer well, said, "There's no way she did this to herself."

"It was a pretty tumultuous time," Jill said. "They were trying to build a case on homicide. I didn't really know what or who to believe. I also didn't understand that if this person was so guilty, why wasn't he in custody? There's no way her thumb could have pulled the trigger. The police were trying to prove that there was no way she could have done it herself. Adam was never arrested or put into custody."

As Jill continued in her quest to mine for answers, she decided to search for Adam because he was the only person who knew for certain how Jennifer died, but she was never able to find him.

Though Jill and others read through a 200-page police report, discovering the bullet entered over her right eyebrow and discharged out the back left side of her head, there was still no hard evidence that she died by suicide. Jennifer, who frequently sat on her heels with her elbows on her knees, was sitting in that position when the gun discharged. She fell forward and died instantly. According to the report, that was an unusual position for people to shoot themselves. When the police arrived, the gun was on the table, not in Jennifer's hand. Why would Adam move the gun and implicate himself? Jennifer didn't have a burn on her temple, indicating the barrel was not pushed up against her skin.

There would have been a bigger shatter pattern on her skull. Nothing added up, and the report brought them no closer to a definitive answer.

Jill had to learn to live with the unanswered questions, which can complicate the grieving process. At some point, it stopped mattering because the outcome was the same. Jennifer was dead.

"That must have been so difficult," I said. I had some depth of understanding of how it feels to live with ambiguity and unanswered questions. When Rocky died, our family had to deal with relentless unknowns because the doctors had no cause of death. It would take a year for us to receive the autopsy report and even then we were left with the haunting question, *If he had been in the U.S., could the doctors have saved his life?* He was left in a hallway for four-and-half hours. When he began to hallucinate, the doctors placed him on the psychiatric ward, before he was finally admitted to the ICU. What if he had received care more quickly? We knew he died from swelling of the brain, but what caused the swelling? Three-and-a-half years after his death, Setiawan sent our family an email. She said she had gone to a tarot card reader. The reader told her Rocky died from meningitis. True? Not true? Though the autopsy report stated there were no signs of meningitis, could the pathologist have missed something? Like Jill, the outcome was the same, and the "why" stopped mattering in the end.

Jill carried guilt over the last conversation she had with her sister, which kept her up at night. Two weeks before Jennifer's death, they talked on the phone.

"I think that was what I struggled with really bad. The last time we talked, we argued, and she hung up on me because of a snide comment I made. It was supposed to be a joke, and she didn't think it was funny. I tried calling her back once, and she didn't pick up the phone. If I had known, I would have continued trying to call her because it was a couple of weeks before her death."

When Jill made the decision to return to school, it helped her to let go of her guilt. As a social worker, she wanted to spare families the pain and anguish that her family went through.

"I figured if I could stop just one family from going through this by putting myself out there and get to the problem before it became a suicide, maybe Jennifer's death would yield something better. I don't know if you ever come to terms with it, but there's definitely some point of acceptance that takes place because you cannot change what happened."

*   *   *

When my days stopped spinning, I discovered a regret I've carried around since my brother's death— not reaching out to him more frequently while I still had the chance. During the last time I saw him on his visit home, my brother said he felt like I had abandoned him in the past year. When Skype was removed from my work/home computer by our IT department, I could have bought an iPad to FaceTime. I could have researched the other numerous ways to communicate with a brother who lived on the other side of the globe, but I didn't—I had PLENTY of time. And yet, there was a little more to it.

The truth was I was furious with Rocky for being angry with me when he was the one who chose to live halfway around the world. The death of my brother, coupled with my guilt, awakened me every night between two and four in the morning. I began sleeping in the guest bedroom so I didn't disturb my husband. I stared at the ceiling, cried, silently punched my pillow, and squelched the screams. I wanted to unzip my skin and rip my own heart out because I thought the pain was going to kill me too.

It was moving through the guilt and pain that helped me to arrive at a place I had never been before. In order to get on the other side of those intense emotions, I had to gain an understanding of what burrowed beneath the guilt. Both the therapy sessions and my volunteer work at the Center for Grieving Children helped me to fully accept and embrace the truth: there was nothing I could have done to prevent my brother's death.

I also had to forgive myself for how I believed I failed my brother, his wife, and his daughter. Even though my last conversation with Rocky had not been a pleasant one, he knew I loved him, and I knew he loved me. As with anger, the guilt was not serving me on my path toward healing. It was prolonging an excruciating process and preventing me from reclaiming joy.

I asked myself, *What would I say to a client who came to me with these thoughts? A best friend? A child?* The answers I received allowed a deeper compassion to take root, which was necessary for me to fully forgive myself and move forward. When lingering thoughts of guilt seeped into my conscious thoughts, I said out loud, "Stop." I wrote letters to Rocky and talked to him in my mind. Though cutting off my relationship with Setiawan was heartbreaking, the boundary I put around our relationship was the most loving and kind action I could take on behalf of my mental wellbeing.

Not everyone feels guilt after the loss of his or her sibling. Several of the surviving siblings I interviewed didn't carry any guilt. For those who did and continue to, whether their relationship with their deceased sibling was strained due to addiction issues, suicide, or not feeling as though they had done enough to save their sibling's life, they understood that dragging a trailer full of guilt behind them was and is a heavy burden. Our deceased siblings do not want us to suffer. They want us to live fully and joyfully.

CHAPTER 10
Blessings in the Lessons

Sisters Yvon Stokkink and Marissa Kerkdijk: interviewed in June 2015, Holland
Mattijs Kerkdijk: 5/17/82-9/7/14
Cause of death: Suicide

The day before his mother's birthday, Mattijs received a text from his sister Yvon, who offered to pick him up the following day and bring him to his mother's birthday party.

My back is killing me, he texted back.

Oh, I'm so sorry to hear that, and I hope you feel better, Yvon wrote. *I assume you're going to tell Mom yourself that you can't come.*

Yvon never received a reply and never expected one. The next day, Yvon, her husband, Hans, her sister, Marissa, and brother-in-law, Marlo, went to their mother's home to celebrate her special day.

"Where's Mattijs?" Yvon's mother asked.

"Didn't he contact you?" Yvon said.

"No." Her mother cried because they both understood his silence meant he had slipped into the darkness of depression.

The following morning, Yvon awoke, riddled with anxiety and worry about her brother's mental health, given his history of depression. She wanted to reach out to him, ask if there was anything at all she could do to help lift his spirits, but chose not to because she feared he'd clam up and not respond, which would have increased her anxiety even more.

Yvon decided she would watch a movie he downloaded for her. She could text him and tell him how much she enjoyed it, giving her a light, breezy reason to check in on him. She'd gauge what next steps to take based on his response. Maybe she'd invite him over, and they could hang out together. If she had to, Yvon would go to his apartment and start banging on his door.

When she attempted to watch the movie, she couldn't open the link. Yvon thought, *This is even better because now he can troubleshoot for me because he knows much more about computers than I do.* Yvon texted him, *You know, brother, please help me out here because I'm getting frustrated trying to get this to download. I'm getting all these fault messages. What am I doing wrong?*

Mattijs walked Yvon through the downloading process and a long and lovely text conversation ensued between them. They swapped jokes, and he sent her an email with another link to make it easier for her to watch the movie. After the two-hour film, she texted him and told him she enjoyed it because it made her feel better.

The conversation rinsed away her earlier concerns. Yvon sighed, relieved he was in a healthier headspace than she had thought. She wrote, *We'll hang out soon. Just one more hug and I'm off to do the dishes.*

He wrote, *Luv ya.*

Back atcha, she texted.

Before or after the texting with Yvon, Mattijs made a grilled cheese sandwich, eating half, while the other half sat untouched on a plate. He inhaled a breath, stood, and got busy making a shrine for his family in his small two-bedroom apartment. Mattijs pushed the coffee table against the window and laid out a cloth at the base of it. Then, he gathered family photos, four of his favorite DVDs that he knew his family loved, and placed them on the altar he had created.

I imagined Mattijs sitting quietly with a notepad and pencil as he wrote the first note to his family: *Dear Mom, Yvon, Marissa, Hans, and Marlo, I am sorry I did this to you. I've been depressed for years. This is because of money issues but also because almost nothing about myself is positive. And always that pain in my back. Life is too hard for me, and I see no other way out. I've been thinking about ending it for years. Your love kept me going. I can't let you pay for my life anymore. I can't go on anymore. I love you.*

The second note was to his mother, and the third one to his oldest sister: *Yvon, I love you. You are sweet and kind. You are smart and intelligent. You have a warm and good heart. Stay strong.* Mattijs penned two more letters, one to his youngest sister, Marissa, and a combined note to her boyfriend, Marlo and his brother-in-law, Hans.

When he finished it, I imagined that Mattijs didn't feel sadness. Though he didn't want to cause his family pain, perhaps a sense of relief washed over him. He decided to write one last note to the whole family, providing them with more comfort after his passing. *You've done what you could. I hid my pain and feelings, mostly to spare you pain. I don't think you saw this coming. I will watch over you. I will always keep loving you.*

Mattijs carefully laid the letters side by side on the altar. Soon he'd be free from his psychological and physical pain, but he still had a few more things to do before he ended his life. To make it easy for the authorities to contact his family, he wrote down his family members' names and addresses and shoved the piece of paper into his pocket. He got on his computer and searched for any insurance he could buy that covered a suicide but found nothing. Next, he checked the train schedule. At 9:30 p.m., he put his coat on, walked out of his apartment, locked the door, and headed toward the station. At 9:45 p.m., Mattijs leapt in front of an oncoming train.

Marissa, the youngest sibling, shivering and in shock, rang Yvon's doorbell at 4:00 in the morning. Her husband, Hans, jostled from sleep, climbed out of bed and opened the door. Marlo, Marissa's boyfriend, explained that Mattijs died by suicide. The police went to Marissa's home first with the tragic news.

Yvon said, "I still remember the scream I gave when he told me. I can still hear it in my head."

As I listened to Yvon, unexpected memories flooded my thoughts. I was back in the kitchen, holding the phone, falling to my knees, listening to Setiawan, as she said, "Brian's gone, Sue. You have to be brave."

Prior to Mattijs' death, Marissa didn't have the same level of patience for her brother that Yvon had. She said, "My way of thinking was 'Suck it up. Put some pepper in your ass. You need to get through, and find a way to get through, and do it.' Maybe it's a bit harsh, but I couldn't deal with him the way Yvon did. She was always so sweet to him and always making sure he wasn't left behind and thought of him. But I couldn't do small talk with him because I was really annoyed by how he got through life. And that's what really bothers me now because now I know how really bad it was. He couldn't get through it any other way."

Since they lost their brother, Yvon and Marissa have each traveled her own journey as they came to terms with their brother's death and how it changed their perspective on life.

Yvon said, "I quite desperately wanted something good and meaningful to come out of this situation. And yet, my problem was, after it happened, so many things no longer had any meaning for me. So many things felt frivolous and a waste of time. Even though I know it's a very useful thing to be resting your body when it's feeling tired, when you're watching TV all day due to health reasons, it just feels like you're killing time. And for me, that particular phrase, to kill time, felt so disrespectful of the gift of life, considering my brother and the way it ended. I very much resented that. At the same time, I was faced with the fact that I had very little energy to do anything. So how do you go through your day without the energy to do much, but at the same time, really want to turn every situation into the most useful thing you can think of? That was really troubling to me."

Marissa, on the other hand, said, "For me, it was a really weird time. I couldn't go through the grief process because I had a daughter. He died on the 7th of September, and my daughter was born on the 13th of October. Having a baby does take up your time. I started working in January/February. I thought to myself,

Wow, we are dealing with this quite well. I'm already at work, things are going fine, and I'm going with the flow. I feel like a super mom. I had energy. I'm thinking of Mattijs but in a good way, and I'm not always crying anymore. If this is grief, it's quick."

A few weeks later, Marissa's energy plummeted, and thoughts of her brother plagued her daily. She thought of questions she wanted to ask him and things she wanted to say to him. Marissa had been pregnant at Mattijs' funeral and felt too emotional to stand up and speak. She said, "My family all had the best words. I couldn't picture myself saying something without totally melting down, seeing all that grief, and holding my big belly. It was too much."

"How do you feel about it now?" I asked.

"I wrote a few things down, and it helped me to try to let it go. Now, I have something written down, and in my mind, I can say what I've written at the funeral. And that's what's important, to know what your feelings are so you can deal with them."

Marissa said one the most important lessons she learned as a result of her brother's death is that people who are hurting and depressed need to reach out for help. If people don't let anyone into their inner world, into their shadow side, "Then no one knows and no one can help you, and no one can understand it, and it builds up inside," Marissa said. "I appreciate life more. I'm very lucky to have all those people around me, friends and family. I always did and now even more because I know there is so much to be grateful for. Maybe it's having a child. I also think it's because of Mattijs. Sometimes I talk to him or see him seeing me. I now run 5Ks. I was never sporty. This is really something for me. When I ran my first 5K, the first thought that came in my mind, I could hear him say, "'Way to go, Sis! Good job! Good on you.'"

Yvon said, "When you relax and allow things to unfold, life knows where it wants to take you. If you really trust that, you stop working so damn hard. It doesn't need to be a struggle. When you're struggling, that's your signal that you're off course. The course back is love. Love for yourself, love for your surroundings, love for life. When I say love, I mean the purest form of love. I get the image of that compass. Anytime you feel a negative emotion, it's a gentle reminder, a tap on your shoulder, that your compass is off and you need to adjust your thinking."

"Yes, that's it exactly, Yvon," I said, thinking about a piece I wrote on Rocky that helped me to understand the splendor of life. *I feel the coolness rise from the earthy depths and know I have a choice, we all do: to climb down, curl up tight inside a hardened heart with each loss we endure like a periwinkle snail, or climb up, spread arms and hearts wide to joy, to heartache, like a parched seedling welcomes the rain and the sun because it needs both to grow.*

Here, thirteen months later, I tip my head to my dimmer sun, open my arms wide to love, to life itself. Gratitude swells and rises up through my body, as I maneuver my way along those cracks because I had time with a brother who has given me the courage to say yes to joy, to heartache. Without you, Rocky, I would not know the full depth of one without the other.

* * *

Shamola Chintamani Kharkar: interviewed in November 2015, Zambia
Salonee Chintamani Kharkar: 7/20/85-8/16/12
Cause of death: An unknown infectious disease.

Salonee returned to her home in Denver after a glorious two-week vacation in Zambia with her parents and her younger sister and best friend, Shamola. Her family surprised her with a mini cruise on a lake. Sadly, while Salonee was in Zambia, her grandmother died in India, and her father flew to the funeral but returned home to say goodbye before her flight back to the States. He embraced his oldest daughter and told her how much he loved her. After Salonee left Zambia, Shamola and her parents flew back to India for the thirteen-day mourning period. Though Salonee knew they were in mourning, she hadn't been feeling well and decided to call them to let them know something just wasn't right with her health.

Shamola asked, "What's wrong?"

"I have a fever," Salonee said. "It's not going away, and I don't know what it is."

After their brief conversation, Shamola hung up the phone, hoping her sister would feel better by her birthday. Shamola couldn't imagine a day going by without talking to her sister, who had been more like a mother. She admired how Salonee could step into a room and infuse it with vibrant colors. While Shamola preferred a safe and steady life, her sister had an insatiable thirst for adventure. If Shamola had a tough day, she depended on her sister to lift her spirits. Salonee had a magic about her, and Shamola couldn't wait to spend a month with her when she started her summer college course in Denver.

A couple of days later, Shamola called Salonee on her birthday, July 20.

"This fever isn't going away," Salonee said. "Do you think it's malaria?"

"It could be," Shamola said. "You just got back from Zambia."

There is a two-week gestation period before symptoms show up, and because the family was from Zambia, they were already equipped with medication needed to cure malaria.

"You're probably right," Salonee said. "I'll take the medication." For her birthday, she planned to go see the opening show of *The Dark Knight Rises* in Aurora—the same cinema, same day, and same screening when James Eagan Holmes killed twelve people and injured seventy more. As fate would have it, she canceled her plans because she still had a fever and didn't want to see the movie until Shamola could join her.

Shamola and her parents were not concerned

about Salonee's health issues. They were sure the medication would heal her. As they headed to the airport to return to their home in Zambia, Shamola tried several times to reach her sister, but Salonee didn't answer her phone. When they arrived at the airport, their flight was delayed and then canceled. The following evening, they went back to the airport, and their flights were delayed again, forcing them to spend another night in a hotel. As the hours passed, they began to worry because they still hadn't heard from Salonee.

In the hotel that evening, Salonee's father Rahul finally received a call from her. "I'm not feeling well at all. I feel horrible," she said. "I think I'm going to go to the hospital." Salonee hung up, drove to the hospital, and admitted herself into the ER.

Meanwhile, Shamola and her parents received a call from the airport, alerting them to return immediately because they had been rebooked on a flight home. Within their six-hour flight, Salonee moved from the ER to the ICU.

When Shamola and her parents landed in Zambia, they called the hospital, and Salonee answered the phone. "Mom, I'm fine," she said. "Don't come and don't cry." She couldn't say much more because she was too weak.

The nurse took the phone. "You need to come," she said. "Your daughter is very sick. Is there anyone nearby who could come see her?"

Salonee was a kind and gentle soul, thinking about others before herself. She didn't want to burden anyone with her problems, so her family called her friends and colleagues and asked them to get the hospital as soon as they could. It was nighttime in Zambia and daytime in Denver. A good friend of Salonee's gave Shamola and her parents a live update, but they lost the power and couldn't Skype. The last words they heard on the other end of the line was, "Oh my God, oh my God," and the phone cut out, leaving the family frightened and confused.

The doctor called and informed the family that Salonee went into cardiac arrest with a multi-organ failure. They were able to resuscitate her within ten minutes and placed her on a respirator to revive her lungs and dialysis for her kidneys.

Shamola and her parents panicked and felt helpless. While Salonee's father talked with the doctor, her mother booked flights, and Shamola canceled the summer college course in Denver. She was supposed to leave the following day, so she already had a booked flight to Colorado. Together, the family flew to Dubai. They were not able to get on the same connecting flight from Dubai to Denver, so Shamola flew to New York, and her parents flew to Seattle. When Shamola arrived in New York, she felt defeated. The flight had been delayed by ten hours. Emotionally and physically exhausted, Shamola fell asleep and missed the closing of the gate by one minute.

Now frantic and desperate to get to her sister, Shamola had a meltdown and tried to break down the gate. Airport staff refused to let her board the flight and re-routed her to Boston the following day. By the time Shamola reached the hospital, Salonee was unresponsive, but when her family talked to her, her heartbeat increased—a sign she could hear them.

For two to three weeks, the family camped out at the hospital, refusing to leave Salonee. The doctors called in two officials from the Center for Disease Control (CDC) in Atlanta and two from Fort Collins. The doctors were stumped. The officials from the CDC put the family through a grueling interview, going over minute details from Salonee's lake cruise in Zambia, and still, they found nothing. She was tested for forty to fifty infectious diseases, including HIV, cancer, and Ebola—all came back negative.

As the hot summer days passed, Salonee appeared to be improving. She moved her head when her family spoke to her. A close college friend came to visit Salonee and stood on the right side of her hospital bed.

The doctor stood on the left side. He bent down and said, "Hey, look, your friend Sage is here."

Salonee swung her head from left to right and began to become more responsive. Shamola and her parents were elated—Salonee was out of the woods. Shamola knew her sister was going heal from the mysterious disease. On August 2, the family was down the hall from Salonee's room when they received a call in the morning.

"Salonee's doing great," the doctor said. "She opened her eyes."

They ran into the ICU and could see her eyes open. They smiled and waved at Salonee, relieved and hopeful that she would fully recover. The doctors were inside Salonee's room, but they wouldn't let Shamola and her parents enter. The family's joy was short-lived when the nurse came out of Salonee's room and said, "We found some blood in her ventilator tube, so the doctors need to check."

Throughout the course of the day, Salonee's health took a sharp turn. The doctors discovered blood in her nose and lungs. The blood was building up. The family, wrought with fatigue and fear, became overwhelmed with the amount of information they were receiving from the medical staff.

In the evening, Salonee was placed back on the respirator, and her fever continued to fluctuate. Salonee was in a Christian hospital, so her mother went to pray in the church downstairs, while Shamola and her father slept in the hospital in the event anything went wrong. The next morning at 5:00 a.m., on Shamola's birthday, they received a heart-crushing call.

"We need you to go to the ICU right away. You have one hour with your daughter, and she's going to pass away," the doctor said. "We can't do anything anymore."

Though Salonee's temperature had risen to 106°F, her father refused to let the doctors give up. He rounded up the twenty-five physicians on Salonee's case and said, "You have to figure something out. You cannot tell us we have one hour. You cannot tell me my daughter is going to pass away on my other daughter's birthday. You cannot give up."

The doctors continued to try various modes of treatment. They put her on a lung bypass machine, which pulled her through the day, and her fever came down. She remained on the bypass machine for three days until the doctors discovered blood was not reaching her toes on her right foot and feared they'd have to amputate.

The doctor said, "Her lungs are doing great and her toes need blood. Let's get her off the machine."

The medical team put her back on a ventilator, but the new concern was clotting. The doctors were trying to get her blood thickness back to normal, but clots developed in her legs and around the lower part of her body. The doctors worried the clots would go to her heart, so they performed a mini surgery to prevent that outcome.

The family was then informed Salonee needed a plasma transfusion. The blood tests showed her white blood count was so low she could have been an HIV patient, but that test had already come back negative. When they looked at the plasma, the doctors said that something was wrong with all the cells in her body. The family watched the plasma going into Salonee.

A close family friend, who used to live in Zambia and moved to the U.S., had dropped out of a pre-med program. He stood at the door with Shamola and said, "Can you see the plasma going in? Look at the bag next to it."

Shamola felt physically ill. Salonee's blood was thick as sludge and looked like red porridge.

Around August 13, the doctors wanted to do a bone marrow biopsy, and the family said, yes, but only when she is stabilized. On the fourteenth, Salonee had been stable the entire night, and the doctors said it was the perfect opportunity to do a bone marrow biopsy.

Throughout this time, Salonee's father had spent several hours on the phone with priests in India and astrologers. He recorded prayers, put them on a disc, and played them in Salonee's hospital room. Her father was not going to let his daughter go but started to panic when every astrologer told him that something was wrong with the date of August 16.

While the doctors did the bone marrow biopsy, Shamola's father told her and his wife to leave the hospital and rest at Salonee's home. The next day, they woke up early and returned to the hospital. When Shamola saw Salonee's colleagues, she knew something was very wrong because Salonee's colleagues only came to the hospital if it was serious.

"What's going on?" Shamola asked, fearful of the answer she'd receive.

Her sister's colleague said, "Don't worry."

Shamola's dad ran into the ICU family room and said, "Something is wrong with her. They are taking her for a CT scan because something is wrong with her brain."

Unable to endure the possible impending death of her daughter, Salonee's mother went down to the church and remained there for the day, believing in the miraculous powers of prayer.

After the CT scan, the doctors came into the room and said, "There's something wrong. Her eyes are fixated, and she's not responding to light."

A half-hour later, the doctors had the CT and bone marrow biopsy results. They said, "We don't know how to tell you this. Your daughter is brain dead."

Shamola, through tears, asked, "What do you mean she's brain dead?"

The doctors explained that due to the blood thinning, the clotting, and the fevers, blood had built up in the space between her skull and skin and pushed her brain through the cavity of her neck, snapping the brainstem. The disease that killed Salonee had also taken her bone marrow. Salonee's heart continued to beat because she remained on the ventilator. Shamola and her father asked the doctors to give them the night before breaking the news to Salonee's mother. Her mother's best friend was flying in the following day, and they wanted to wait for her, so she could help break the life-shattering news to Salonee's mother.

On the afternoon before shutting the ventilator off, family and friends sat with Salonee and sang all of her favorite songs. They Skyped Salonee's grandparents and her younger cousins. From 4:00 p.m. to 9:00 p.m., they sang songs. Friends came in to say their final good-byes. At around 9:00, they decided it was time to let her go because her vitals were dropping.

Shamola doesn't believe in mourning and sitting and crying. She told every person in that room, "Cry if you want to, but we have to celebrate life. We can't sit around for days crying. The person who passed away celebrated life to the fullest. She did whatever she wanted to do. She enjoyed life so much, and we should be celebrating everything she did and all of her milestones." Shamola believed those words motivated her parents to not give up.

As I listened to Shamola cry as she told me the heartbreaking ordeal they'd been through, I imagined myself in Rocky's hospital room, holding his hand, playing his favorite Grateful Dead tunes, or one of his more recent favorites, *Climb* by Miley Cyrus.

Though it was painful for Shamola's family to witness the demise of Salonee, they had the gift of saying goodbye. Salonee could hear their voices, offering them some measure of comfort. My brother died alone in a foreign country, in a foreign hospital room in the ICU. For me, Rocky dying alone has been one of the most haunting images to live with.

As I interviewed Shamola, I realized I still clung to the sadness that no one flew out to Hong Kong when we learned Rocky was in the hospital. Though I wanted to be with him, I didn't listen to my intuition because everyone assumed he would make a full recovery, including me. Rocky's death changed my perspective on the world, and I wanted to know if other siblings had this same experience.

When I spoke to Shamola about her sister, who was eight years, two weeks, and two minutes older than her, she said, "We were inseparable. We were two souls into one."

"How has her death changed you?" I asked.

"I went from being the younger child and not worrying about anything to feeling like I have to take care of my parents. I have to do things right. I have to take care of my future. Her death motivated me to push for more in my life. The only thing I can do right now is help my mom feel better and help my dad feel better because they had to go back to Zambia. They were alone. I was alone. I had to be there for them on Skype. I had to do as much as I could do as a daughter to fill those two shoes. I honestly don't talk about my feelings about my sister because whenever I'm talking to my parents and my sister comes up, I know my mom is going to end up in tears."

"I think that's what makes sibling loss different from other kinds of losses," I said. "This belief that we can't talk to our parents because it will cause them more pain. But you know, I've learned at the Center for Grieving Children, the opposite is true. Our parents want to talk about their child. It's impossible to cause them more pain," I said, "because the loss is always on their mind. It's not as if they forget about it and we remind them."

I encouraged Shamola to talk to her parents, believing it would create an even closer bond than the one they already shared. It would offer the space and freedom for her parents to grieve and talk about Salonee; it would offer Shamola the same. They were the three people who knew and loved her most in the world.

When we finished the interview, I shared a story with her about my experience when I opened the floodgates for my father to talk about Rocky. I too tried to never bring his name up in front of my parents for the same reasons as Shamola. I told her one evening after returning home from the bereavement group I facilitate, I called my father and explained to him what I learned at the center about the grieving process. I said, "I'm sorry I've not given you the space to talk about Rocky. I was scared it would hurt you."

My father's voice cracked and he said, "I'll talk about him anytime anyone will listen."

At the end of our interview, Shamola thanked me for sharing the story and said she'd begin to talk more about her sister with her parents, so they could walk through their grief together and mine for the golden nuggets of joy that Salonee would want for all of them.

*   *   *

Emily Gary: interviewed in September 2015, Virginia Beall Dozier Gary known as Nap: 7/19/58-5/10/15 Cause of death: Massive heart attack

On Mother's Day, Nap awakened eager to begin his thirteen-mile run and relieved he already fulfilled his duty as a son. The previous day, Nap took his mother out for a Mother's Day lunch with his wife, Amy, and his youngest sister Emily. This year, he made the decision to celebrate a day early, so he could attend the local festival and listen to his nephew Sam play music with his high school jazz group. He was grateful he lived close to his sister Emily again. Moving to Virginia had been the right choice. They loved to run together, share stories, and make each other laugh. A month ago, on one of their runs, Emily asked him what his wishes were if and when he died.

At fifty-six years old, Nap was in better shape than most men his age, so he never reflected on his post-death wishes. Nap said, "I want my ashes spread on Timpanogos." It was a mountain in Utah that he climbed every year and had become a special place to him.

I could picture Nap's blue eyes twinkling, his smile wide as he thought about their lunch together. Nap needed the run to work off yesterday's feast. They splurged and ordered big at the Restoration Restaurant. After his jog, he'd meet up with Emily at the festival. Maybe he'd take a different running route today. It was going to be a good day.

While Nap went on his run, Emily buzzed around her house, preparing for the festival, excited Nap cleared space in his day to watch her son play his music. Yesterday's lunch had been bearable because of her brother's ability to make her stomach ache with laughter. She, too, relished in her own ability to swap jokes as her amused brother chuckled.

When she walked out of the restaurant, she thought, *I'm as close to my brother as I've ever been.* He looked so handsome in his sky-blue shirt that matched his eye color. Emily smiled, as she thought about their next era together. Rather than seeing him twice a year, she'd now get to enjoy their "every day" friendship. After he moved to Virginia, they became peers, and she was no longer just Nap's baby sister. Nap was her hero, her rock, and he had supported Emily throughout her life. Now older, she wanted to pay it forward and support Nap, doing her part to help him care for their ailing mother. She couldn't imagine a world without him in it.

As the oldest of four, Nap carried a heavy burden, managing their mother's financial affairs. Soon to be the CEO of his company, he already had an overflowing cache of responsibilities, but he never complained, at least not to Emily. Nap told her if he had to move again due to his job, he didn't want to strap her with the added tasks given the load she already carried as a single mother of three boys. Emily felt a lightness as she drove to the festival, steeped in deep gratitude for the joy her brother brought to her life. She rolled down the window, cranked the radio, and breathed in the sweet fragrance of the magnolias. It was going to be a good day.

Meanwhile, Nap ran across the breathtaking Virginia countryside, magnolia trees in full bloom, exhilarated. He had plenty of time to finish his run, get home, dash in the shower, and make it to the concert on time. As he came upon a red picturesque barn and glistening, still lake, a sharp pain ripped through his chest, sending him to the ground.

Twenty minutes into the concert, Emily stood next to another proud mother as they listened to their kids spill music into the open air. In the back of her mind, she wondered what could be keeping her brother and sister-in-law. It wasn't like Nap to be late or to blow anything off, especially when it came to family. He had looked forward to the concert all week. When her cell phone rang, she was relieved it was Nap's wife, Amy.

"Hi, Em. I'm sorry, but we're going to be late. Nap isn't home from his run yet. He must have taken a longer route and lost track of time." Amy paused and added, "I think I see his car. Let me go."

When the show ended, Emily began to feel anxious as her heart rate accelerated. *It's nothing,* she thought as she strolled by the vendors, looking at the arts and crafts. She walked all the way to the other end and stopped at a booth that sold Bonsai plants. She picked one up to buy for Nap because he collected them when she was a little girl. It reminded her of their childhood and his wood-paneled room with his velvet Elvis poster hanging on the wall. She set the plant down when her phone rang again. She glanced at the caller ID. It was her other brother Loren. *Oh, how sweet,* she thought. *He's calling to wish me a Happy Mother's Day.* She answered the call and said, "Hey."

"Sit down," Loren said. "I have some really awful news."

Emily could tell he'd been crying. Her stomach twisted. She knew. "No, no, no," she wailed.

"It was a heart attack," Loren said, through his own tears. "He died, Emily."

"No, no, no," she said over and over again. "Where's Amy?" Emily was confused as to why Amy hadn't called her when she lived ten miles away, and Loren lived in Boston. She learned later that Amy didn't want Emily to find out the tragic news through a phone call, so she called Emily's friend Martha and asked her to go the festival and tell Emily in person.

Emily cried, held her head, and caught a glimpse of Martha walking toward her. She held the phone in her hand, collapsed to the ground, and looked at her friend. "I know," she said. "I know."

Through sobs, Emily said to me, "I remember things falling out of my purse, and strangers stopping and asking me if I was OK. The jazz-group mother that I had been standing next to during the concert came up to me, and I said for the first time in my life, 'My brother died. Today. Just now. This morning.' I remember I didn't use the word 'died' for a long time after that. I still don't use it that often. Died, to me, meant such a finality, and I couldn't even comprehend it then."

With each interview, I relived the three-minute phone call with Setiawan. I had not anticipated the visceral response I'd have to their losses while holding my own in the space between us. My brother died all over again with each raw story, and I was left haunted by his half-open eye.

As Emily shared the details of Nap's death, I could see him jogging toward the stunning Virginian barn, the pristine lake, and hoped his last thoughts, before he died, were comforting and peaceful.

"I don't think people really understand the profound depth of loss we feel when our sibling dies," I said. "I remember reading once (I don't recall where) when a sibling dies, parents lose the past, spouses and children lose the future, but siblings lose both."

"Yes," she said. "It's difficult losing a sibling because everyone is more concerned about the parents and the spouse and children left behind. It's like there's no space for a sibling to grieve. My friend came up to me, literally moments after I just found out Nap died, and said, 'You have to be strong for Amy.' I was stunned and thought, *He was my brother. Don't tell me anything I'm supposed to do.* It was the beginning of feeling like my grief was secondary. There was little acknowledgment of my grieving process." She continued, "I'll never forget when the kids were finding out and coming home, and the heartbreak of having to retell the story a thousand times. My cell phone filled with messages from people. Then I went into this fog."

We talked for three hours that day. Emily had lost her brother four months earlier at the time of the interview and remained in the thick fog of grief for two years. After more time passed, I had a follow-up conversation with her and asked, "Throughout your two-year process, have there been any blessings that have come from such a tragic loss?" I asked.

"I believe the universe gave me two gifts the April before he died. The first was when I asked him on our run what he wanted for his body when he died," Emily said. "A month later, I realized I was the person who knew the answer to the question of what he would have wanted. In some way, I feel this was a gift to me from the universe, though I never thought I would need the knowledge so soon after."

On another April day, Emily called her brother to relay her depth of gratitude and appreciation for all he did for their family. She said, "You may think when Daddy died that you lost your biggest fan. But you didn't. I'm your biggest fan, and I love you so much."

In retrospect, she believed the universe had a higher plan and knew the crushing blow of her brother's death would tip her world upside down. She was grateful for these two sweet memories to hang on to, grateful she had the opportunity to thank her brother for all he did, and grateful to know where to spread his ashes.

"I spent the first six months after Nap's death just weeping and walking. On my walks alone, I would wail and beg God to give me a heart attack too. At the time,

I felt so grief-stricken and paralyzed that I didn't feel I was enough for my kids. They were so gentle and understanding, though. I remember my youngest saying 'Mom, I know what he meant to you.' They grieved so tremendously for me and for themselves. Our house was so dark for so long."

"When did the light shine again?" I asked.

"I remember vividly the first time after his death that I looked forward to anything. Four months after his death, friends came to town for a music festival, and I knew seeing them would soothe my aching heart," Emily said. "That feeling of looking forward to something really struck me because I realized it was the first time I had looked forward to anything at all since Nap's death. I remember the first time I laughed after he died. My oldest son began to show me videos he thought were funny and would tickle me. For many months, I binge watched Ellen DeGeneres to help remind me of the good in the world and learn how to laugh again. But still, I mostly wanted the heart attack."

Out of desperation, Emily made an appointment with a medium for the first time in her life. She vowed to enter the session with an open mind and heart. After her first experience, she scheduled several more appointments.

"Those experiences with the medium, plus reading books about grief and the afterlife, especially *Journey of Souls* by Michael Newton, led me to a new belief system," she said. "Prior to Nap's death, I wasn't sure what I believed. Two years later, I believe he is still with me and that I will see him again when it's my time to join him. This is the deepest blessing of all."

* * *

In my early social work years as a behavioral home health therapist, I worked with families with complex mental health issues and traumatic histories. Often these families had little hope that their lives would improve because they were unable to see the blessings that came into their lives as a result of their challenges. It was much easier for me to identify those blessings through the remarkable courage and resilience they mustered, as they coped with their personal struggles. I used to say, "I know you don't have any hope for the future, so I'm going to hold hope for you until you can hold it on your own."

After my brother died, I needed someone, anyone, to hold hope for me, believing I would feel good again and happy to be alive. I did everything I could to maneuver my way through the darkness. I read spiritual books about the afterlife, went to mediums, and asked my brother for signs, but what I found to be the most helpful on the path toward healing was to open my heart wide to the blessings that I had always believed arrived following a tragedy.

Rocky's death expanded my capacity to hold the space for people who are in pain, to listen to their stories, and to be that holder of hope in a way I couldn't have been before I went through this life-changing experience. Grief work isn't pretty. It's messy, frightening, and, at times, ugly, and cruel. I know this firsthand. Metaphorically, I've crawled on hands and knees through the cave of despair, bloodied and bruised. I curled up inside myself with all my pain and with our memories sitting next to me. The blessings flowed into my life because I didn't run away from myself or numb my emotions with busyness, alcohol, or drugs. I just let myself feel. Though this wasn't my experience, there are circumstances when prescription medications are necessary for those who are struggling with debilitating symptoms of anxiety and depression.

Three-and-a-half years later, I recognize that I'm stronger than I ever could have imagined. With that strength came newfound courage to engage in the world in a more meaningful, loving, and peaceful way. The majority of the siblings I interviewed, in one way or another, said they don't get upset or stressed out over minor inconveniences that life throws their way. This, too, has been my experience. What used to have the power to send me hurtling into a tailspin, no longer does. Grief strips us down to our core and removes the illusions in our lives. It provides a window into what matters. Grief hurtles us into the unknown and invites us to ask, What is this life really about? What is my life about? Why am I here? What is my purpose? What do I want to do with the time I have left?

Seven months after I bought a new iPhone, my husband and I were invited on a boat ride. I placed my handbag on the dock, backed up, and hit it, sending the bag into the ocean. My husband grabbed it, but not before my phone fell out and sank. I just stood there and said, "Great. Now I get to upgrade to an iPhone 7."

My friends and husband were a little stunned that I didn't react in a negative way to losing the phone. Was it a bummer? Sure. Did it create a hassle? Yes. Was it a big deal? No. It was a phone. It was a minor inconvenience. Rocky's death gave me an acute understanding of how trivial experiences used to have the power to upset me or negatively impact my emotional state. Now, I'm more loving with myself, which in turn allows me to be more loving and forgiving toward others. If I get cut off in traffic, I no longer curse. If someone is rude, I no longer react negatively. I have no idea what kind of day that person is having or what he may be going through. Instead, I ask myself, *How would love respond?* And I respond from that place, not from anger, not from fear, but from a place of compassion for myself and for the other person.

My purpose, our purpose, is to serve ourselves and humanity through love, kindness, and compassion. Although I've held this value throughout my lifetime, it wasn't until I kissed the bottom of the river of grief, with an open and bleeding heart, that I understood. Love is the only life force that matters, and that elevated awareness has been the most profound blessing of all.

CHAPTER 11
Beauty in the Pain

Katie Stickney: interviewed in July 2015, Maine
Timothy James Stickney: 11/11/1994-1/11/2011
Cause of death: Drowning

Tim was no ordinary sixteen-year-old. He was special and had a heart that knew only love. Though he was diagnosed with autism at four years old, it didn't define him. He felt nothing but joy and infinite love for his sisters and parents. Tim's mind was alive with sights and sounds that he revealed with peals of laughter, a shining smile, and a twinkle in his eye. But as much as he connected with his inner world, Tim was deeply attuned to his surroundings. He was always the first to spot a rainbow in the sky or to announce a beautiful sunset. He was proud of his role as manager of his varsity hockey team and of the gold medal he won in the hundred-yard dash at the Maine Special Olympics.

It was Tuesday evening, and his heart skipped a beat as he stepped into the hot tub, which he did every day. The water was his friend, and he could swim for hours at the lake or in a pool. While Tim reveled in the soothing heat of the water, his younger sister Katie, who was in the eighth grade, zipped down a snow-covered mountain trail at Shawnee Peak. She always looked forward to seeing her brother at the end of the day because he brought her nothing but love, joy, and smiles.

Though Tim was older, she worried about him. When he was little, he had seizures until he had an operation. He had an intracerebral hemorrhage on the brain. The surgeon cauterized the bleeding, and Tim had been seizure-free for more than a decade. At fifteen years old, he started having grand mal seizures again, and the doctor prescribed Dilantin.

Katie remembers the day well because her parents

were out of town and her older sister, Morgan, baby-sat her and Tim. Sound asleep, Katie heard a big bang that startled her awake. She almost lay back down but had an intuitive feeling to check on her brother. Katie went downstairs and saw Tim passed out on the kitchen floor. He'd had a seizure while eating his breakfast. She snatched the phone and called an ambulance, as she ran over to check on him.

After that event, the seizures became more frequent. Every time he had a seizure, the doctor raised his dose of Dilantin, and the family had to wring hands, wait, and pray the new dose worked. *He'll be OK,* she thought as she skied down the mountain.

In the hot tub, Tim seized. As his mother walked out of the kitchen to check on him and ask him what he'd like for dinner, she found Tim, lifeless under the water.

"I was fourteen when he died. Experiencing such a traumatic event at such a young age shifted and shaped me into the person I am today. No one really experiences a personal death, like an immediate family member's death, until much older. I was always older than what my age was. I understood things and caught on quickly. I was really mature for my age."

Katie said her brother's death was the most devastating event in her life, and as a result, her perspective on life shifted. Through her grieving process, she gained a new understanding of trivial events that may have, prior to Tim's death, caused a more emotional reaction than was warranted. Now, if she receives a low grade on a test, or breaks up with a boyfriend, she remains grounded, knowing life heals our bruises over time. Through Tim, because of the person he was, Katie is able to see the bubbles of joy in life and cherish and appreciate them.

"I take everything with a grain of salt now. I think I would have been a lot more anxious in high school or anxious about getting into college. I think all of those big experiences would have been more stressful or more heightened, but now I always know that, whatever happens, it's going to be OK. School-wise or job-wise, those things don't matter as much to me anymore. Nothing matters more than being with family and friends, growing relationships with people, and being kind. They're more important than how much money I'll make, or if I'm going to go to graduate school, or anything like that."

Katie no longer takes any of her relationships for granted because she doesn't know how long the people will be in her life. "I really put forth all my effort in the *now* because we don't know if there is going to be a later or tomorrow."

As a Christian, Katie was furious with God after Tim drowned. She couldn't understand if God loved her, why he would take away someone she loved so deeply. Early in the grieving process, she went to the Center for Grieving Children, where she could share stories and memories about her brother. The center gave her a safe space to talk about her sadness without feeling obligated to make someone else feel better, like her sister or her mother.

When kids who had survived a tragic loss surrounded her, she didn't feel alone in her grief, but she continued to cling to her anger toward God. At the end of her eighth-grade year, her friend invited her to a program called Young Life, a non-denominational Christian ministry that talks to high school teens about Jesus and God in innovative and interactive ways. The ministry's goal is to inspire and engage more kids to get involved in their faith. Every year, Young Life leaders take teens on a trip to Saranac Village or Lake Champion. Katie went to Saranac Lake her sophomore year because her friend had a life-changing experience when she went on the trip. Katie hoped she would have a similar experience so she could release her anger toward God and feel at peace.

"I went to Saranac and one night during the week, we went off and had quiet time with God," Katie said.

"I was just trying to marinate with my thoughts and think about Tim and ask God why he took him away from me. Then I had a realization that God didn't take Tim away from me. God gave me Tim for fourteen years of my life, and I had the privilege of having him as my brother. My mind shifted to gratitude from then on out. In another life, I wouldn't have had him as a brother. I wouldn't have anything that I've had. I have amazing memories with him that overruled the sadness at that point. It helps me to become more at peace."

As Katie and I talked about her revelation, I was reminded of a letter I wrote to Rocky on the first anniversary of his death, ending with, *I've waited for four seasons to pass as I was told to. And I did it, brother. I was numb through winter. Clawed my way through spring. Dragged myself through summer. Said goodbye to the person I used to be in the fall. Now, a year later, I stand barefoot in the snow, awake, alive, and changed for good and for the good because of you.*

Because of you, I take more chances. I live more fearlessly, love more deeply, and say "YES" to joy, to life. On this day, I embrace our memories and feel your spirit fill the room because now, after four seasons, I realize you carried joy into—not out of—our lives.

As Katie and I were finishing the interview, I asked her if there was anything she would have done differently during her grieving process if she could turn back the clock.

She said, "I probably would have taken more time before jumping into everything again. Once high school started, I joined everything I wanted to do and got super busy. I think I just pushed my grief to the side because I didn't like to deal with it. It brought up a lot of pain, and I didn't want pain anymore. I was tired of crying and not being able to function. But looking back, I still had a little more grieving I could have done. I think I stunted my grieving process by weighing myself down with a ton of clubs, and sports, and voice lessons, and AP classes, etc. I purposely made myself so busy I wouldn't have time to think about it. I would give myself a little more time to process it and relish in it."

*   *   *

Melissa Doughty interviewed in July 2015, Maine
Alnah Doughty: 12/9/1969-10/10/2005
Cause of death: Cancer (Small-Cell Carcinoma)

Alnah's mantra was "It can be done and how are we going to get it done," which often came in handy, like tonight, when all of her pipes froze in the sub-zero temperatures. I imagined Alnah mumbling under her breath as she got to work on de-icing the pipes before they burst because then she'd really have a problem on her hands. She was a tough Maine woman and a single mother. She didn't have a man around who could help her out with these kinds of tasks, and she didn't need one. Alnah could do anything she set her mind to. At thirty-four years old, she snagged a solid job with an insurance company with securities and annuities. It was the best time of her life, and she relished in motherhood, raising her son, William.

Drano, she thought, that should do the trick. She tipped the bottle and poured it down the drain, hoping it would break up the ice. Next, she had to siphon the Drano back out of the drain. It was a pain in the ass, but if it saved the pipes, it was worth it.

Over the next few days, she began wheezing and thought it was due to her exposure to the toxic chemicals, but she continued to wheeze several days after she used Drano. Alnah decided with her great insurance that she'd go to Maine Medical Center and get checked out. She wasn't deeply concerned as they ran a myriad of tests. There had to be a simple explanation.

Her older sister and best friend, Melissa, was home when her phone rang. When she picked up the call, Alnah said, "They found a mass and you need to come in, and you need to call Mom and Dad."

Melissa felt light-headed. *Please don't take my sister.*

You've already taken my brother. She calmed herself down and thought the mass could be benign. It was too soon to panic. She just had too much knowledge of that horrific disease. Melissa attended nursing school and worked at the Barron Center on the skilled unit with end-of-life patients. She knew cancer, the way it ravaged the body and stole joy and dignity from the patients. After four years of that, and privately working for a family for another eight years, she ran out of fingers and toes to count how many people she helped through cancer to pass over to the other side. If her sister had cancer, she believed, it would be a long and painful process.

When Melissa and her parents arrived at the hospital, the news they received was devastating. Alnah had small-cell carcinoma, which was rare in a person so young who had never smoked.

"Don't worry," Alnah said. "I'm going to kick cancer's ass."

Melissa felt blessed she had some savings tucked away and worked very part-time, so she could take care of her sister and help with Alnah's six-year-old son, William. Before Alnah could begin treatment, the oncologist said they had to start by shrinking the tumor. When she went into the hospital, her lung collapsed because they burned it during radiation.

Alnah was determined to put herself through any treatment she had to so she could live to raise her son. After the burning incident, she went to the National Institute of Health in Maryland to get Lung Reduction Surgery. Their hope was to get rid of the now-diseased tissue that would cause more harm than good. Alnah was nervous about the surgery because the surgeon had to cut her ribcage open to access the lung.

After a slow two-month recovery, she was ready to leave the hospital. Alnah wanted to go home and be with her son. She felt so much better, stronger, and more alive than she had in months.

Both Melissa and Alnah felt like celebrating when she was declared cancer-free in the summer of 2004, a year after she'd been diagnosed. Still, she agreed to brain radiation as a precautionary measure because the majority of brain metastases originate from lung cancer (40–50%) [Schouten *et al.* 2002].

At Christmastime, Alnah said, "I'm not feeling that great. I'm cranky, and I have no energy. I feel something in my throat."

Melissa was terrified the cancer had returned. "Go to Maine Medical Center."

"I already have an appointment."

Alnah hated the feel of the scope down her throat but relieved she'd soon learn whether or not the cancer had reinvaded her body.

"No, there's nothing there," the doctor said. "There's no cancer."

Alnah wasn't convinced. "I know there's something there. I can feel it in my throat. I can feel it."

The doctor reassured her the cancer had not returned and offered alternative possibilities of what could be causing the sensation in her throat.

One month later, Alnah rubbed her fingers over her neck and felt a lump. Each day, she checked it. Two weeks later, it was the size of a golf ball. Alnah called her doctor, who scheduled an MRI, which revealed the cancer had spread throughout her body. It was in her lungs, neck, and liver; she was full of cancer.

No matter how dire the news, she wasn't ready to give up on a life with her son. She agreed to go on ICE, an exceptionally strong chemo, so strong it would turn Alnah into a hemophiliac. The risks were great. Alnah was aware she could bleed out or sustain a hemorrhage in her brain, but she was strong. She could do this for herself and for William.

As she received the treatments, Alnah became sicker and sicker. She couldn't eat or she'd vomit incessantly. Another scope showed the tumor in her neck had closed off her esophagus.

Melissa didn't know how much more her sister could go through. Alnah underwent another surgery so the doctors could drill through the tumor, but it was too hard to penetrate. The mass moved over to the only lung she had left.

After the failed surgery, her oncologist said, "You need to get your affairs in order and get them together quickly. You don't have a lot of time."

Alnah swallowed her grief and said, "I want to take my son to camp one last time."

"Do what you have to do," he said, "but just keep in mind, your life is very short."

Heartbroken, Melissa took her sister home and packed up everything Alnah would need to go to camp with William. Melissa collected Alnah's nebulizer, tubing, oxygen, and medications.

Alnah, William, Melissa, her father, and her nephew Chris drove to camp on Columbus Day weekend. Sunday night, Alnah wrestled with sleep and got off the couch to use her nebulizer. In the wee hours of the morning, Melissa awakened and said, "Why didn't you wake me up?"

Alnah closed her eyes and shook her head. Melissa stayed by her sister's side throughout the night. Monday morning, Melissa packed up camp while Alnah went to the outhouse. When she came out, Melissa thought she had a funny look on her face and asked, "Are you OK?"

"Yeah," she said. "Let's get ready to go home." Alnah didn't know how much time she had left but feared the end was near. *How could she say goodbye to her son?*

Chris, William, and Melissa piled into her car, and Alnah drove with their father. There was a torrential downpour as they headed home. Melissa followed behind her father. When they were close to Augusta, coffee flew out of the passenger side window of her father's truck.

Hairs raised on the back of Melissa's neck. Something was wrong. Her father pulled over to the side of the road, and Melissa pulled in behind him. Melissa got out of the car and ran over to the passenger window.

Alnah held out a coffee cup full of blood. She said,

"I have to get out of the car. I have to go to the bath-room. I have to get out."

Melissa said, "Let me help you." *I have to keep it to-gether. I have to be the anchor.* "OK. Let's get you out." Me-lissa helped her out of the truck and pulled her pants down, as Alnah tried to go to the bathroom. "I'm in so much pain," she said as she gripped her stomach, rocked, and writhed.

Helpless, Melissa watched cars whiz by, furious that no one stopped. She had to get Alnah back into the truck to protect William from witnessing his moth-er's agony.

Melissa called the doctor and said, "I'm an hour away." She turned to her sister, "Do you think you can make it to Portland?"

"Yes. Let's try to get to Portland," she said. Though Alnah didn't know how much more pain she could take, she didn't want to leave her son. She wasn't ready.

When they made it to the Lewiston exit, Melissa's father pulled over again. This time, Melissa called 911 because she wouldn't let her sister die on the side of the road. She called her family. Then she called a friend and said, "Get my mother and brother to Central Maine Medical Center." Melissa drove like a crazed woman be-hind the ambulance.

It was going to be a long night, and Melissa needed coffee. She asked the doctor, "How much time does my sister have? Does she have hours? How much time do we have here?"

He said, "No. No. She has days."

"Are you sure?" she asked.

"Yes," he said.

An hour later, Melissa sat in the waiting room with her parents while her other sister took Alnah to the bathroom. Minutes later, she ran out into the waiting room and said, "Alnah wants you, Melissa. She wants you now."

Oh dear God. Alnah was bleeding out of both ends; she was hemorrhaging. There was no place in the hospital for the family to be together, so they placed Alnah on the pediatric unit. The nurse took her off the morphine pump because the plan was to administer medication through her port.

Melissa marched upstairs to the nurses' station and said, "You get that morphine. And you get it now."

Alnah sat in a chair, rocking back and forth in pain until the nurse finally gave her the morphine, and she went limp.

"Oh my God, she's dying," Melissa said. "We have to get her into bed."

The nurses stood around like they had no idea how to transfer a patient. Melissa wrapped Alnah's arms around her neck, got her into bed, and held her until she died moments later.

"That was hard," Melissa said. "But what was harder, after she died, William went to live with his father, and then I wasn't taking care of him every day. I wasn't taking him to school. I wasn't taking care of Alnah. All of sudden everything just stopped, and I was working two days a week. All my family was on Chebeague Island. My mother went into a depression, and I had to figure out how I was going to live my life without my little sister who was always there, and who I took care of and protected. My job was done. But the interesting thing that got me through it is I had to make myself get in the car and go to work. I could have curled up and died with her, but I couldn't because I was alive."

When I was nineteen years old, Melissa's twenty-four-year-old brother drowned. He was a friend of my brother Jim. It was tragic news, but I had no understanding of the way the world crumbles around us when we have a deep loss until Rocky died. Like Melissa, I wanted to curl up and die too, but that wasn't my soul's plan. Listening to Melissa talk about losing not one, but two siblings gave me an overwhelming sense of her strength and courage.

"When Alnah was sick and she was dying, we had really frank talks. She asked me one day, 'What are you going to do when I'm gone?' It was the strangest conversation to have, but I said, 'I'll expand my business. I'm going to learn how to spin wool and have a herd of sheep.' I've done everything I said I was going to do. It's taken me a decade to do it and to be OK with the fact that she's gone."

Melissa embodied her sister's spirit and grew in unimaginable ways. She quit smoking, started mountain climbing, and learned to spin her own wool, and knit hats and mittens. She clipped negative people out of her life who were jealous of the new life she had created for herself.

"My life is so precious," she said. "I'm not wasting any more time with people like that in my life. If you're not positive and good, if you're going to be a negative force in my life, you're out. I'm not one to tolerate cattiness, or gossip, or any of that. I won't play the game. So that's how my life has changed. I'm really trying to be positive and make the best of my life that I can. If that means shedding people I've known all my life, sometimes that's what you have to do. You have to move forward, embrace life, and take the good with the bad."

Melissa went on to say that many people drown in their grief and stay there for years, but she was able to emerge as a new and better version of her former self in honor of her sister.

"I couldn't lay down and die. She wouldn't let me, and she still won't let me. OK, so I'm a warrior now. I've been through hell a couple of times. I know the way. And when I send love and light, I send love and light because those are the things you need. Sometimes that dark place can overtake you, and you can't lose sight of the real reason you're here. So that's my action, just by living, thriving, growing, and teaching."

* * *

Dave Walsh: interviewed in June 2015, Virginia
James Whitten Walsh: 7/29/1959-1/17/2014
Cause of death: Cancer (Multiple Myeloma)

Jim was an architect and project manager. He was a person who people depended on because he was bright, fair, and calm. Even in a crisis, which happened frequently in construction, he remained levelheaded—a noble characteristic he inherited from his father. It gave him a great sense of purpose to lead community events, like re-building projects for a charity organization, and he could fix anything that was broken. On his time away from work, he was an avid sports fan. As a kid, he was a star soccer player and had a line of trophies to prove it. But what he cared about most was his family, his beloved wife, Sharon, and three children, Nick, Ben, and Cara. He was content. At least he was until he was diagnosed, at the age of fifty-two, with an aggressive form of multiple myeloma.

At the onset, Jim was determined to beat the cancer. He couldn't imagine his children being fatherless and his wife, a widow, left alone to launch their children—the youngest of whom was still in high school—into adulthood. First, he completed a round of chemo and then underwent a stem cell transplant. They extracted his bone marrow, killed the cancer cells, and then re-injected him, and it worked. When he was declared cancer free, he was grateful he had been given a second chance at life. Six months later, Jim was crestfallen when he learned the cancer had returned.

Jim was one of nine children, all of whom were tested as potential donors for his second attempt at a bone marrow transplant. His brother Dave was four years younger, and they shared a room growing up in a houseful of constant activity. Jim was the one who showed off his Easter suit, while Dave wouldn't stand still for the family photo. As adults, Jim and Dave grew closer. Each with three children of similar ages, their families spent numerous holidays together and became close friends. After Dave was tested, the doctor said to Jim, "Dave is a perfect match." Hope was high for a successful bone marrow transplant, which would be the cure for the cancer that was threatening to steal his life. Before Jim could undergo the transplant, they had to get the cancer under control.

Once again, Jim went through months of grueling chemotherapy treatments. At times, he had to go several days a week to the cancer treatment center. Dave took time away from work to help out when he could, driving four hours to Jim's home to take him to his transfusion appointments and offer his brother the opportunity to talk about his experience and concerns.

After he was diagnosed, he said to Dave, "I've done a lot of research on this form of cancer, and I don't want to do a whole bunch of crazy stuff because I want a quality of life." Yet, his family needed him, so he used his levelheaded approach and continued to work with the physicians to fight the cancer.

As the fall of 2013 approached, the markers in Jim's blood tests were looking promising for the transplant. Dave again traveled four hours to Johns Hopkins Hospital to undergo his own thirty-day preparation work for the procedure, which was scheduled on November 1, All Saints Day. The only remaining test was a final bone tap test to assure the cancer levels in Jim's bone marrow were low enough for the transplant to succeed. The day of the test, Dave, hopeful and eager to save his brother's life, awaited a call from Jim or his wife Sharon, which never came. Several days later, Jim called with the disheartening news that Dave feared. The bone tap showed that the cancerous cells were all through his marrow. The transplant was canceled, and Jim's doctors continued to explore other possible treatment options.

For many years, Jim and Sharon hosted a Thanksgiving dinner for the extended family. Several of Jim's siblings, including Dave and his family, would gather with all their children and the thirteen cousins of the next generation. Everyone looked forward to this annual tradition, which was always a lot of fun and brought great joy to Jim and his siblings. Due to Jim's illness, another brother, Tom, filled in as host. Though Jim was weaker than he'd been in a long time, he was able to taste the turkey. He said he really enjoyed the meal and the company of the large and loving family.

For two years, he took the medicine his oncologist prescribed, but everything the doctors tried, failed. Jim was tired and no longer felt he had any quality of life. Around Christmastime, he made a big decision to stop treatment and wasn't sure how to break the news to his wife, but he was done with pills and blood transfusions.

Dave and his wife immediately put their lives on pause to be with Jim and Sharon and helped arrange for the other seven siblings to come in time to visit. Two weeks later, Dave had one work commitment he had to attend. While he waited for the train to return to his brother's bedside, Jim transitioned out of this world and into the next.

Dave and his wife stayed with Sharon and her children for a week after his death, providing comfort, stability, and support during the most devastating time in their lives. Dave drove Sharon to the funeral home to pick up Jim's ashes, and his siblings asked Dave to write and share a eulogy at the memorial.

When Dave went to Johns Hopkins, preparing for the bone marrow donation, the professionals warned him that transplants don't always work. They said if the transplant failed, "survivor's guilt" was a possible donor reaction. Dave dealt with his own version of this, sharing with his wife at one point, "I was supposed to save him, and I didn't even get the chance to try." While Dave hadn't "followed in Jim's footsteps," as his next oldest brother, he did serve as a role model, and they shared a strong connection.

When Dave turned fifty-two, the same age as Jim when he learned he had cancer, he began to experience a fear of being diagnosed with a life-threatening illness. Instead of pushing the fear away, running from it, or denying it, Dave recognized it as a part of his grief work. He took on Jim's levelheaded calmness and was patient and understanding with himself. Dave reached out to his other siblings and continued to nurture a connection with his sister-in-law, nephews, and niece.

"I have a way of confronting some issues," Dave said. "With Jim, I asked him, 'What do you want to do?' He said, 'If we're not actively working toward some sort of successful intervention, I don't want to not be able to drink a beer.' Toward the end, I talked to him a lot about dying."

Since his brother's death, Dave tries to carry the best of his brother inside of him. Jim was gifted at communicating with people. He made them feel important and listened to, like they were the only person he was interested in.

"At some point, about nine months past his death, I decided that I would carry that forward and represent that for him," Dave said. "I would try to be very intentional when I talk to people. I want to know what they have to say, and what they say is important. I want to hear people. Maybe it's a sense of responsibility to act honorably and mindfully. I don't give myself the same slack to be self-absorbed like I used to."

As Dave took his solitary grief walk, he allowed the sorrow over his brother's death to open him up, rather than shut him down, or hide away from it. He said he didn't always handle the grieving process well and that was OK.

I listened to Dave, and it seemed we shared commonalities in the way in which we approached the grieving process. Instead of closing down, I, too, allowed my agony to open me up and sink fully into my grief. One sleepless night, I tiptoed down the stairs, slipped outside, and stared up at the low-hanging moon, so close to me it looked pinned against the black canvas with a thumbtack. I reached out a hand to snatch it from the sky, tuck it inside my heart, feel its warm steady glow burn through my body, filling the empty places my brother's death left behind. Perhaps, I thought, I'd be able to float, or fly into the midnight sky, join him there in the crook of a star, swing our legs, and whisper all that he gave to me in his short life. How he inspired me. Expanded me. I'd tell him my favorite parts about being his sister and the infinite ways he changed my life and is changing it still. I stood there and cried under that moon, aching to hug him one more time.

"What's changed for you as a result of Jim's death?" I asked.

"My appreciation for life has intensified, but that's been going on. Having gone through the experience of this ability to be fully who you are with other people seems to increase. Not necessarily with everybody. A lot of people are still behind a mask. When my dad got sick, I couldn't be with him, so I did hospice volunteer work as kind of a proxy thing ten years ago. When you're with someone in that position, there is no bullshit anymore. They're fully there and this is what's happening with me. After Jim died, I'm more like that more of the time. I'm ready for deeper connections."

* * *

As soon as I learned my brother died, I wanted my soul to knock down the walls of my bone and skin and join him there on a fat downy cloud in the sun, dancing to his favorite Grateful Dead tune. I was unable to see any beauty in the heartbreak. Season after season slipped by without notice. I didn't care when autumn turned green maple leaves into rich jewel colors. I numbed out during Nor'easter snowstorms that socked me in, as I huddled by the woodstove. I walked past the gifts that spring brought to me: buttercup yellow daffodils, azaleas, rhododendrons, and magnolias. Throughout the warm summer months, I passed on invitations to walk along the beach, squishing sand between my toes, as waves crashed against the rocks.

My grief had become a shade that I pulled down over my life, blocking out the sights, smells, and sounds that used to bring me joy. About two years after Rocky's death, I slowly pulled the shade up, and when I did, my perspective of the world had changed without my knowledge. It was quieter, softer, gentler, and more colorful. I was confused. My brother had died, so how could I feel this way instead of feeling more bitter and viewing the world as an ugly and cruel place? I realized, if we allow it, grief could truly transform the darkness into light.

There was a bleaker day than subsequent days when I asked myself, if given a choice, would I erase my memories of Rocky if it would eradicate this pain from my body?

I searched a cloud-filled sky for the answers, as they drifted and wove themselves into shapes. Animals. Waves. Faces. Winged creatures. I closed my eyes and became still, so I could feel the question in my body. I placed a hand on my chest, wishing I could massage the bruised heart muscles. "No," I screamed. "No. I wouldn't trade a single second with my brother." I would rather feel the intensity of the pain and loss for the remainder of my life than trade it for one hug, one memory, or one phone call with him. Like Katie, who lost her brother Tim in the hot tub, I shifted into a state of gratitude for experiencing this lifetime with Rocky.

When we love, it's not contingent upon how long we have a person in our lives. If I knew Rocky was going to die young, would I have done anything differently? Yes. I would have taken the trips to Egypt and Thailand. I would have scheduled more calls, not fewer. I would have shared more of my secrets and thoughts.

The true beauty in our pain is to understand that we have hearts with an infinite depth to love wholly, which makes the pain that much greater, the hole that much wider and deeper. We could never feel the beauty of love without feeling the depths of our pain and heartache. Without the pain, we would not have had the experiences with our siblings because they wouldn't be dead; they never would have existed in the first place. We can express our gratitude for the heartache we experience after a loss by saying, "I am grateful that I had the chance to know, experience, and love my sibling in this lifetime."

CHAPTER 12
Messages from the Other Side

Amy Boles: interviewed in June 2015, Tennessee
William Clinton Davis: 7/1/86-5/24/2010
Cause of death: Opiate Overdose

Amy loved many characteristics about her twenty-three-year-old younger brother's personality. She enjoyed how Clint was deadpan about everything with hilarious sarcasm and marvelous wit. He was so bright, and life always seemed to work out for him no matter how bad things got. She admired how intensely people loved him. Though she respected his sense of loyalty, she thought there were times he could be loyal to a fault. Once he cared about someone, his loyalty was unshakeable.

Amy always thought of Clint as the cool kid on the block by the way he held a cigarette and gestured with it in the air as he spoke. Tall and lean, he hunched his shoulders, put his hands in the pocket of his ripped jeans when he walked, his dark hair always in his eyes. Physically, Clint was beautiful with his straight, white teeth that showed on that rare occasion when he smiled or laughed.

Both Amy and Clint were raised in a Christian home. Though Clint believed in the Lord Jesus Christ and accepted him as his savior, he loathed going to church because he felt like a fish out of water amongst the church crowd. Amy never felt that he tried to fit in because he was always kind of a rebel. If she told him the sky was blue, he'd look her in the eye and tell her it was green. But Clint didn't thrive on controversy or go looking for it. He was content to stand against the wall and observe the action around him, dropping a few funny lines that would leave the crowd in stitches, which was why people naturally gravitated toward him.

Amy didn't understand how her talented brother got into drugs in high school. He was laid-back and casual. Things didn't seem to get to Clint the way they got to other people, but both Amy and her mom knew he was a softy and arrows could pierce his heart even when he pretended they didn't. Amy had been excited about the future because she and Clint shared the same passion for the holidays, especially Christmas. They always talked about having large families, getting together over the holidays, and whipping up huge feasts. Clint had so many dreams, and it hurt Amy to watch him throw them all away.

As much as Amy loved her brother, she harbored anger and resentment for what he had put their mother, Diana, through and now he disappeared shortly after Mother's Day. *How could he do this to our mother?*

As Clint's drug addiction spiraled, he began stealing money from his mother, giving Diana no other choice but to ask her son to leave and have the locks changed. Amy knew her mother struggled with the decision and questioned whether or not it was the right one, but what other options did she have? It was hard for Amy to watch how torturous this was for her mother. Her mom would have done anything to help Clint, but Diana knew the choice was up to him. Amy feared how her mom would survive if anything happened to Clint because Diana lost her own brother, Clint, when she was in college and named her son after him. Her son was the same age as her brother when he died in a plane crash in Alaska while Diana was in college.

When Amy stopped by for a visit with her mom, Diana was worried because no one had heard from Clint for four or five days.

"I'm going to call the police," Diana said, "and file a Missing Person's Report."

Amy listened as her mother filed the report, describing Clint's physical characteristics and what he was wearing the last time she saw him. Amy wished he'd just pick up the phone and call her. *Was he in one of the seedy places in Nashville, shooting up drugs?* Though she tried to push the disturbing images out of her mind, she was worried too.

After Diana filed the report, the locksmith showed up to change the locks at the same time she received a phone call from the police. They refused to provide any information over the phone and asked if they could come to the house.

When Diana hung up, she was in shock because deep down in her gut, she already knew what they were going to tell her. Her daughter had left earlier, and Diana couldn't face what was coming without Amy. She called her and asked her to return to the house as soon as possible.

When the police detective and a police chaplain arrived, Amy was on her way. Diana asked them to wait for her daughter before they gave her any information.

After I learned about Rocky's brief cocaine use, I feared my parents would receive this same call in the wee hours of the morning. When I talked to his ex-wife Kristen, she shared a story with me. One night when he snorted too many lines, his heart raced, and he went to the ER. Now that he's gone, I wonder how many brushes with death my brother had before his chances ran out. I struggle with the question of why addiction takes one life but not another? People who suffer from addiction don't want the illness. Addiction changes the wiring of the brain, and some people can and do become drug and alcohol-free, but the addiction never goes away. It's always there lurking, waiting for its chance to sink its claws in deeper, dragging the person down into darkness and despair.

Amy felt sick the whole drive over to her mother's, fearing the worst-case scenario. When she pulled into her mother's driveway, she rubbed her pregnant belly and said a silent prayer with one thought on her mind: *How would her mother survive if something happened to Clint?* She inhaled a breath as she walked into the house and heard voices in the living room. Amy went in and sat down on the couch next to her mother.

The detective greeted Amy and said, "I'm sorry to have to tell you this," he paused. "We found a body in a car. It seems he'd been in there for three days." He held a picture in his hand.

Amy put her arm around her mother, who started to cry.

"I have to ask you to look at the picture and tell me if this is your son," the police detective said.

Diana shook her head. "I can't," she said. "I can't do it."

Though Amy didn't want to do it either and couldn't stand the thought that it could be her dead brother in the photo, she had to do it for her mother. "I'll do it," she said.

Amy's mother left the living room, unable to stay while her daughter looked at the photo. She simply couldn't bear it and prayed to the Lord to give her strength.

The detective held out the photo for Amy. She trembled as she stared at a body lying on a table in the morgue. This person could not possibly be her brother. This person didn't look anything like her beautiful brother, Clint.

"Did he have a lip ring?" Amy asked. *Please, God, don't let that be Clint.*

The detective nodded. "Yes, he did."

"I think it's my brother, but I can't honestly say with a hundred percent certainty."

Amy's whole body shook when the detective said, "You're going to have to get your mom."

As Amy went to retrieve her mother, she felt she failed her in the most horrific way. How could she put her mother through this?

With a trembling hand, Diana took the picture and looked at her once-perfect boy, lying still on a table. She let out a wail, fell to her knees, and said, "Yes, that's my son."

Amy had no idea how to console her mother, and

Diana didn't have a partner to support her through the devastating loss, just a daughter who was preparing to have a baby. Amy stared at her favorite picture of her brother, hanging on the living room wall. The Clint she wanted to remember was sitting in the cockpit of an airplane, arm slung over the side with an easy smile. *He was beautiful,* she thought, with his tousled blond hair, ripped blue jeans, and forest green jacket. *What you could have done with your life.*

"I was in shock for a while," Amy said. "I don't think I cried for a really long time. It didn't sink in. You kind of feel like people are looking at you and saying, 'Why is she not crying? What's the matter with her? Did she not love him?' I felt that way."

As Amy bore witness to her mother's deep grief, she became angry thinking about the person responsible for getting her brother hooked. Though Clint's high school friends told him to stay away from Teddy, her brother was drawn to his charismatic personality. Teddy was manipulative and had the ability to suck people into his dark world of booze and drugs. The more Clint hung out with Teddy, the less he saw his other friends until he stopped seeing them at all.

"He (Teddy) had the audacity to show up at the memorial service. There was a ripple effect, and people were talking. I looked at my mom, and she had her fist balled up, trying not to come apart. I was furious," Amy said.

As with my relationship with Rocky, Amy, too, shouldered guilt and regrets. Though different from mine, they were still painful for her. She wished she'd been more compassionate toward Clint when her parents were in the midst of a turbulent split. Amy believes Clint's problems stemmed from their father's death. "I could have been there more for him, and I tried to be at the end."

While Clint continued to sink deeper into his opiate addiction, Amy, for her own self-preservation, snipped him from her life. During the last phone call she had with her brother, she screamed at him, told him she was done with him, and expressed her contempt over what he'd done with his life.

"Have you forgiven yourself for the last phone call?" I asked.

"No," she said. "I'm really bad about putting things out of my mind that are unpleasant. It didn't get through to my brother. It just helped me get my aggression out. It was selfish."

I explained to Amy that often our anger at a loved one engaged in a life-threatening behavior comes from a place of deep love, just as a parent will scream at their four-year-old child for running into the street. As the interview continued, I asked Amy what helped her the most in her grieving process.

"After his death, it actually helped me to get closer to God. My husband and I joined a church, and we started going to a bible study group. I felt like I healed faster by doing that," she said.

Amy explained that her brother's death reinforced her, and her mother's, commitment to God. Diana also joined a bible study group. Both Diana and Amy receive comfort in knowing Clint is with the Lord now.

"Do you believe you've had any communication with Clint since his death?" I asked.

"I never believed in dreams or ghosts talking," Amy said. "I used to make fun of people who did that, and I was like, 'That's not true. That doesn't happen. Whatever.' A couple of months after my brother's death, I was sleeping next to my husband. I thought this was really happening, but apparently, it was a dream. I woke up in bed. I remember sitting up and thinking, *Am I dreaming or is this real life?* I looked over at my husband, and he was snoring just like he always does. I thought, this has to be real life, but why do I feel weird? And then all of sudden, my brother is sitting on the end of my bed, and I said, 'You're dead.'"

Amy heard her brother speak to her. Clint said, "I need you to tell Mom that I'm so sorry." His voice shook, and with tears in his eyes, he said, "I need her to know that I am OK."

"Why don't you tell her yourself?" Amy asked, but he didn't respond. She had a deep sense that he could not stay and continue to talk to her. He had to go, but he worried about his mother. Before he left, Clint said, "I'm sorry for what I did to you, too."

"I was like, 'It's OK.' It just came out as a polite response because I was kind of in shock, like, am I having this conversation with you right now because I don't believe in this stuff," Amy said. "Even in my dream, I remember thinking, I don't believe in this stuff. And then he left."

Amy shared the dream with her mother the next day, and they had a moving conversation. Diana believes it was God who used the dream to communicate with Amy. She believes God chose Amy because if he had chosen to go directly to Diana, she wouldn't have believed it was true. She would have just thought it was her psyche trying to make her feel better about the loss of her son. Diana said to her daughter, "I know you're very pragmatic, and you would never have believed in this stuff, and that's why I think God communicated to you in a dream instead of me."

"After Clint died, it really made me appreciate my family, even their bad habits," Amy said. "I don't care. I love them and take them as they are. I'm so glad I have the family I do. I'm grateful for every single day I get to spend another day on this earth with them."

*   *   *

Julie Brown: interviewed in June 2015, Vermont
Keith Richard Brown: 7/25/51-11/10/81
Cause of death: Testicular cancer

At thirteen years old, Julie was a free-spirited freshman, enjoying the newness of high school. Her brother Keith, fourteen years older, had always been her role model because he was off living his passion. After graduating from Rosary Hill College in Buffalo, New York, with a Bachelor of Arts degree, he pursued an acting career, despite his parents' attempt to discourage him.

"It's hard to make a living as an actor," his father would say.

For Keith, life wasn't about chasing the cash. Life was meant to be lived with purpose and passion, and when he was performing on stage, an electric energy coursed through his body. When he returned home for visits, Julie laughed until her belly ached, mesmerized by her brother's impersonations and his ability to capture an audience, keeping them in hysterics. He possessed an inherent gift for the stage. Nothing would deter him from pursuing his dream, and Julie, like her brother, vowed to follow her heart no matter where it led her. They had the same brown hair and brown eyes. Julie, the youngest of five, shared a special bond with her brother. When it came to Julie, she felt Keith possessed X-ray vision and could see inside her soul, her strengths, and beauty that Julie was never able to see in herself.

Keith's life was on fire, and he met the love of his life, a gorgeous actress named Cheryl that he hoped to marry. They had big plans. First, a career and later a family until Keith's back started bothering him, and Cheryl encouraged him to go see a chiropractor. He probably pulled a muscle or maybe his spine was out of alignment. What could possibly be wrong at twenty-six years old? He was in great shape, ate right, and exercised. It was nothing.

When Keith went see the chiropractor, he discovered a growth in Keith's midsection and said, "You need to see your physician."

Still, Keith wasn't concerned. "I will," he said. "I'm sure it's not a big deal."

He made an appointment and had tests and X-rays. When he returned for the test results, the doctor's expression told Keith everything he needed to know. It wasn't good. "Just tell me," Keith said.

When the doctor told him he had advanced testicular cancer, and it had spread to his kidney, Keith fell silent before he finally asked, "Is it treatable?"

The doctor explained available options, and that they were going to be aggressive with treatment. "We'll schedule surgery to remove the mass," he said. "Then you'll do a year and half of chemo. The goal is to reduce the size of the mass and save the kidney."

Keith felt heat rise in his body, cheeks flushed. "Can I still act?"

"As long as you feel up to it," the doctor said.

Keith left the appointment optimistic, believing he'd beat the cancer no matter what it took.

When Julie's parents explained that Keith had cancer, she was young and didn't really understand the extent of the diagnosis. She knew he'd get better, and everything would work out, but she still felt confused.

Keith protected his family from how brutal the treatments were. The oncology team decided to try a potent drug, sis-platinum, as part of his regimen, in addition to the two he was already taking. Though he only had chemo three days a week, he was too weak to go home after treatment. He would spend five to seven days in the hospital and take a week off, but he was too fatigued to accomplish simple tasks. He'd have a week and a half when he felt pretty good before he had to start the process all over again. Thankfully, Keith had Cheryl by his side throughout treatment. She was his beacon of hope and did everything she could to buoy his spirits. She'd tell him they'd kill the cancer. They had a future awaiting them. He was going to regain his health and return to his acting career. They'd get married and have a baby. As Keith grew more fatigued, he tried to maintain a positive attitude and wouldn't allow himself to give up.

Despite the doctor's best attempts, he couldn't save Keith's kidney and removed it. A year and a half later, Keith and Cheryl received the news they were waiting for—Keith was in remission. It was a glorious day for everyone.

Julie had been given limited information from her parents throughout Keith's treatment because they wanted to protect her, so when she received the news, she was overjoyed but always knew her brother was going to recover.

Cheryl and Keith didn't waste another precious day. They got married, started trying to have a baby, and plan their future together. Keith felt stronger by the day, returning to his pre-cancer self. They worked temporary jobs during the day to support their passion for theater. Life had become sweeter for Keith, as he no longer took anything for granted. He was energized and excited by the acting gigs he was offered. Both Cheryl and Keith felt their path was free and clear. They were going to grow old together and have grandbabies one day.

Two years later, at twenty-eight years old, Keith woke up and just didn't feel that great. It couldn't be cancer, right? Just to be sure and to put his concerns to rest, he made an appointment with the oncologist. Keith's skin turned ashen as the oncologist shared the news that the cancer had returned with a vengeance.

The surgeon operated on the mass, and Keith considered doing chemo treatment again, but the cancer was too far advanced. Together, Keith, Cheryl, and his doctors made the decision to stop treatment. The couple naively thought they had more time until the doctor informed them that Keith only had about one week to live.

Cheryl had to make the dreaded call to Keith's parents. It was time for them to come and say goodbye to their son. Ten days later, Keith died in the early morning hours in Cheryl's arms. Julie, a senior in high school, was not able to go and say goodbye to her brother. After his death, her world fell apart.

"I played it safe after he died," Julie said. "I phased out and faded in. I did things that were required of me. At first, it was ugly and so devastating and made me very fearful about life. It made me feel unsafe and unsure because I thought, *You're following your heart and living a joyful life and then you die?* I didn't get that. I was young and I was like, *What's the point?* I drank a lot that first year. I started a family pretty much right after high school. It was the best time of my life being a wife and mother. But I was in denial and, worse, I was painfully aware that my girls would never know him. It wasn't until my thirties that I started tapping back into the emotion."

Julie's true transition happened in her early forties as she began to delve into the murky waters of her delayed grief. She dug through the archives of what her parents saved from her brother's life. They had squirreled away playbills from every play he was in, photographs marking time, letters he had written, and clipped news articles reviewing his performances. She put it together in a video, added music, and gave it to her other three siblings for Christmas. The process gave Julie the opportunity to get to know her brother's life and spirit on a different level through her adult eyes.

"I could see that he lived a life of passion, and I hadn't been. I remember I caught a glimpse of myself in the mirror and said, 'Is this it?' I felt that I was supposed to be doing something, and I had forgotten what it was. It was a very strong feeling. Very quickly, I became intrigued with this untapped potential that was seeking to surface."

I cried as Julie described her process to me. I worked for a behavioral healthcare company for fourteen years, and I felt like something more fulfilling was awaiting me, if I only had the courage to give my resignation and make the space to welcome new opportunities into my life. It was a good job with good pay and good benefits. Good. It was good, but I no longer felt I was living my purpose.

Like Keith, my brother, too, followed his passion for the spa industry and won the award for the most influential spa leader in Asia. I, too, looked in the mirror and made a declarative statement that I was going to live a more courageous and passionate life, but I had no idea what that meant. It took my brother's passing for me to have the courage to resign from my position. On the first anniversary of Rocky's death, I collected my last paycheck with no compass to help me find my way.

Julie's shift happened when she began reading books by the spiritual gurus of our time: Marianne Williamson, Neale Donald Walsh, Gregg Braden, and Deepak Chopra. The more she read, the more she paid attention to the stirrings of her soul.

"It's like I woke up," she said. "These great teachers help you to think outside the box, and if you've been living in one your entire life, you're going to need a little help to get out." She added, "I had a beautiful life, but I realized I was supposed to be doing something innately. Something that was already in me, and I had no idea what it was."

She began writing her first novel, *The Brownstone*; it would be one of a trilogy that seeks truth around death, grief, the afterlife, and reclaiming joy. In her first book, she wrote: *Have you ever stood in a place that should be familiar and yet felt lost? You've walked the same street for years, seen the same people, done the same things, but my impassiveness was lost in the faint idea that I didn't belong here. Everything that made sense to me simply didn't anymore. I had to believe there was more.*

As Julie wrote, she outgrew the box she'd been living in and tried to spread wings in a space that had become too small. Transformation requires courage to handle the emotional turmoil necessary for true metamorphosis to take place. Julie shed her old skin. She left her husband, her big beautiful home, the cars, and the financial security. She moved into a tiny apartment in the mountains of Vermont and wrote two of her three books.

"I was going to learn one very important lesson. It's not everyone's lesson, but it was mine. I was going to learn how to make decisions and live life from my heart, my intuition, and my passion. I was going to learn to not be afraid of living life. I was going to learn more about myself than I ever had. I had to see me through my own eyes. Although my grief has shaped the person I am today, I wouldn't trade it for anything. If I had, this book would have never been written."

I smiled into the phone, thinking about the blessings our siblings leave behind. Yes, I thought, and *Rock On: Mining for Joy in the Deep River of Sibling Grief* would never have been written either.

Julie's beliefs about the afterlife changed significantly through the process of reading the thoughts of her spiritual teachers and writing her books. Prior to her brother's death, she believed in God, in heaven, in hell, but she also believed that when we die, it's the end of life.

"Now," I asked her, "after all you've learned and all you've been through, have your beliefs changed?"

"I believe in God, but I also believe in myself, and I believe God wants me to trust my inner voice because God is a part of us, not just with us," Julie said. "I don't believe in places like heaven and hell. I believe the soul never dies. I believe the spirit lives on with the soul, and together they continue onward and upward. I believe we have guardian angels with us all the time. I've seen them, and we can ask them for help anytime."

Julie learned the most important thing we can do for ourselves and humanity is to be in the stillness, the silence, and quiet ourselves every morning. She discovered the only thing that creates a barrier between us, no matter the realm of existence, is noise.

"I used to believe grief should be avoided or at the very least ignored. Today, I believe grief is not meant to be transcended, rather grief should be embraced," Julie said. "Grief is the burden you carry and the flower you plant."

Julie read Doreen Virtue while she was in the midst of creating a character in her second book, a character that could talk to angels. Doreen offered meditations to help people connect with the angels and to loved ones who have crossed over.

"And I did," Julie said. "I have seen Keith, always in my peripheral vision. I was on the deck one beautiful summer morning. I saw him sitting on the picnic table, and he had his head in his hands. I said, 'Oh my gosh, what's the matter, Keith?' And he said, 'It's Andy. It's bad.' I didn't know what to do, so I called my sister an hour after that happened and asked how Andy was, my nephew and godson. She hadn't talked to him in a few days and thought he turned off his cell phone. Several days later, I found out that Andy was in the hospital with his jaw wired shut. It would be four days before he could communicate with anyone. He was attacked at an ATM in Washington, D.C. I firmly believe we can all do it, but it's a process. You have to quiet yourself. I was enjoying nature and listening to the birds. I was in a nice quiet place."

Julie had not only lost her brother, she lost a sister-in-law, too, as Cheryl had her own pilgrimage. Though Julie had tried to track her down a few times, she was unsuccessful. Last year, she looked her up on Facebook and reconnected with Cheryl. Julie visited Cheryl and went to Keith's gravesite for the first time. Their walk together continues, as they share memories of Julie's beloved brother.

* * *

Andrea (McLaughlin) Stiernstrand: interviewed in June 2015, Virginia
Paul McLaughlin: 8/3/73-6/24/2014
Cause of death: Heart failure due to alcoholism

Paul sat on the couch, lifted the vodka bottle to his lips, and took a long haul because he was unaware of his talents, his beauty, and the laughter and joy he brought to his friends, his parents, and to his only sibling, Andrea. He had no idea how many women had fallen in love with his quick wit and his intellect when he was younger. It was his insecurity and depression that warped his sense of self, crushed his confidence, and drove him to the bottle to numb the shame. He never felt he could measure up to his own expectations or to his sister.

Andrea was the good student, the traveler, and the ambitious one. Though he knew he was somewhat smart, he was never a good student. And travel? He had no desire to leave his home, never mind the state. Paul got into trouble here and there, but not his sister. Her life was good. She'd be getting married soon to her soul mate, and they'd probably have a couple of kids.

What did Paul have? Sure, he thought, once upon a time, he was a decent athlete. Now he was overweight and smoked. He would never marry because he wouldn't put a wife or a child through the experience of being wedded to an alcoholic. It didn't matter what other people told him or what they saw in him because when he looked in the mirror, he didn't see a funny, handsome, charismatic guy. Through his eyes, he saw a forty-year-old man who was an overweight and unemployed alcoholic.

Nobody knew the depth of Paul's depression because he hid it behind his quick wit and smile. Nobody knew the extent to which he drank because he hid that too. Alone in his apartment, he tucked himself away from those he loved the most.

As Andrea shared the story of her brother, a memory of Rocky's last visit home leaked into the interview. Rocky, too, hid the depth of his emotional pain behind his charismatic personality, enchanting stories, and humor. He woke up one morning, went downstairs, and poured himself a glass of vodka, stating it was 4:00 p.m. somewhere. I knew his drinking was an attempt to mitigate the vertigo, to quiet the worries, and numb the depression caused by the three-year illness. Like Paul, alcohol became a crutch for Rocky. And though it wasn't the cause of his death, I believe it was a contributor.

When Paul went to his cousin's wedding in May,

his appearance blew the lid off his Pandora's box of secrets. He looked terrible, and his sister and parents voiced their concern. Two weeks later, he contacted his sister and mother, texting, *I can tell my body is failing and I only have a few more days to live.* He knew how sick he was getting and believed he would die soon.

I also believe my brother knew his life would be cut short. He wrote Kevin an email two years before his death. In part of his note, he wrote: *I want you to be the person entrusted with my wishes if anything should ever happen to me before my time of old age arrives...again, I am 100% healthy. just thinking a lot! If I am to pass away unexpectedly for any reason, my wishes are to be cremated in Bali and have my ashes spread there where my wife and daughter will live forever. This is where my home is and would want Anna and Setiawan to always know I am close to them.*

When Andrea and her mother received Paul's text, they organized an intervention. They rushed to her brother's house in New York, and that's when Andrea realized how dire the situation had become. Her brother had always been a neat freak, but when she arrived, the apartment was a disastrous mess, and it was apparent he'd been getting sick.

Andrea was frightened at the condition of both her brother and his living space. She had to do something fast, so she arranged a professional intervention that motivated Paul to admit himself into a rehabilitation facility. Though he ran from the airport the day of his departure, a good friend was able to convince him to go.

Andrea's hope for her brother's recovery vanished when she learned he checked himself out of rehab before completing the program. She couldn't bring herself to talk to her brother for a week because she was disappointed, angry, and emotionally drained. She also thought about what all the professionals said: *You have to cut the person off.* Still, she refused to give up on her only sibling. Andrea was able to track Paul's spending because she had access to his bank accounts and email.

When Paul was in rehab, he gave his sister all of his passwords, hoping she could get him on a medical insurance plan.

As she scanned his spending, her anxiety grew, realizing Paul ordered less and less food and only ordered vodka. She was determined to get her brother back into rehab. She called and pleaded with him to get the help he needed to save his life. After a few days, he agreed to go back to the rehabilitation facility. His flight was scheduled to leave on Tuesday, June 24, but Paul never boarded the flight.

Andrea, again, was crestfallen because she thought he changed his mind. When she checked his spending, she saw he charged another bottle of vodka on Tuesday night. When there were no new charges on Wednesday, Andrea called the police on Thursday, and they found Paul dead.

"It was awful. We didn't know when he died, but we were tracking down the charge that hit and a few other things. We're ninety-nine percent confident that he died before he was supposed to go to rehab, which weirdly makes us feel better. Just because he really did seem like he wanted to get help, so I think we all felt good about that despite him dying a sad, lonely death." Andrea cried as she said, "His last text to me was, *I'll wash the floor on my hands and knees. I will do whatever they tell me to do. I promise you I'm going to get better.*"

Though Andrea felt guilt for not rushing over to see her brother when she learned he stopped going to work in April because everything in her body told her to go, she said, "I was fortunate because my brother and I probably had some of the most heartfelt and loving conversations in the last month of his life than we had in twenty years. And we weren't distant at all. We talked all the time."

Given the nature of Paul's death, Andrea continues to process guilt, plagued with what if questions, like, *What if she had flown up to see her brother the day before his death?* Though she carries guilt, she said, "I am at peace with the fact that he died because I really believe that's what he wanted. But he kept saying, 'I don't want to kill myself. I don't want to kill myself.' But he was sending me a text saying, *'I know I'm going to be dead in the next couple of days, so please get help.'*

It would take six months before Andrea felt as though the haze lifted, and she realized how new everything was with her parents and the stress she felt, feeling it was her sole responsibility to support them emotionally. What has helped Andrea feel a sense of peace was the conversation she had with Paul since his passing. Andrea had been going to acupuncture, which she believes has been the most helpful during her grieving process. After her brother passed, she was in a session, half asleep, and it was the first time he had spoken to her.

"It was amazing. My brother is very funny, and all of a sudden I saw him sitting in the chair he always sat in, laughing at me maybe because he would have thought acupuncture was crazy. So he's sort of making fun of me for that and I said, 'I don't know what to do for you this month to memorialize you.' And he said, 'Oh stop, I couldn't be happier here. Don't be sad. Don't do anything sad.' And I said to him, 'You need to be with Mom.'"

Andrea began to cry. "He said, 'I'm with her every day.' I said, 'It's so sad without you.' He laughed and said, 'Stop. I'm fine and you should be too.'"

"The weird thing about that was I did call my mom on my way home from acupuncture," Andrea continued, "and I told her what happened. Mom said, 'Oh my God that is so strange because today I held his picture and asked him to send me a sign that he's OK.'"

After the conversation with her mother, Andrea said, "I had this weird conversation with him. Right after he died, I had a dream. I saw him. And I said, 'Paul you're here, you're here.' Paul had this huge smile with new bright white teeth. Almost like sparkly cartoon teeth. My brother had terrible teeth, and he was always very embarrassed by them. It was like him saying, 'I'm OK.'"

Andrea had two more dreams, but Paul didn't speak in either one. She talked to someone about the symbolism and what it might mean. The person told her that it may be his way of asking Andrea to let go. Now Andrea feels that her brother's spirit has traveled to wherever he is meant to be.

I asked Andrea, "If given one more chance to talk to Paul, what would you say?"

"Paul, I hope with every part of my being that you are at peace and you no longer have to suffer with whatever demons plagued you," she said. "I hope, despite our heartbreak, now you can see how much you were loved by so many people, but especially by me. I'm sorry if you couldn't see that while you were alive. I will always cherish our last conversation. Your very last words to me were, *I love you, Sissy.* I can hear your voice saying those words every day, and it brings me so much comfort. Please stay close to us, Bubba. Please continue to communicate with me. Stay close to Mom and Dad. They need to feel your spirit; it's the only thing that will let them move forward. I miss you more than words can describe, but I know now you can be a better big brother to me than you ever could while you were on this earth, and I feel grateful for that."

*   *   *

Micah Brown: interviewed in June 2015, Maine
Laurie Leigh Wile: 8/9/1970-12/23/88
Cause of death: Cancer - Primitive Neuroectodermal Tumor (PNET))

It was New Year's, and seventeen-year-old Laurie couldn't have been happier. Though her world temporarily blew apart when her parents divorced two years ago, she forgave her father, Rick, and loved her younger stepbrothers, eleven-year-old Micah and fourteen-year-old Jeremy. She adored her stepmother too and felt fortunate because she had a friend who hated her own stepmother. Everything worked out for the best. Plus, there were so many experiences to look forward to: her high school graduation, followed by an American Field Service student year abroad, and then she'd attend Hampshire College in Massachusetts to study international relations. Maybe she'd be able to get her dad to fly over while she was abroad, but her mother was a different story. *But,* she thought, *miracles do happen.*

Life was magical, except for the stupid cyst on the back of her head that she was getting removed over February school break. She had it since she was twelve years old. Dr. John, as she liked to call him, said it was a harmless sebaceous cyst. She traced her fingers over the lump. In the fall, it had grown twice the size and with her short-cropped hair, she could see the protrusion jutting out of her head. She started to feel self-conscious and couldn't get rid of it soon enough. Tonight though, Laurie would forget about it for a while. She and her two friends, Arthur and Jennifer, were going to New Year's Eve Portland with her dad, stepmom, Micah, and Jeremy. She was psyched to hang out with Jeremy because she didn't get to see him very often. He chose to live with his dad in Colorado, Laurie lived with her mom, and Micah lived with his mother and Laurie's dad.

Laurie knew her stepbrothers looked up to her because she was the cool, artsy older sister. It thrilled her to pieces that she was able to get Micah interested in creative art. She felt most comfortable in her skin when she held a paintbrush or felt the cool, moist clay in her hands as she manipulated the earthy material into a sculpture. It was an inherent talent. She had a gift and had already won numerous contests. She was teaching Micah how to paint with watercolors, how to sketch, and how to make creative things. He hadn't known much about art until he met Laurie.

I imagined Laurie, her friends, and family gathering

in Portland for an enchanting evening out. To kick off their night's festivities, they sat around her dad's kitchen table and feasted on delicious holiday food. They licked sticky sugarcoated fingers, cleaned the dishes, and layered their bodies in coats, hats, and gloves, preparing for a chilly Maine winter night.

When they arrived in Portland, Laurie felt giddy. The city buzzed with holiday cheer. They walked along the cobblestone roads in awe of the twinkling Christmas lights and the shimmering sequined gowns in display windows of expensive boutiques. Jeremy, in his glory, tagged along with Laurie and her friends, while her dad, stepmom, and Micah went to concerts by Duke Robillard and Holly Near. Of course, Micah wanted to hang out with the older teens, but he was too young.

As the evening wound down, they headed back to Laurie's dad's apartment to spend the night. I could almost smell the piping hot cups of silky hot chocolate with marshmallows they cupped between their hands as they gathered around the Christmas tree, sharing stories about the night out. Her dad and stepmom sipped brandy, and Laurie was sure they felt grateful the bad feelings had dissipated over their divorces to their previous partners. Laurie's heart filled with joy and gratitude for her life and her new family. It had been a perfect evening to begin the New Year.

Over February break, Laurie went in for surgery and had the cyst removed. Finally, she didn't have some foreign bump on her head. She was relieved and focused on finishing up her senior year. Then, the most exhilarating chapter of her life would begin. Soon she'd be on a plane flying overseas, headed toward new adventures that awaited her.

Four weeks later, Laurie sank into the soft couch cushion with a tight knot in her stomach as she held her pug, Penny, rubbing her behind the ears. Something was up, and it couldn't be good because her father had driven 120 miles on a school night and arrived unannounced. Though Laurie was nervous as her parents grabbed chairs, positioning them to face her, no news could be worse than when her parents told her they were getting divorced.

She ran her hand over Penny's belly, feeling the soft pink skin, grateful for her companion, as she await-ed whatever it was her parents had to tell her.

"Laurie," her mother said. "We don't know how to tell you this..."

A silent terror settled in her bones, as her parents detonated a stick of dynamite on her world. *Cancer? But how could she have cancer? She was only seventeen years old!* She stared at her parents. "I don't believe this," she said, tearful. "This is like a dream." She held Penny tight. "I keep waiting to wake up."

Her parents cried, hugged her, and attempted to comfort her. They assured her they'd get through it to-gether. It was going to be OK. They would be beside her all the way. Laurie melted into her parents' arms, de-ciding she would do whatever she had to do to beat the cancer and go on to chase her wild, beautiful dreams.

With a renewed sense of purpose, Laurie spent the summer driving herself five days a week to Eastern Maine Medical Center in Bangor, Maine, for radiation treatments. Her mother took her to her chemotherapy appointments every couple of weeks. After radiation and chemo, she lay low from exhaustion until she felt strong enough to work on her art. Laurie understood she had an extremely rare and progressive cancer, so she had to be equally aggressive in fighting it. As she drove home one day after radiation, she sank back into a memory. The previous winter, as part of her work for Amnesty International, she went to the Ellsworth Library and folded several paper cranes. Laurie strived for world peace, and she knew the story of Sadako, the little girl who died of leukemia due to being exposed to radiation in World War II when the bomb was dropped on Hiroshima.

Sadako's father told his daughter, according to legend, whoever had the patience and fortitude to fold

1,000 paper cranes would be granted one wish. Sadako managed to fold 644 paper cranes before she died. Her friends folded the remaining 356 and erected a monument in Hong Kong, expressing their desire for peace and to comfort Sadako's soul.

If I had known this story, I would have folded 10,000 paper cranes for Rocky. If I had, could I have combined my ten earned wishes into one giant wish? A wish to save his life as he lay dying in the ICU. If I could hold my brother's hand, hear his laugh, and walk along a wooded path with him one more time, I'd give up everything I own. I'd say to him, "I love you in the only way an older sister can. I will roll in a bed of coals for you or give you my heart if either would save your life."

By early July, Laurie's hair started falling out until she was nearly bald. Every time she looked into the mirror, she ran her hands over her head and wept. During one of her visits to see her father, she hung out by the pool with Micah and his friend and overheard Micah tell the kid not to say anything about her hair loss. Laurie was so angry she could have spit rocks, but she still felt bad about turning it into drama. She just wanted to be normal again and do normal teenage things.

As an optimist, Laurie worked hard to maintain a positive outlook and hold on to her faith that she would recover from the disease that was stealing pieces of her life. Though she already had to give up her dream of traveling abroad, her art teacher, Mr. Mike, had been her savior, and he was able to get her a late acceptance to the Portland College of Art. She still had dreams to look forward to, and she clung to them, believing they were still a possibility.

At the end of August, Laurie had renewed hope. She was responding well to the radiation and chemotherapy treatments, and the tumor on the back of her head had disappeared. Excitement sizzled through her body as she and a friend made the 120-mile drive to a Grateful Dead concert in Oxford. As they swayed to Dead tunes, Laurie felt she was reclaiming her life. She giggled when she told her father she and her friend were pulled over by a cop for going forty miles per hour in a twenty-five-mile-per-hour zone at 2:30 in the morning on their drive back to Yarmouth, Maine, after the concert. It felt good to laugh over normal teenage troubles.

A week before Laurie would begin classes, she enjoyed a lovely day with her mother and her mother's boyfriend as they strolled along Sand Beach, nestled in a small inlet between the granite mountains and rocky shores of Mount Desert Island. Out of nowhere, her leg gave out as a sharp pain traveled up her leg and into her hip. Laurie bit back tears and saw the fear in her mother's eyes.

The doctors weren't able to pinpoint what was causing the leg pain, so they sent her to physical therapy, which intensified her extreme discomfort. Laurie was *over* being so tired and weak all the time. She could no longer climb the stairs and slept on the pull-out couch in her father's living room when she visited. Finally, she had to succumb to using a walker. In the middle of October, the pain became so unbearable, Laurie was admitted to the hospital for a week, but still, the doctors couldn't figure out the source of Laurie's debilitating pain.

Later in the fall, Laurie's world crumbled around her again when she learned that the cancer had spread from the back of her head, down her spine, and into her pelvis. At the end of October, she was readmitted to the hospital, where she would stay until the end of her life.

A month before her death, several of her friends folded 1,000 paper cranes, each one holding a wish and a prayer for her recovery. Laurie cried, overwhelmed that her friends cared enough about her to spend hours and hours of their lives folding all those paper cranes.

"When they found the tumors, it was chemo, chemo, chemo, and everything started failing after that," Micah said, who was twelve when Laurie died. "What my mom, to this day, can never forgive herself for is they never told me Laurie was dying. On some level, I knew. I was pretty much in charge of the house. Laurie was at Eastern Maine Medical Center in Bangor. On the weekends, we went to the Ronald McDonald House, and we visited Laurie. I became friends with some of the regulars at the Ronald McDonald House who were about my age."

Laurie's father, Rick, took a leave of absence from work and spent all of his time at the hospital with his daughter.

"I would do what I could to make sure everything was ready for Mom when she got home," Micah said. "I tried to make sure everything was cleaned, picked up, organized, and ready for getting dinner on the table. She was a teacher, so while she was grading papers, I'd fall asleep on the living room floor, and wake up, and everyone would go to bed."

"Were you at the hospital when she died?" I asked.

"No. In fact, it was my dad's year to have me for Christmas, so I was in Colorado when she died. I didn't go to her funeral. They let us know the morning it happened. Although I remember knowing it had happened before because my dad told me," Micah said. "My dad came home from work early and talked to us. My brother went upstairs to his room, closed the door, and didn't come out for twenty-four hours. They were closer in age. They got along really well. They really liked each other."

One of the most difficult challenges for Micah was watching his parents flounder and bearing witness to their profound grief. Though he knew on some level that Laurie was dying, he was continually being told that everything was going to be fine. Micah felt he stopped being a kid as he endured the process of illness and death because he no longer wanted to be around other kids. He'd been the victim of bullying for years. Once his sister died, he stood up for himself and refused to allow the kids to push him around anymore.

"I think the result of being told that everything's

going to be fine, I became very blunt," Micah said. "I don't like games. I don't like not knowing things. I don't like surprises. I just want to know what is going on."

The last time Micah saw Laurie, she was in the hospital, rapidly declining. Two days later, Micah would head to Colorado to spend Christmas with his father. Laurie looked at her stepbrother and said, "It's OK."

"No, no, don't talk," Micah said, because Laurie's throat was raw.

She smiled, hugged him, and said, "I'll always say goodbye."

The day Laurie died, two days before Christmas, Micah believes she visited him.

"I choose to believe this happened," Micah said, "as opposed to something that happened in my head. I don't analyze it. I choose not to. I remember very clearly waking up in Colorado. Laurie was sitting on my bed, and I was confused as to why she was there. I sat up in bed, half awake, and I asked her, "What are you doing here?"

She said, "I promised I'd say goodbye."

"I lay down," Micah said. "She tucked me in, kissed me on the head, and I went back to sleep."

*   *   *

Oftentimes when I was writing, I would feel a strong presence in my office. I believe this was Rocky's spirit. One of the first signs I received from Rocky arrived when I returned from Asia. I had to forge ahead and go on a dreaded shopping trip to find a dress for his memorial. I didn't have the energy to go to more than one store. Before I left the house, I talked to him and said, "I'm going to Banana Republic, Rocky, and I really need you to help me find a dress that you like."

I walked around, scouring the racks, trying on dresses that were too big or too small. After forty-five minutes, I was over the shopping scene. As I opened the door to leave, I turned my head and saw a dress on the mannequin that I hadn't noticed before. It had a nautical feel to it with cream and navy-blue stripes. Given my brother's love for the ocean, I thought it would be perfect. I went into the dressing room and pulled the dress over my head, zipped it up, and cried. It was too big, and I didn't have time to get it altered before the memorial, but I bought it anyway.

At home, I tried it on for my husband and he said, "You have to get that altered."

"I don't have time," I said. Standing five feet tall, I frequently had to get my clothes altered. The only place I knew that provided alteration services close to my home was a dry-cleaning business, and they were always backed up two to three weeks. I Googled alterations in Topsham, one town over from where I lived, and a business popped up that I'd never seen before. It was called *Asian Touch. It's a sign,* I thought. When I called to make an appointment, she scheduled me to come in the following day. I hadn't looked up the street address, and when I did, I sat stunned, as I read *5 Rocky Road,* which was the first of many signs I've received since my brother's passing.

Our loved ones can and do try to send us messages, but they can't get through if we don't believe their spirit lives on and has the power to communicate with us. The deceased also have trouble getting through to us when we are deeply entrenched in our grief. Our energy vibrates at a much lower frequency when we're sad and depressed. The spirit world vibrates at a much higher frequency. We can all work on elevating the vibration of our energy through meditation, but it's important to give ourselves the time to grieve the physical loss.

The deceased attempt to speak to us through several mediums. They visit us in our dreams, play meaningful songs on the radio, place coins in odd places, move objects, and play with electricity and clocks. They communicate through nature, birds, butterflies, and dragonflies. When we smell a fragrance out of nowhere that reminds us of our sibling, it's a sign. When we feel our deceased sibling's presence, believe it's a wink from them, letting us know they love us and are watching over us. We must remember to thank them when they send us a sign. A reputable medium is another easy and powerful way to speak to our deceased sibling and for them to speak to us. Believe and know our sibling's spirit lives on, and we can talk to them anytime we feel the need for their support and presence in our lives.

CHAPTER 13
Honoring Our Siblings

Morty Ballen: interviewed in July 2016, New York
Anne Jaye Ballen Gaynor: 1/24/1963-10/18/2000
Cause of death: Hit by a car

Anne was, in a word, content. She sowed her wild oats in college, ripping it up in New York City while she earned her degree in journalism. She satiated her thirst for travel and met and married her husband. Dreams achieved make room for new ones to emerge. At thirty-seven years old, she was living her dream as a mother raising her two daughters. They brought a deeper level of meaning to her life. She was proud of her accomplishments and could have gone places with her career in television production, but no achievement compared to being a mother. She and her husband moved from New Orleans to a suburb of San Antonio two years ago. Anne had just begun to take on freelance writing gigs. She recently had an essay published by the *San Antonio Express-News*. It was an article on adjusting to life in San Antonio.

Though she envisioned herself working behind the scenes in television, she was young and could return to her career when her girls were older. The way Anne moved and lived in the world embodied the basic tenet of Judaism: Tikun Olam, the repair of the world. Her new life design gave her the time to immerse herself in the mother role, to volunteer at the school, to tuck little notes and pictures into her daughter's lunchbox, to keep meticulous scrapbooks of their family getaways and journals of the girls' developmental milestones. It also offered her the time to walk Moriah, her five-year-old child, to the bus while strolling Tess, her eighteen-month-old.

It was a full-sun, blue-sky Tuesday morning in

Terrell Hills, Texas, and her heart brimmed with gratitude that she had the good fortune to be able to be a stay-at-home mom with her beauties. She smiled as she thought about how Tess would awaken, stand in her crib, and clap her tiny hands together when she saw her mommy's face. It was Anne's daily standing ovation. For Anne, life could not have been any richer or more fulfilling.

When they reached the bus stop, Anne kneeled down and enveloped Moriah in her arms, gave her a kiss on the cheek, and told her to have good day. She stood and waved at her daughter as the bus left the curb.

On her way back to the house, strolling Tess, Anne hadn't noticed she drifted toward the center of the 500 block of South Vandiver, devoid of sidewalks. She didn't hear the BMW sedan behind her, squealing the breaks, and felt nothing when it struck her from behind. Tess, strapped in her stroller, was miraculously unharmed.

Anne was rushed to Brooke Medical Center, placed on life support, and declared brain dead due to massive head injuries. She was surrounded by her three other siblings, her parents, and spouse, who had to make the excruciating decision to take Anne off life support.

"She died on my birthday," her brother Morty said. "And the year that she died, everything felt to me like, *This is the first time I'm feeling this thing without my sister in my life.* The first time it became spring, or the first time I saw a robin, or the first snowfall, or the first Thanksgiving, or the first Hanukkah. It was a year of painful, painful firsts. It was 365 days of firsts. I thought, *So this is what THIS feels like when I don't have a sister.*"

On the year anniversary of Anne's death, Morty went out with his friends and got drunk, ordered a fat, juicy steak, and said, "I felt this amazing relief. I actually feel privileged that I can celebrate life with this special connection to my sister. My birthday has turned out to be a special time to celebrate Anne. It's also the passage of time. It's not as fresh. It's folded into my life. I lost a sister on my birthday, and it's calcified into this way of being."

Yes, I thought, a year of firsts. Every Christmas Eve we spent at my brother and sister-in-law's, and we Skyped Rocky, Anna, and Setiawan so Anna could share what Santa had dropped off for her in the wee hours of the night. I remember the first Christmas Eve without my brother, the empty space, the longing to erase events that required celebrations: Christmas, Thanksgiving, birthdays, and especially Valentine's Day, which ceased to exist after Rocky died. It became the day to shut out the world, gather with my family to honor Rocky's spirit, and hold the space for my parents to grieve and celebrate their beloved son.

"I can't imagine what it would be like to lose a child," Morty said. "I don't have children. I don't know what that's like. So given that, my question was, how do I most empathize with and support my parents? Not only was I dealing with my own grieving of Anne, but I also had to figure out my role with my parents, who were going through this very difficult time. Alternatively, I'd be like, *You need to take care of me because you're my parents* and recognizing how that's not reasonable for me as a grown adult. I actually had to take care of them."

Many of the surviving siblings that I interviewed struggled with providing themselves the space to grieve their loss while juggling their self-imposed role of helping their bereaved parents come to terms with the loss of their child. We're taught there is no greater tragedy than a parent losing a child. However, groundbreaking research issued in *The New York Times* in July 2017 found that surviving siblings have a much higher mortality than children who've not experienced the loss of a brother or sister, making it imperative that surviving siblings find a support system where they are free to grieve and take care of themselves through the process. Https://mobile.nytimes.com/upshot/when-children-lose-siblings-they-face-increased-risk-of-death.html

As Morty shared his grieving process, he felt proud

of the way he dealt with the traumatic loss of his sister. "I'd cry, and go to the beach, and listen to music. I wrote voraciously in my journal. I feel I processed it in a healthy way. I openly grieved and, looking back, it was a very organic way to deal with something so traumatic. I think we had a strong foundation for me to ultimately accept her death and move on and keep her with me, too, at the same time. I felt comfortable and confident that I was really doing good, hard, honest work around how I processed her death."

The majority of the siblings I had the great privilege of interviewing believe it's the way in which we honor our siblings that can help us, to not only heal but also mark their life, like their names engraved on their tombstones. Morty's family established, through the San Antonio Jewish Federation, the Anne Ballen Gaynor Endowment Fund, to benefit children's charitable and educational organizations. They believed the fund was the perfect memorial to Anne's devotion to the wellbeing of our children and the world.

In addition, Morty started a charter school that opened in 2002. "I created a library in her honor, in her memory, for this one school. It's called Anne's Book Corner, and we set it up. We also set up an Amazon list. Friends and family have a way of honoring Anne and buying all these books. Fifteen years later, we now have ABC Day (Anne's Book Corner) once a year."

Morty invites authors to talk to the students about the process of writing and reading. He explains to the kids every year why they have the event. "I tell them Anne's story and that she was killed in a car accident. Many of our kids have one parent, so it kind of resonates with them," Morty said. "When I opened up the school, I knew how important it was to read, and if you want to achieve your goals, the two things I know are to work really hard and to read. So we have ABC Day to celebrate reading and, selfishly, when we have ABC Day, I get to think of my sister who was a great, voracious reader. I'm really proud of how I could get satisfaction in thinking about my sister in an ongoing way but also use it in an authentic way to support the students that we're teaching."

For Morty, one of the most important ways he's honored his sister's life is through the time and energy he invests in building a close bond with his nieces, Tess and Moriah, and to have a substantial relationship with them and with his other sister's children.

"I really want them to know me as Morty, and I want to know them as individuals. I don't honestly know if I'd be quite as engaged with my nieces and nephews if Anne hadn't died," he said. "When her daughter Moriah graduated from high school, I flew her up to New York City, and we had tea at the Plaza and went to see a show. I wanted her to feel Anne because I so much associate New York City with Anne, and I wanted my niece to feel the city through how I experience it and also get to know Anne through New York City that way too."

Though life is busy and Morty doesn't live in close proximity to Tess and Moriah, when they're together, he said, "I want them to feel really safe and good about themselves when they are with me. I do a lot of listening and a lot of complimenting them. I put lots of money in the piggy bank (metaphorically) with them. When and if time should be hard for whatever reason, there is a strong foundation that we have, and they just feel safe. They feel like I'm a consistent support. They understand who I am, my essence, and my aura, and they feel good and comfortable. I'm very cognizant of that being a way for me to continue the values that Anne was building with them."

Morty could not have known at the time of the interview that the following year Moriah would accept an internship at a public relations firm in New York City. She spent the summer living with Morty and his husband, creating an even closer bond. A year after completing her internship, Moriah accepted a position as a media coordinator and lives only a couple of subway stops away from him. Morty said, "Anne would be so proud of her!"

*   *   *

Debbie Steiman: interviewed in September 2015, Indiana
Ben Steiman: 9/17/1952-4/2/2001
Cause of death: Sepsis - complications with surgery regarding an aneurysm.

On a Sunday afternoon, Debbie spent the day packing up her family's belongings in her rental house in California. She was ecstatic to move into a new home she and her husband recently purchased. When the phone rang, she picked it up. It was Georgia, her brother Aron's wife.

"Ben's been taken to the hospital," Georgia said. "He's being prepped for emergency surgery."

"What happened?" Debbie asked. The excitement and energy of the move evaporated in a flash. Her oldest brother had a tendency to drive fast, and Debbie always worried he would be involved in a car accident.

"This morning, Ben called Aron because he wasn't feeling well. He said, 'I feel really bad and my leg hurts a lot. I can't get a hold of Idrienne [his wife]. She's at the gym and not returning my calls.' Aron told him he'd come right over." Georgia is a nurse practitioner and the family's medical go-to person. She took the phone from Aron and when Ben informed her the pain was in his groin, she told him to call 911 and not to wait for Aron.

By the time Aron arrived at Ben's house, nobody answered the door and his worry increased. A neighbor across the street saw Aron trying to get into the house, and he went over and told Aron that an ambulance had arrived right before he got there. They tracked down Idrienne, Ben's wife, and she met Ben at the hospital. The doctors thought Ben's problem was simply thrombosis (clotting of the blood in a part of the circulatory

206

system) until Idrienne mentioned that there was a lot of heart disease in the family. The emergency room staff further explored the cause of the blood clots. They discovered that Ben had an aneurysm in the ascending part of the aorta. When his aorta dissected, it threw off blood clots, causing the thrombosis. The surgery was scheduled for 11:00 p.m. that night.

Shaken, Debbie hung up the phone and booked a red-eye flight to Indiana.

While Debbie boarded the flight, she thought of her brother being wheeled into the operating room and pictured him on a stainless-steel table illuminated by bright lights, fighting for his life. The airplane trip stretched out through a restless night. Fears of losing him and concern that she wouldn't get there in time caused her to second guess everything. Given the late hour that the surgery started, she stressed over whether or not the surgeon could stay awake for the twelve-hour surgery at that time of night.

Her mind was stuck in a constant loop of questions. *Was her brother still alive? What part were they working on now? Was the surgeon still sharp and awake? Would she get there in time? Was an aneurysm a part of the family's heart history? Did her father die of an aneurysm and not of a massive heart attack, as was suspected at the time of his death twenty-five years earlier?* As the plane finally descended, Debbie inhaled a deep breath. *What was awaiting her?*

When Debbie arrived at the hospital, she learned Ben's surgeons had repaired his aorta and replaced the aortic valve since it was also damaged, which most likely happened when the aorta dissected. The last piece of the surgery involved dealing with the blood clots in his leg. Ben had been a smoker, and after the long, grueling surgery, they had trouble getting him off the ventilator. The ICU staff preferred to slowly bring a patient off a vent, as they wanted a patient to start breathing on their own first. In the end, the slow method didn't work, and they ended up pulling the vent, which required them to fully wake up Ben. On Tuesday, he was exhausted and weak, but Debbie was hopeful. He was groggy but able to talk. The family members were all encouraged because he interacted with them.

They were limited to twenty-minute visits four times a day. During those times, Debbie went into the room along with other family members. Beatles music played on a CD player that her sister-in-law had brought in. Ben had always loved the group. He was very musical and played several instruments, including four-, six-, and twelve-string guitars. He formed a musical group with his friends called the *Mesmerizing Eye,* and they played at local parties.

Ben's talents were not limited to music. While still in high school, he figured out how to build sound systems and music synthesizers on his own. He was technically way ahead of his time. He earned an engineering degree from IUPUI and received the Purdue Senior Design Project Award. He was the first person Debbie knew who had a computer and could write software programs. Years after his first computer, Debbie entered the field of software engineering. In the hospital, she told Ben a little of the new software project she was working on.

In between time at the hospital, Debbie visited with her three- and five-year-old nieces. Ben had shared his love of music with them. He was a great dad and loved his time with his kids. They had created a band called the *Steiman Cats.* His daughters performed for her without the sweetness of Ben's guitar joining in. When Debbie went into the garage, she saw Ben's 1971 Pontiac T-37 that her parents bought for him when he was in high school. His first car meant so much to him that he kept it through adulthood. He babied it, washing and waxing it until it shined. He had bought a special plate for it since it was now considered vintage.

By Friday morning, Ben was having trouble breathing again. Debbie didn't want to leave town, but she had to get back to California due to work and her imminent house move. She left Indiana with a heavy heart and called the nurses' station regularly to get updates on Ben's status. His breathing ability decreased through the day, and by the time she arrived home on Friday night, they had sedated him and put him back on the vent.

The news continued to get worse. Ben had developed pneumonia and was running a fever. As Ben's health continued to decline day by day, Debbie made the decision to fly back to Indiana to be with him and the rest of the family. He was on a feeding tube and developed sepsis. Although Eli Lilly (drug company) was just coming out with a medicine for sepsis, it wasn't on the market yet.

On Saturday, fourteen days after the aortic dissection, Debbie stood by her oldest brother's bedside, along with Idrienne, Aron, Georgia, and their son, when Ben died. Her brother quietly passed away at the age of forty-eight with his immediate family with him. Her mother left the hospital earlier, as she had been utterly exhausted.

"The rabbis of our congregation had visited Ben and the family earlier that evening. When Ben died, Idrienne called them, and Rabbi Dennis came right over to be with us and say a prayer."

As Debbie described the last few hours of her brother's life, a wave of grief washed over me as I thought, again, about how Rocky was alone when his brain swelled and pushed through his brainstem. Was he frightened? Did he call out for anyone? Did he wonder where his family was? *You abandoned me, Sue.* I pushed the thoughts aside and wiped away tears as Debbie continued talking.

"I am alive today because of Ben and what happened to him."

After his surgery, both Ben and the surgeon told the immediate family to get checked and make sure they didn't have an aneurysm because they can be hereditary. When Debbie returned to California, she underwent testing, and the doctor discovered she had a small one. Her cardiologist monitored her closely. They didn't want to perform the surgery prematurely because it's risky, and they didn't want to do it until it was necessary. As an aneurysm gets bigger and the wall of the aorta gets too thin, there is a much larger risk of it dissecting or rupturing. It is a fine balance between going in for surgery when it is absolutely needed but before it becomes critical. Debbie had two young children at the time near the ages of Ben's two daughters. Witnessing what Ben experienced and the complications that developed as a result of his aorta dissecting, she wanted to pre-empt going in under an emergency situation but only wanted to go for the surgery if it was required. She ended up having the surgery about a year after her brother died, and it went well.

"I owe him my life, and I can never thank him. I can never tell him what he did for me. I often think about him, particularly if I'm driving or doing something we shared an interest in. When I'm having a great time with my kids, I think, *He gave this to me*. It breaks my heart that he can't be with me to share my life and me, his. It makes me so sad that he hasn't been able to watch his girls grow up and be a part of their lives. I try to appreciate everything they do and accomplish on two levels, one for me as their aunt and one for my brother. It was so hard for my other brother Aron. He didn't only lose a brother; he also lost a best friend. After Ben died, my husband, kids, and I moved back to Indiana to be closer to our families."

Ben's death deepened her appreciation for life itself and how she lived it. The first to go was her high-stress job. She yearned for more creativity in her life, which led her back to her photography and creative writing. She returned to school for her MFA in fiction writing.

"Ben's memory helps remind me to enjoy my life and not take things too seriously. He found the humor in life, and I try to do the same when I get too stressed. Even when he was in the hospital after surgery and they limited him to ice chips, he joked about how stingy they were with the water. He had this great smile. I can still close my eyes and see his face with that beautiful smile. He had such a great sense of humor and always loved telling jokes."

"That's a beautiful way to honor your brother's spirit," I said. "Did you do anything else to honor his life?"

"My husband and I wrote a cookbook, and we dedicated it to Ben and to my husband's brother, who also passed away."

Her families also made a donation to the congregation where her father was a rabbi. He died when she was eighteen. Debbie explained there had been an electrical fire a few years ago in the ark where the Torah scrolls were kept. The ark was opened at different times during the service, and the Torahs were removed from the ark and read. They had vestments that included both metal and cloth (the mantel) to cover them.

Before the firemen arrived, the rabbi ran into the sanctuary and grabbed the ten to twelve precious Torahs out of the ark in an attempt to save them. Not only was the ark damaged, but also the room itself was affected by the smoke and water.

"Standing in front of the ark like that was an emotional experience. I couldn't help but flash back to all the times I had stood in front of it. I thought a lot about my dad," Debbie said. "The Torahs had been moved to a different room, and they were all laid out on a table. The metal vestments were horribly smoke- and soot-covered. The mantels covering the Torahs were all destroyed. I had chanted from those Torahs. My father, mother, brothers, and I had carried those Torahs during services at different points in our lives. It was a very sad thing to see. I told the rabbi that when they got ready to replace the covers to let me know."

In early summer, he contacted Debbie. They were in the process of replacing the vestments, which was a huge expense. The temple had full-sized large Torahs that were kept in the ark and two smaller, lighter Torahs that sat on either side of it. Women, kids becoming a Bar Mitzvah, or the elderly typically carried these.

"Whenever I've been given the honor to carry one, I used one of the smaller ones because the large, full-size Torahs are too heavy for me. When the rabbi contacted me, he said it would be nice if we could donate the money for the vestments of one Torah, but they had these two smaller Torahs that are displayed on either side of the ark. As soon as he said that, I felt like taking care of the vestments for the smaller Torahs was exactly the thing to do. We could donate one in memory of Ben and one in memory of my father. The synagogue had all the new Torah covers commissioned by a talented seamstress. She designed them with a similar theme, so they all coordinated. I saw the new Torah covers right before the high holidays, and they are beautiful. The Torah covers we donated in memory of my dad and Ben are so lovely, hugging either side of the ark."

* * *

Morgan Callan Rogers: interviewed in June 2015, Maine
John Michael Rogers: 2/4/1957-3/18/1994
Cause of Death: Complications due to an unsuccessful bone marrow transplant.

One day, eight-year-old Morgan and her brother and sister went with their mother to her mother's friend's house. Her mother's friend had a passel of kids for them to play with, but Morgan noticed someone she didn't know—a little guy who had the most gorgeous brown eyes and the longest lashes she'd ever seen. He was playing trucks by himself while all the other kids ran around, screaming like miniature hoodlums.

As Morgan and her family were leaving the home, the boy latched on to her mother's leg and wouldn't let go. Morgan would learn later the boy's father, who was in the service, left him with relatives who passed him around. Conversations ensued between her parents about the little boy's fate, and they made the decision to adopt the three-year-old toddler.

Morgan and her siblings adored their new little brother. He was quiet and kept to himself at first but began to open up as time went on. John entertained them at the supper table as he built villages and waterfalls with his vegetables, mashed potatoes, and gravy. Once, she caught him outside flogging a tree with a stick like a sword. A child herself, she didn't understand how it felt for John to be abandoned by his biological parents.

When John was in the fourth grade, he came home one day and dissolved into a puddle of tears. He said, "For Show and Tell I told people I was adopted, and they kept asking me all these questions, and I didn't know what to say."

Adoption didn't mean much to Morgan because, to her and her siblings, John was their brother. John and her older brother went everywhere together and became best friends. As John grew up and matured, he had a love for philosophy. He was into occultism a little bit and spiritualism.

Morgan looked forward to the deep conversations they'd have together. Their bond strengthened through their in-depth talks about life and the afterlife. John was sensitive and humorous, and Morgan could spend hours with him.

One night, Morgan went to a bar with a friend who didn't know her limit and got staggering drunk. Morgan called her brother and said, "Can you please come help me out?" She explained the situation and John showed up at the bar. Morgan drove his car and followed him as he drove her friend's van home, even though he didn't know how to drive a standard shift. They brought her into the house, tucked her in, and the two of them drove to Popham Beach in Phippsburg, Maine, at 2:00 a.m. The moon, full and high, looked pinned against the inky sky.

The two clambered up a dune that had been chopped out by the ocean below. Their hearts pounded, high on adrenaline. After that adventure, they became thrill seekers, going out in hurricanes. They drove a car into a parking lot during a blizzard and did donuts. They did crazy things. Deep talks and storm chasing came to define their relationship. Those talks covered everything from reincarnation to the merits of the band Genesis.

After high school, John went directly into the Air Force. He wound up being stationed on a base near Lakenheath, near Suffolk, England. It had been Morgan's dream to live in England, so she hopped on a plane and lived with her brother in a shared half-cottage. They had more adventures together in a little black English motoring car that John called Bug Buggy. They went to a rock festival and saw Genesis, Tom Petty, and Jefferson Starship. They saw Electric Light Orchestra in London. Morgan watched with pride as John marched in formation in his blue uniform at an Air Force base show, knowing he had the heart of a soldier. She admired John's determination to be fit and strong by boxing and running five miles a day.

Living in England was a special time for both of them, but in the fall, Morgan had to return home and figure out what she was going to do with her life. John also returned home after the Air Force, enrolled at the University of Southern Maine, and graduated. Around that time, Morgan noticed that her brother looked tired, with circles so dark around his eyes, they looked bruised. Not long after, he told his family he had terrible news. At twenty-five years old, he was diagnosed with leukemia.

After the announcement, John and his siblings piled into a car and went to the beach as they tried to absorb what the diagnosis meant and how much time they had left with their brother. When his treatment started, the oncologist put John on a series of drugs instead of chemotherapy. He went into what would turn out to be a ten-year remission.

John was determined to live his life, to live out his dreams before his time ended. He attended Syracuse University and received a master's degree in Public Service. He worked at the State House in Augusta, Maine. When he began to show signs of illness, his colleagues and contacts at the State House helped him obtain complete disability with the Veterans Administration, after it was determined that his job, handling and packaging jet fuel waste, had caused the leukemia.

He kept working. He kept striving. He even built a little house for himself. Then he began to get sick and started bleeding, and he knew he'd have to try a bone marrow transplant match or face death. All of his siblings rallied and lined up to get tested. None of them was a match.

He had no other choice. "I have to search for my birth family," he said.

Morgan hoped he'd find them and one would be a perfect match. When he located his mother, she, too, was not a match, and she lied to him. She told John his biological father had been an airman who was killed in Iceland. When John researched this, he discovered it wasn't true.

But there was still hope. He had a half-brother who agreed to get tested. John was crestfallen when he learned his brother was also not a viable donor. John was running out of time and options, so he chose to go with the nearest match they could find. Out of the six criteria needed for a successful match, the match John chose only met three.

He traveled to Dana Farber Institute in Boston and had the bone marrow transplant and experienced a painful recovery. Morgan and her family went to Boston by bus several days a week to visit him, wearing gowns and masks for numerous months to keep any possible germs at bay.

They were eager to get John home where they could take care of him. When he was released from the hospital, he moved in with his parents. John hoped that he'd continue to recover, but his health declined when he developed pneumonia that led to kidney failure. He was forced onto kidney dialysis for about a year. Then one day, he walked out of dialysis and decided he didn't want to be on it for the rest of his life. This would mean that fluids would build up in his body and eventually kill him. He understood the repercussions and a short time later, he went into Maine Medical Center in Portland and made a plan for the week he was to die.

Each night, he would eat one of his favorite meals. He arranged who he would say goodbye to and when— friends first, then close friends, then family. His parents would be the last ones to say goodbye.

Morgan recalls the last week of her brother's life like a well-remembered movie. "I see myself walking down endless hospital corridors. I saw a new father enter the hospital with a baby carrier so that he could bring his wife and his newborn home, and I remember thinking, *How ironic.*"

John's doctors had determined that John would die on March 17. Morgan and her siblings were to stay at the hospital until 11:00 p.m. and leave when their parents arrived. At some point during the evening, her siblings couldn't take the pain of watching their brother die, and they left.

"I hadn't had any experience with someone dying. I remember sitting there, reading, listening to his breathing become labored because his lungs were filling up," Morgan said. "I panicked and asked a nurse to please clear his lungs before I realized he was going to die from a very fast pneumonia. I continued to listen to him as he struggled to breathe some more. It didn't get easier. At 11:00 p.m., my parents came into the room. I kissed John and as I left the room, I shouted, 'Goodbye.' To my amazement, he shouted back, 'Goodbye!' I'll never forget that. I waited in our hotel room, but I was restless. My parents called me about an hour later. He died at 12:05 a.m. on March 18, 1994."

During the last week of his life, John and Morgan sat in his hospital room and had one of their special talks.

He said, "You know you have to stop messing around and decide what it is you want to do."

Morgan knew her brother was right. He had a significant influence on helping her come to terms with what she wanted to do with her one precious life. John pushed her toward getting an MFA in creative writing and kept her on course.

Two published novels later, she said, "His death and his life made me a different person, and I think that person is better. The way he lived his life with courage and determination gave me the confidence to move forward. He did major things with his life, even when he was sick. He got his master's degree, he worked a full-time job, and he built a house. He was a remarkable man. It shifted my whole paradigm of who I was and what I could attain. I was blessed to have somebody so brave who allowed me to be present throughout his struggle and to bear witness to how he handled it. He was a real man," Morgan said. "That's my definition of one, anyway. I miss him more every year. For the longest time, I expected that he waited just around a corner, or I'd be looking at a doorway and expect him to appear. I don't expect that anymore. I think he's in a better place now. I think he's at peace."

As Morgan talked about her brother's bravery, I thought about my own brother's courage to live halfway around the world and the legacy he left behind as a result. I remember how humble he was when he was recognized by the spa industry and received his award and was promoted to Senior Director of Spas for Four Seasons, overseeing all twenty-two spas in the Asia Pacific. Later, when he joined the Mandarin Hotel, he was deeply committed and passionate about Corporate Social Responsibility (CSR) initiatives and giving back to the community. They provided support to 800 orphans by donating vegetables from their own organic garden every week, and they worked on giving them employment opportunities if they were interested in hospitality. Rocky, too, was a remarkable man.

"He did sound like a special man, Morgan. Thank you for sharing a piece of your brother with me," I said. "Did you do anything special to honor his life?"

Morgan took his Tree of Life ring to Ireland, along with the ring of another friend who had died in a car accident. She traveled to the largest Aran island, Inis Mor, and walked the length of it to a prehistoric fort, Dun Aengus. The fort, a circle on the edge of a very high cliff, rose above the sea. The rocks located around the fort were fissured and worn. Morgan placed the two rings in a crack in those rocks.

"It is one of my favorite places," she said. "He would have loved it, and he would have liked where his ring ended up. Me and my siblings also met in Arizona because John loved that state, and we scattered some of his ashes in a state park near Phoenix."

Morgan believes being part of his illness ultimately has made her a more patient, understanding person. Now she cares for her elderly parents.

"I love spending time with them, and it's a place I never thought I'd be. I always thought I'd be living quite a ways away when they grew old, but I'm here and it's good," Morgan said.

Lastly, one of the most important ways she honored her brother's life was by pursuing her dreams the way he pursued his. "He made me realize that my imagination, which I always kept in a back closet, is the best part of who I am. It's my superpower, and I honor it every day."

* * *

I've taken several action steps in my life since Rocky's passing to honor his life. I flew to Asia to support his wife and daughter, spread his ashes in the Indian ocean, helped to structure the memorial service, got a tattoo, quit my job, became certified to run a bereavement group, and wrote this book. I share stories about him, light candles on the anniversary of his death, keep pictures of him on my desk, talk to him, and, most importantly, I have committed to living the best life I can, a life that would make him proud.

When we take steps to honor our sibling, it keeps their spirit alive in our memories, fosters a sense of peace as we celebrate what they brought to our lives while accepting the death, and gently lets them go without letting the memory of them go. We can honor them through big and little ways: read books they enjoyed, play their favorite songs, cook their favorite meals, and include their memory in celebrations, like weddings and anniversaries. We can try their favorite hobbies, make a quilt out of their clothing, buy a piece of jewelry in their memory, write them a letter, plant a tree, finish a project they were working on, live a more passion- and purpose-driven life, or climb their favorite mountain. If they were cremated, we can spread their ashes in a place that brought them peace. Volunteer for a cause or a population that mattered to them. Travel to a place they always wanted to visit but never had the chance to go, or set up a foundation in their name.

The list of what we can do to honor our siblings is endless. One of the young women I interviewed said she bakes a cake on her sister's birthday and gives it away to someone in need or donates it to a local shelter.

CHAPTER 14
A Journey Worth Taking

I'm a therapist, a graduate of Martin Seligman's Authentic Happiness Coaching course, and a Passion Test facilitator—helping people to identify their top five passions so they can shift their lives into high gear. I have dedicated my career to inspiring clinicians to search for the exception to their clients' problems. "When you help your client to identify the exception," I'd say to the therapists, "you can help them expand what's working in their lives. Focus on their strengths rather than on their problems. Human beings are stronger and more resilient than you can imagine."

In the aftermath of Rocky's death, it was as if God dangled me over a fire pit as flames singed my skin, and asked, "Do you still believe in human resilience? Do you still believe people can rise up out of the ashes and live a joyful life? Do you still believe that life is worth living?" These questions rolled around in my head for months and what frightened me the most were my answers, a resounding NO every time. I didn't feel resilient. I didn't believe I'd rise up out of this heartache. I felt hopeless and weak in a world where I no longer belonged. Where did that leave me? My career, my beliefs, and the foundation I had built my life on were swept away in a tsunami of grief. I wandered around in a hollow body, living a hollow life without anything solid to hang on to. If someone pried my jaw open and yelled, "Hello" inside my mouth, they'd hear an echo.

In those early months, I sat on my kitchen stool and stared out the window at the barren maple tree, its crooked, knotted limbs blanketed in snow. When I couldn't bear to look at it any longer, I closed my eyes and sank into memory where Rocky lived, where I could reach for him, where I could listen to his voice and weep.

It was ten months before I heard my own laughter again. I attended a leadership course with my colleagues in Virginia. I don't recall what was said, only the deep guttural laughter in the room. I turned around to see who was laughing because I didn't recognize the sound when it rose out of my body. I locked eyes with my supervisor, and she winked and smiled, recognizing that my laughter was foreign to me. I was both stunned and guilt-ridden. How could I have allowed myself to find humor in the wake of my brother's death? As a person who loves to laugh at the silliest things, I hadn't even let out the tiniest giggle since February 14. When Setiawan released the truth from her mouth, "You have to be brave, Sue. Brian is gone," each word carried a hundred-pound weight and crushed my will to care about the good and the bad events happening around me. I was sure that I'd never find humor or joy in this lifetime again. If I reclaimed joy, wouldn't I be dishonoring my brother? How could I laugh and enjoy life when his life was taken?

I took my guilt-ridden self back to my hotel room, lay down, closed my eyes, and landed in my parents' backyard twenty years earlier when Rocky was twenty-four and I was twenty-eight. It was a gorgeous summer day in July, and we were celebrating my mother's birthday. We descended on the occasion with an abundance of food—one of our greatest joys. My brothers grilled marinated chicken, bourbon steak tips, and sweet Italian sausages. We sautéed mushrooms, caramelized onions, and roasted red and yellow peppers with numerous side dishes: pasta, potato, and green salads. We munched on horseradish-deviled eggs, chilled shrimp cocktail, and corn tortilla chips and mango salsa.

After we stuffed our bellies, drunk on delicious food, laughter, conversation, and Harpoon IPA, we played croquet, pushing each other out of the way, reciting our favorite movie lines, and enjoying each other as we always do when my siblings and in-laws get together.

When it was time for presents, I handed my mother a gift. I bought her a bright pink sun hat from L.L. Bean. I should have known she wouldn't like the hat, preferring denim jeans and black, gray, or white T-shirts. Though she looked beautiful in deep jewel colors, she refused to wear them, and I refused to give up on her.

Mom opened the gift and said, "Thank you." She put the hat on, danced around the lawn, flapping her arms, mockingly.

"OK," I said. "I get it. I'll take it back and buy you a gray one."

Rocky plucked the hat from our mother's head, put it on his head, and said, "I love it. This is just what I've always wanted, Sis." For the remainder of the cookout, he pranced around in the blazing pink hat that stood out even more against his bronze skin and jet-black hair. I erupted into laughter and he said, "What's so funny, Sis? You don't like my hat?"

In the hotel room, I smiled from the memory. Rocky was a prankster and loved to entertain us with his elaborate tales and jokes. I sat up in the bed and thought, *He'd hate all these tears.* Then I remembered something his three-and-a-half-year-old daughter, Anna, said to me when we were in Bali the morning after we released his ashes into the ocean.

Anna came into the kitchen and said, "Daddy doesn't want any more tears."

I held her and said, "It's all right to cry when we're sad, Anna."

"But Daddy doesn't want you to be sad anymore." She laid her tiny hand on my cheek. "He wants us to be happy."

That evening, I thought about Anna's words. Had Rocky come to her? Had he passed on a message to us from the other side? No more tears? How could I magically stop mourning the absence of my brother? I could hear my friend's words like a prayer to my question. It was shortly after my mother's stroke, and I cried for three days straight, standing vigil by her bedside in the

ICU. One night after leaving the hospital, I met one of my best friends for a glass of wine and she said to me, "You don't wear sad well."

She was right. I didn't wear sad well just as my mother didn't wear colorful clothing well. It's not that she couldn't do color, or that I couldn't do sad, it just wasn't our preference. I had, of course, experienced deep sadness over loss but not for long stretches. My bounce-back time had always been short. Even after my mother's stroke, I moved through the grieving process relatively quickly and jumped into gratitude and hope. Gratitude that she was alive and hope that she would continue to make strides in her recovery. When I got divorced, I threw myself into my graduate studies, said goodbye to the past, and looked toward the future.

I didn't want to wake up sad every morning and go to bed sad every night. Sad slung its arm over my shoulder and led me around. Sad slammed its fist down on all the activities that used to bring me joy. I wanted to take a shovel, dig a hole through the frozen earth, jump in, and hibernate until the despair was leached out of me, and I could awaken my old self when most days were either mediocre, good, great, or fantastic, not sad and hopeless.

I rolled off the hotel bed, walked over to the mirror, looked at my ashen skin and swollen eyes, and said, "You are not going to be sad anymore. You have to reclaim joy. Rocky would want you to laugh. No more tears."

As I've learned through this process, it's not quite that clean and easy, but it was a start. I could shed the guilt that snatching moments of joy was somehow dishonoring my brother. There were no clocks or calendars when it came to my grieving process, but I had to allow myself the space to experience tiny moments of joy until those tiny moments expanded as the months and years marched on. Over time, laughing and living again was the path to honoring his life and my own. His life was taken and mine was not. Memories of

Rocky now—instead of triggering tears each and every time—bring me both comfort and great pleasure. I love to conjure snippets of our time together when he made me laugh till I couldn't breathe.

I still continue to talk to him about anything tricky that's going on in my life and imagine what advice he might offer as he did two years before his death when we Skyped. He told me about his vertigo, and I shared my health issues. He said, "Sue, go to a spa for a week and take care of yourself. You deserve it, Sis."

"I can't," I said.

"Why not? It's only a week," he said.

"Work is too busy right now," I said. "Plus, it would be very expensive."

"Sue, we're talking about your health. If not now, when?" he asked. "Work can live without you for five days. And money is meant to be spent. You take care of everyone else. You have to take care of yourself too."

The truth was I didn't know how to take care of myself. I was burned out and yearned to slip away somewhere quiet and toss my cell phone into a drawer, but I rationalized that I didn't have the time. What astonishes me now is after Rocky died, I spent close to three weeks in Asia and emails, phone calls, meetings, and deadlines waited until I returned. I could clear off my calendar for a tragedy, not caring a whit about my job, but when it came to nurturing my weary self, I couldn't or wouldn't carve out the time.

One of the most powerful lessons I learned close to three years after Rocky's sudden death was the meaning of the quote, *If not us, who? If not now, when?* When my husband asked me if I wanted to go to Costa Rica for twelve days for my birthday I said, "YES." And while I was in Costa Rica, four of my best friends texted me and asked, *Do you want to go to Mexico to celebrate our fiftieth birthdays?* My old default answer was, "Of course I can't go to Mexico. I can't take two big trips within months of each other." And then I heard Rocky's voice, *If not now, when?*

I looked at my husband as we ate scrambled eggs, rice, and beans in our bathing suits by the pool and said, "Karen G, Karen P, Annie, and Amy want to go to Mexico for a week to celebrate our fiftieth birthdays." Before my husband could respond, I said, "And I just want you to know that I said yes."

"Good," he said. "You guys will have a blast."

"Thank you," I said and kissed him on the cheek. I looked at my husband, thankful he gave me this trip. After losing Rocky, I squirreled away my emotions, my fears of losing another family member, of never feeling happy again, of walking through life purposeless, of never earning another penny because I had no desire to work. I shoved my dream aside of one day making it as a writer and gave up on querying agents to represent my novel. I hid my anxiety attacks when I awakened sweat-soaked in the middle of the night, asking myself, Is Rocky really dead or did I dream it?

I tucked all the messy, frightening feelings that grief brought into my life way deep down inside the hidden pockets of my heart where they were only mine, which created a crack in the foundation of our marriage. I pretended to listen to my husband when he returned home after a grueling twelve-hour day at our pub. I feigned compassion when he discussed issues he had with his staff. When he returned home from golf, I asked him how he played even though I didn't care. I asked him the same questions over and over about things going on in his life because I couldn't remember asking him in the first place and therefore had no recollection of his answers. It became a game of pretending, and the chasm grew between us. By the time I noticed, the fissure was so wide and deep, I didn't have the emotional capacity to fill it in. Between my grief and caring for my bereft, aging parents, there was no room for Steve and our relationship.

As I slowly moved through the days, months, and eventually hit the one-year, then two-year mark, I cared a little more each day about Steve's life, my friends' lives, and about my own until I was ready to rejoin the living. Two weeks before the third anniversary of Rocky's death, I packed my suitcase for Costa Rica with an excitement that tickled my insides. I was ready for adventure. I was ready to yank the padlock off the door to my heart, swing it wide open, and let joy walk through it.

Prior to our flight, I vowed that I was going to strap courage on my back and try new activities in the spirit of Rocky. If he could ride camels in Egypt, elephants in Thailand, and scooters in Bali, then I could muster the nerve to go surfing, zip lining, and kayaking through alligator territory. Steve and I did all three, and I felt more alive, free, and open than I could ever remember feeling before.

On our way home, I realized how much Rocky continued to expand my life even after his death. If not for him, I never would have seen Hong Kong, squinting at blinking lights during the Night Market; I never would have eaten fresh fish under a smoke-filled sky in Bali; I never would have jumped off a cliff, fastened to a zip line, careening hundreds of feet above a Costa Rican jungle; and I never would have understood how the loss of a brother could change the trajectory of my life.

Because of him, I've not only learned to say *yes* more, I've also learned how to say *no* more. Yes to life-giving activities with friends and family, and no to soul-sucking obligatory events and employment that don't bring more joy into my life. It was Rocky's death that gave me the courage to leave a company and a job that no longer felt fulfilling. I stayed two years longer than I wanted to because it paid well, and I carried the insurance for our family. I held onto the mistaken and limiting belief that I'd never find another job that would pay as well.

After I left my job, my husband encouraged me to take some time off and write *Rock On: Mining for Joy in the Deep River of Sibling Grief* before I re-launched myself into the work world. He secured insurance, and I wrote my way through grief. I've laid down the worries

I used to carry around about the future because I understand at a soul level that each moment is all I have; it's all any of us have. Each breath I inhale is a true gift and a blessing. I don't take my life or those I love for granted, and I share hugs, thank yous, and I love yous in abundance.

When it was time to leave for Mexico, I had been in my new job for exactly one week. I also had this final chapter to write. Had I known either one of those pieces of information when I was in Costa Rica, would I have said "yes" to the Mexico trip? I'd like to believe I still would have.

I optimistically packed my journal with the intention of penning notes for *A Journey Worth Taking*. But five women together on a beach didn't lend itself well to quiet writing time. I didn't write a single word, but I did mine for nuggets of joy and found them.

Three of us strolled down the tranquil beach in Troncones, Mexico, as our feet sank into the warm, soft sand. We were light and carefree, feeling eighteen all over again as we reminisced and resurrected stories from our high school years together. Waves crashed against the rocks. Surfers sat idle on their longboards, waiting to catch the perfect wave. Birds flew in the blue sky. It was a spectacular day. As we walked, my friend Karen, who had lost her father the previous year, talked about signs she received since his passing and the odd places she found pennies when she needed her father most. When she finished, I held out my hand and showed them a silver ring with four dolphins I bought a couple of years after Rocky died.

"My brother had two beautiful dolphin tattoos on his back," I said. I proceeded to tell them what I've coined as the "dolphin story." One of my colleagues and dear friend Sharon went through a horrendous divorce and needed to find a new home for herself and her two children. She located the perfect rental on a lake in Oakland, Maine, but she was number six on the waitlist.

227

Sharon called me and said, "It's on Rocky Ridge Road. I've been praying to your brother. I feel like it's a sign."

Sharon got the rental on Rocky Ridge Road. I'll never know if my brother had anything to do with it, but a few days after Sharon moved in, she texted me and said she felt tugged to go out on the porch. She had an intuitive sense that she needed to convey a message. On the porch, a stained-glass dolphin hung in the window. She took a picture with her phone and sent it to me. Sharon wrote, *Does this have any meaning for you? I feel like it's a sign from Rocky.*

Yes, I texted back. *He loved dolphins. I asked him for a sign this morning. Thank you.*

After I finished telling my friends the dolphin story, we sat on a piece of smooth driftwood and gazed out at the ocean. Karen screamed, "Sue! Look! It's a school of dolphins."

Their glistening bodies swam in front of us. "Wow," I said, knowing it was a wink from my brother.

"You don't get it," she said. "We've never ever seen a dolphin here. They don't like the temperature of the water."

Karen owned the property on Troncones Beach and had been there several times since they purchased it in 2015. As Karen said, "That's probably the first and last time we'll ever see a dolphin," one jumped in the air, followed by a second one, and then they were gone.

We fell quiet, absorbed in the spiritual rhythm of the ocean and the magnitude of what we had just experienced. I could feel his presence in the wind, in the crash of the waves, in the joy of the jumping dolphins. I thanked him silently and wiped tears from my face that were not from sadness but sprang from an overwhelming depth of gratitude for being alive.

Later that evening, we walked down the beach to watch the turtle hatchlings. The turtle eggs were in a fenced-off conservation area next to a wide-open restaurant on the beach. Once the turtles hatched, Antonio, the person in charge of the conservation area, gathered the babies and placed them in a plastic tub to carry them closer to the water. A guard dog stood by, ready and alert, to chase off predators before they could attack and eat the hatchlings.

"You seem pretty enthusiastic," Antonio said to me. "Would you like to release them?"

"Me? Are you kidding? I would love to. Thank you." He handed me the tub, and I gently tipped and jiggled it to slide the babies onto the sand. We watched the tiny miracles waddle toward the ocean and swim away. We thanked Antonio as we followed him into the restaurant.

"Do you work here, too?" I asked.

"I own it," he said. "Have a seat and I'll bring you all some margaritas."

Before we sat down, we stood in a circle, talking about the splendor of the turtles and our good fortune to have had the opportunity to witness the hatchlings when a four-year-old Mexican boy trotted over and began dancing in the middle of us. He latched on to my leg until I leaned over and picked him up. He wrapped his arms around my neck, squeezed me tight, and kissed me on the cheek. My friends and I were a bit dumbfounded as to why this little boy would have shown me such affection when I was a stranger to him.

Antonio walked over with a tray full of our drinks and said, "I've never seen him do that."

"Is he your son?" I asked.

"No. He's my nephew."

"What's his name?" I asked as the little boy gave me another kiss.

"Brian," he said.

My eyes welled. *Maybe your wife was right, Rocky. Maybe you do prefer to be called by your birth name, Brian, rather than by your nickname.* I kissed Brian on his forehead and thanked him. I put him down, and he ran off to play. My friends and I sat down at a table, drinks in hand, awestruck that we met a Mexican boy named Brian.

Even for the non-believer at the table, it was too powerful to be brushed off as a coincidence.

"I still can't believe his name is Brian," I said as a woman walked over to our table. She seemed to me like a sage with her long, loose gray hair and sparkling eyes.

Although we had never met her before, she struck up a conversation with us and said, "I love Troncones. I come every year and stay four to six months."

"That's incredible," I said.

"I can't stay that long this time though," she said. "I just spent six months over in Bali."

"What part," I asked, even though I knew what she was going to say.

"Ubud," she said.

I hugged her. "That's where my brother lived," I said, thinking, *before his soul left his body*. But now he lives in my heart. He's in the wind, the ocean, and the rocks. He's everywhere.

I know I can call out to him, and he'll walk beside me as he did in Troncones. I always believed it, and now I know it through my personal experiences. It was one of the nuggets of joy I took home with me from Mexico.

After the trip, I sat at my desk to begin this chapter. I picked up a photograph of Rocky cradling his newborn son Michael, both asleep on the couch. I ran my thumb over the infant's sweet face. In the photo, he was two weeks old. At the end of May 2017, I imagined Rocky sitting next to me as I watched Michael cross the stage to receive his high school diploma. In his graduation card, I wrote that he inherited the best of who Rocky was at his essence: his physical beauty, his sensitive and compassionate heart, his kindness, athletic skill, and hilarious sense of humor. I looked at my brother so peaceful in the photo. "You would be so proud," I said, smiling. "Your legacy lives on through your son." I glanced over at a picture of Anna, dressed in a beautiful maroon and gold sarong. "And through your daughter."

Before I went to bed that evening, I wrote a note

to my brother in my journal. "Dear Rocky, do you remember the song, *For Good*, that we played at your memorial? It's a song about compassion, love, and for-giveness. I truly have been changed for good because of you. Thank you for helping me to emerge from the deep river of grief a stronger version of my former self. It's been a bumpy, jagged road that I'd never wish on anyone but one worth taking. I love you, honey."

Thanks for making the trip, Sis. I love you too.

Acknowledgments

Rock On has been both a joyful and heartbreaking journey. There would not be a book on sibling loss if I had not lost my brother Rocky. The space he left behind was so vast, there were days I thought I'd fall into the abyss and never return to myself. I feel as though my brother's spirit was with me as I wrote my way through grief. This book would also not have been possible if it were not for the never-ending support I've received from so many remarkable people in my life.

To the twenty-one brave and courageous people I interviewed for this book who shared their grief and loss with open hearts and raw honesty. I will forever carry your deceased siblings' spirits and stories with me. I am infinitely grateful to each and every one of you for trusting me with your siblings' stories. Thank you, Amy Boles, Yvon Stokkink, Andrea Stiernstrand, Julie Brown, Emily Gary, Morty Ballen, Micah Brown, Debbie Steinman, Maryann Garcia, Jill Williams, Shamola Kharkar, Katie Stickney, Diana Davis, Kim Sisto Robinson, Marissa Kerkdijk, Morgan Callan Rogers, Darra Gordon, Dave Walsh, Jeneen Gallagher, Melissa Doughty, and Miki Gonzalez.

To the Center for Grieving Children and the facilitators who taught me what the grieving process was all about and for the light and love the center shares with abandon. It was a true honor to run bereavement groups and be amongst some of the most loving and healing people on the planet.

To my writing group, who tirelessly read draft after draft of book proposals, synopses, query letters, and chapters and pushed me to complete the manuscript on those days I wanted to throw it out the window and smash my computer screen. Thankfully, I pulled myself together with their steady reassurance. Thank you, Jean Peck, Nancy Brown, Gro Flatebo, Rita Saliba, Rick

Wile, Barbara Walsh, Pat Hager, Steve Lauder, and Amy Carpenter.

To my Stonecoast mentors in my MFA program who pushed me to become a better writer and helped me to find my voice. Thank you, Suzanne Strempek Shea and Lesléa Newman. I will forever be grateful for your insights, guidance, and critical feedback on my early work.

To my two soul-sisters and early readers of the manuscript: Taryn Bowe and Kerry Herlihy. I am grateful for the feedback and insights you offered to help make *Rock On* the best it could be. And I am grateful for your friendship every day and for the powerful writing you offer to the world.

To Amy Amoroso, Lisa Wilson, and CC Robinson for your support and all the time we spent at writing retreats with Taryn and Kerry. You all inspire me with your talent, love, passion, insights, and infinite wisdom. Each of the powerful and talented writers in my life not only makes me a better writer but a better person.

To my dear friends, Denise Lessard, Candy Allen, Laurie Pizzo, and Paul Baribeault for proofreading later drafts.

To my sisterhood, Melissa Smith, Anne-Marie McKenzie, Julie Viola, Kathy Viola, Meg Wilson, Karen Douglass, Karen Gallagher, Catherine Carrington Rand, Jackie Stowers, Wendy Howard, Amy Sheehan, Suzanne Roberts, Susan Douglas, Kristen Hursty Edson, Angela Menendez, Dr. Stem Mahlatini, Crystal Hathaway, and Sharon Fowler. Thank you for your friendship always and for your unwavering support during my grieving process. Thank you to those who listened tirelessly as I talked about *Rock On*.

To Anne Moss Rogers for so generously sharing her wisdom and knowledge on how to maneuver through the marketing and social media world and inspiring me to maintain stamina.

To Tracy DiMillo, who has walked with me every inch of this journey. You told me enrolling in the MFA program was not an option but a must. You held me accountable to ensure I sent out queries. You have picked me up a thousand times and refused to let me contemplate giving up. Your belief in me kept me striving and pushing toward the finish line. You've been my sister, my friend, and my coach. My gratitude is endless, and I will forever cherish our friendship.

To my endorsers, who I both admire and infinitely respect for the gifts they bring to the world: Barbara Walsh, Tasha Walsh (they are not related), and Aimee Mckee.

To my amazing and talented publicist, Susan Schwartzman. Thank you for all your guidance and hard work, and for offering me opportunities of a lifetime.

To my publisher, Library Tales Publisher and CEO, Usher Morgan, who held my hand throughout the publishing process and made it a little less scary every day. Thank you for taking a chance on me and for helping me to bring my life-long dream to fruition.

To Setiawan and Anna, for the love and joy you brought into Rocky's life and continue to bring into my father's life.

To my siblings, Jim, Paul, Rocky, and Kevin Hathaway, who I love with such abundance, it would be impossible to describe the depth of my love and gratitude. I would not be who I am today without each of you and how you've helped to shape my life. To my sisters-in-law, Gayle, Pam, and Jessica Hathaway, who are more like blood sisters than in-laws and who have supported our family through deep hardship, sadness, joy, and endless celebrations.

To my beloved mother, Judith Hathaway, who passed away on March 8, 2019, four months before I received a book deal, and to my father, Brian Hathaway, Sr. Thank you both for never giving up on me and holding my dreams as if they were your own. Thank you, Mom, for always knowing, since I was in the 6th grade, that one day I would publish my work. I know you walk beside me every day. I love you both.

Lastly, to my husband, Steve Casey, who told me to quit my job after Rocky died and take a year off to write *Rock On*. We've traveled a bumpy road together and, just when we were about to jump ship, we held on. Thank you for believing in me and never giving up. I love you.

Made in the USA
Monee, IL
10 March 2021

62415280R00142